the series on school reform

Patricia A. Wasley
Coalition of
Essential Schools

Ann Lieberman
NCREST

Joseph P. McDonald
Annenberg Institute
for School Reform

SERIES EDITORS

This series also incorporates earlier titles in the
Professional Development and Practice Series

TEACHER LEARNING

New Policies, New Practices

Milbrey W. McLaughlin
Ida Oberman

Editors

TEACHERS
COLLEGE
PRESS

Teachers College, Columbia University
New York and London

Published by Teachers College Press, 1234 Amsterdam Avenue, New York, NY 10027

Copyright © 1996 by Teachers College, Columbia University

Library of Congress Cataloging-in-Publication Data

Teacher learning : new policies, new practices / Milbrey W.
    McLaughlin, Ida Oberman, editors.
        p.   cm. — (The series on school reform)
    "This collection grows out of a summer 1993 seminar on teachers'
professional development sponsored by the Pew Forum on Education
Reform"—Introd.
    Includes bibliographical references and index.
    ISBN 0-8077-3495-0 (cloth : alk. paper). — ISBN 0-8077-3494-2
(pbk. : alk. paper)
    1. Teachers—In-service training—United States—Congresses.
2. Teachers—United States—Congresses.   3. Constructivism
(Education)—United States—Congresses.   4. Learning—Congresses.
5. Educational change—United States—Congresses.   I. McLaughlin,
Milbrey Wallin.   II. Oberman, Ida.   III. Series.
LB1731.T4186   1996
371.1'46'0973—dc20   95-44592

ISBN 0-8077-3494-2 (paper)
ISBN 0-8077-3495-0 (cloth)

Printed on acid-free paper
Manufactured in the United States of America

03 02 01 00 99 98 97 96   8 7 6 5 4 3 2 1

Contents

PART III: NEW STRUCTURES FOR LEARNING AND CHANGE

PART IV: NEW ROLES FOR TRADITIONAL STRUCTURES

PART V: AN EMERGENT PARADIGM FOR PRACTICE
AND POLICY

Introduction

Teacher Learning: New Policies, New Practices

Milbrey W. McLaughlin and Ida Oberman

The nation's schools confront unprecedented demands for reform, calls for change in their very core. Challenges to do better, and to do differently, issue from disparate sources and describe new foci and frames for teaching and learning. A steady stream of reports, beginning with *A Nation at Risk* (National Commission on Excellence in Education, 1983), declare that what most students know is not enough. The perceived mismatch between what society expects and what students can do has unleased an avalanche of initiatives to raise standards, change curricula, tighten educators' accountability, and restructure the way schools do business. Moreover, efforts at state and national levels aim to make these changes systemic and bring coherence to the nation's education system for the benefit of all students. In a nation fond of reforming, the end of the 20th century arguably witnesses the most comprehensive reform agenda ever undertaken. Few schools remain untouched by new standards, structures, or ideas about practice.

Equally as significant as the scope of reform is the perspective on teaching and learning it embraces. These policy reforms occur in the context of a "revolution" in cognitive science and new theories of learning (Damasio, 1994; Gardner, 1985). Contrary to the teacher-dominated, transmission-oriented practices that have characterized American education, current theory holds that students learn best when they have an opportunity to actively construct their own knowledge. New theories of learning frame new conceptions about important outcomes of learning and, by extension, of school: higher-order thinking skills and deep understanding of the conceptual structures of knowledge domains. A central aim of education, in this view, is to produce young people who know how to learn (Bruer, 1993).

The new classroom practices that reformers imagine, often described as "teaching and learning for understanding," assume fundamental change in the ways teachers interact with students. Not surprisingly, teachers' capacity and opportunity to enact this complex, far-reaching reform agenda have taken center stage. At root, the problem of reform is a problem of teachers' learning—understanding how to translate new standards, curricula, and theories of learning into effective educational experiences for all their students.

In this reform era, old models of "staff development," "inservicing," or "teacher training" are well and truly understood as inadequate and wrongheaded (Lieberman & Miller, 1990; Little, 1993b). To begin with, ideas have changed about where teachers learn most effectively. Ideas about teachers' learning and growth have evolved from the hierarchical, laboratory-based models of the late 1960s, which assumed practitioners could simply transfer knowledge from workshop to classroom (e.g., Gagne, 1968), to approaches that recognize the importance of embedding teachers' learning in everyday activities (e.g., Case & Bereiter, 1984; Tharp & Gallimore, 1988). An emerging body of cognitive and social science research offers robust evidence that context and cognition are inextricably linked for all learners, be they children or adults (e.g., Lave & Wenger, 1991; Peter, 1991; Rogoff, 1993).

Reformers' vision also frame new ideas about what teachers need to learn. Teachers' learning no longer is viewed as comprised primarily of accumulating fact-based knowledge, but as comprehending new conceptions of content and pedagogy, and the new roles assumed by practitioners of teaching and learning for understanding.

But if professional development is not a "program" offered after school or on weekends, an event composed primarily of "how-tos" and "shoulds" conveyed by experts, what is it? What kinds of professional development can facilitate the difficult changes expected of teachers and students? While the "old" approach finds little favor in any quarter, the policies and practices necessary to enacting a new paradigm for professional development are not well articulated. In all arenas of education, efforts are underway to identify and further professional development activities that encourage habits of critical inquiry and foster classroom practices grounded in deep understanding of how students learn. For example, nearly every major foundation with an interest in education has launched an effort to identify successful approaches to teachers' professional growth. These private efforts, like those found in most federal, state, and local education agencies, reflect the struggle to develop new policies and practices that support teachers' career-long learning and capacity to teach for understanding.

This book joins that effort. It is not another autopsy of failed workshops or critique of mandated, generic training sessions, but an attempt to illuminate the principles and policies necessary to foster professional development in a reform era, as well as to learn from successful experience.

This collection grows out of a summer 1993 seminar on teachers' professional development sponsored by the Pew Forum on Education Reform (see the Appendix for a list of participants). Participants spent a week discussing the implications of changed policy expectations and theories of learning for instructional practices and professional development. The organization and content of this volume reflect the content and direction of that dialogue: The design of this book follows the constructivist model it examines.

PART I

NEW PERSPECTIVES ON PRACTICE

Departing from conventions of providing theory first and following with examples of practice, we begin this collection in the multidimensional context of the Center for the Development of Teaching at the Education Development Center, a community of learners whose goal it is to reconceptualize teaching. In Chapter 1, Barbara Scott Nelson and James K. Hammerman describe the Center's ongoing effort to build new practices based in new theories of teaching and learning. They explore what it can look like to create practices of professional development together once traditional roles of outside experts, as well as traditional inside structures, have been reexamined. The chapter provides an introduction to the lessons learned and the psychological, social, practical, and policy-linked challenges of professional development as experienced and addressed through the Center's work-in-progress.

What is the profile of classroom practice that draws on and in turn supports the reconceptualization of teaching—one in which teachers and students create meaning together? In Chapter 2, Beverly Falk turns to the classroom to probe dimensions that provide an environment of cooperative and context-responsive learning and peer teaching.

Taking a step back from classroom practice, Martin G. Brooks and Jacqueline Grennon Brooks, in Chapter 3, examine the assumptions underlying the new vision of learning. The authors open up the question: What does this vision mean for professional development of both experienced and new teachers?

Chapter 1

Reconceptualizing Teaching

Moving Toward the Creation of Intellectual Communities of Students, Teachers, and Teacher Educators

Barbara Scott Nelson and James K. Hammerman

In the United States there is broad agreement that we need to develop educational programs that will provide all students with more conceptual, flexible, and critical habits of mind. This is particularly, though not exclusively, true in mathematics and science, where the argument is made that a technology-based economy needs the skills that such an education would provide (LaPointe & Mead, 1989; National Council of Teachers of Mathematics [NCTM], 1989). And it is possible to provide all students with such an education. To take mathematics as the case in point, a significant body of research conducted over the past 20 years provides substantial guidance about how students can learn mathematics in ways that promote flexible and rigorous thinking. Every student should do mathematics. They should make and test conjectures, investigate patterns, model and represent real-world problems, and construct mathematical arguments (NCTM, 1989; Lampert, 1990; Putnam, Lampert, & Peterson, 1990). While many teachers share these goals, they are often frustrated because it is not clear to them how to provide such an education. They may see that what they have been doing is insufficient. But what to do instead?

The problem is complex. Much conventional staff development is oriented toward helping teachers assimilate new techniques into an existing system of ideas about pedagogy and subject-matter knowledge. However, contemporary ideas about reform in mathematics education are undergirded by a new conception of the practice of teaching itself (NCTM, 1989, 1991). It involves sharing with students a curiosity about mathematical phenomena, animating students' interests and analytic capabilities, assessing the nature of students' understanding, and guiding inquiry and discussion so that students can achieve a deep understanding of mathematics that they can use broadly.

The current reform agenda requires not only that teachers master new technical skills but also, more important, that they reconceptualize and reinvent the overall nature of their teaching practice. Teaching needs to become an intellectual endeavor, one in which teachers and their students inquire deeply into the nature of knowing, rather than a technical craft in which teachers arrange activities that lead students to having the "right" concepts.

The movement toward conceiving of teaching as an intellectual, rather than technical, enterprise coincides with the emergence into the field of education of a set of ideas about the nature of knowledge itself— ideas that have long been percolating in the academic fields that buttress education. These ideas are stated most explicitly in the NCTM *Standards* documents but inform the standards movement in other disciplines as well. Their inherent epistemological position is a socio-constructivist one. Knowledge is considered to be the dynamic and conditional product of individuals working in intellectual communities, not a fixed body of immutable facts and procedures. Learning proceeds through the individual construction of understanding, not by accepting facts and rules from teacher or textbook; teaching is the facilitation of knowledge construction, not the delivery of information. For most teachers, developing a practice based on such a view of the nature of knowledge, learning, and teaching will not be accomplished merely by adding new techniques to their current repertoire of ideas about teaching and learning. It will require a set of epistemological shifts—changing their beliefs about the nature of knowledge and learning, deepening their content knowledge, and reinventing their classroom practice from within the new conceptual frame.

If we are to understand what it is in innovative professional development projects that makes this process of change possible for teachers, and why it works, we must specify the nature of the change that is at issue and advance a theory of the process by which teachers make these changes. Within the mathematics education community are several research programs that explore and offer theoretical explanations for the nature of the transformation that happens when teachers change beliefs, deepen their knowledge, and reinvent their practice. Carpenter and his colleagues (Carpenter, Fennema, Peterson, & Carey, 1988; Fennema, Carpenter, Franke, & Carey, 1993; Peterson, Fennema, Carpenter, & Loef, 1989) suggest that teacher change is a matter of acquiring and using new knowledge about the development of children's mathematical thought and developing enriched and restructured conceptual structures (Franke, 1991). Terry Wood and Paul Cobb (1991) posit that as teachers and their students renegotiate the norms of the classroom to legitimate students' construction of mathematical concepts and discussion of mathematical ideas, teachers encounter and resolve conflicts between their prior beliefs and what they observe happening in their classrooms. Finally, Schifter (Schifter, 1996; Schifter & Fosnot, 1993; Schifter & Simon, 1992) argues that change in teachers' ideas about the nature of learning requires a process of disequilibration of prior ideas and the reconstruction of more powerful ones. In all these programs, teacher education itself proceeds according to a constructivist view of teachers' intellectual development.

FOUR INTERACTING STRANDS OF CHANGE

At the Center for the Development of Teaching in Newton, Massachusetts, our work with teachers is based on the essentially Piagetian view that they, too, develop their understanding of mathematical and pedagogical ideas through a process of disequilibration and reconstruction (Confrey, 1985; Pulaski, 1980; Steffe, Cobb, & von Glasersfeld, 1988; von Glasersfeld, 1983). Teacher education consistent with this view requires creating activities for teachers that challenge them to confront their old ideas about the nature of mathematics, learning, and teaching with new data, ideas, and experiences. Thus teachers are challenged to build on their previous knowledge to develop new and more robust understandings (Simon & Schifter, 1991).

When teachers engage in such a process, they experience an interrelated set of four changes—in their beliefs about learning, in the nature of mathematical knowledge, in the depth and flexibility of their own mathematical knowledge, and in their repertoire of instructional practices. The speed of these changes is considerably enhanced when teachers are part of a group working collaboratively on these issues within a supportive school system; that is, when they are part of a professional culture that supports inquiry into how students' mathematical thinking develops and how to facilitate that thinking. In the Center's work with

teachers, all four strands of conceptual change are viewed as interwoven, though one or more strands may be in the foreground for research purposes. As teacher educators, our role is to provide experiences that will engage teachers with essential issues in all four strands
and to provide opportunities for them to reflect on their own learning
and the implications of this for their teaching. In exploring these ideas,
the culture of inquiry that teachers begin to construct in their classrooms and among themselves bears a strong resemblance to the culture
of inquiry that teacher educators/researchers in the center, themselves,
are building.

Teachers' Beliefs About Learning and Teaching

For most teachers, conceptions of teaching and learning tend to be
eclectic collections of beliefs and views developed over time (Clark,
1988; Cohen & Ball, 1990). Nonetheless, substantial numbers of teachers hold a view of learning that is not based on a learner-centered,
constructivist view of learning, but rather on the view that children
absorb what they are taught; that the sequence of topics in a class should
derive from the structure of mathematics itself; that mathematical skills
can and should be taught independently from problem solving; and so
on (Peterson et al., 1989; Schifter & Simon, 1992). For such teachers,
changing their teaching to better facilitate students' mathematical thinking appears to require several interconnected changes in belief about the
nature of learning. Among these are the following:

- The belief that students are "empty vessels" waiting to be filled,
  which evolves toward the belief that students are intellectually generative, with great capacity to pose their own questions and develop
  their own solutions to problems
- The belief that students learn by being told what to do and how to do
  it, which evolves toward confidence that students will learn through
  their own effort and can take greater responsibility for their own
  learning
- The belief that the subject (for example, mathematics, science, or
  history) consists of a series of isolated facts and topics which should
  be taught in a certain order, which evolves toward a view of the
  subject as a flexible network of ideas, with many interconnections,
  which can be approached in a variety of ways
- The belief that instruction should follow the textbook and that the
  teacher's responsibility is to cover the material, which evolves to-

ward the belief that instruction should build on what students know and can do, and focus on important questions and ideas in the field

- The belief that students' confusion should be relieved by the teacher, which evolves toward the belief that confusion and frustration are part of serious learning and that students need to experience them
- The belief that mathematics, writing, physics, or history is something mathematicians, writers, physicists, or historians—but not teachers—do, which evolves toward confidence that teachers themselves can use the discipline's modes of reasoning to generate and validate knowledge (Carpenter et al., 1988; Fennema, Carpenter, Franke, & Carey, 1993; Lampert, 1987; Schifter & Fosnot, 1993; Schifter & Simon, 1992; Thompson, 1991; Wasley, 1991; Wiske & Houde, in press)

Of course, teachers' starting points vary, and the evolution of beliefs is a complex process that unfolds in different ways for different teachers, as they relate new information and experience to what they already know, believe, and do.

Changes in teachers' beliefs about teaching and learning appear to take place not only in the intensity of summer programs or workshops, but also in ongoing interaction with changes in their classroom practice (Guskey, 1986; Richardson & Anders, 1991; Wood & Cobb, 1991). As they explore new ideas and experiment with changes in their classrooms, teachers often encounter surprises that further challenge their beliefs about students' knowledge and skills. Sometimes teachers are surprised at how much their students understand and how complex their thinking is. Other times they discover that although students can produce the correct answers, they understand much less than was assumed. Both discoveries can motivate teachers' further experimentation.

Teachers' Mathematical Knowledge

Teachers' capacity to pose questions, select tasks, evaluate their students' understanding, and make instructional decisions all depend on how well they understand their subject (Schifter & Fosnot, 1993; Shulman, 1986). However, because of the way they were educated, many teachers do not have conceptually based and flexible subject-matter knowledge. In mathematics, for example, because their own education has often been primarily algorithmic, teachers may not have had the opportunity to think through the mathematical ideas and meaning that underlie formal mathematical expressions or the algorithmic procedures for arithmetic operations (Borko et al., 1992; Schifter, 1993). They also may not have approached mathematical ideas from several different directions, exploring their interconnections. They need such understanding if they are to help students understand why algorithms work the way they do (Ball, 1991). Teachers also need to be able to recognize both the power and the limitations of their students' mathematical ideas, as well as to see how a particular student's approach to an idea could be connected to other important mathematical ideas. Even teachers with undergraduate majors in mathematics may have an inadequate understanding of basic concepts underlying school mathematics (Ball, 1988; McDiarmid & Wilson, 1991).

But reconstructing and deepening one's own mathematical knowledge is not easy—in particular, it is not simply a matter of taking more standard mathematics courses. What is involved is working through a number of fundamental ideas at both concrete and abstract levels, exploring ambiguities and persisting with one's puzzlement until the mathematical ideas *really* make sense. This mathematical exploration typically takes a long time, since ideas often mature in relation to the development of other ideas. It also is multidimensional—in the process of change, variations of the same ideas, strategies, and issues are interwoven in multiple cases, very like the way teachers access and use knowledge in real teaching situations (Barnett, 1991).

One mathematics teacher describes the difficulty of rebuilding her understanding of a concept based on misconception:

> Because it has already managed to survive a test of time, it's hard to undo that entire structure or network that has been built around the misconception. The process is as much emotional as it is intellectual, as it calls your own competence into question. There is a period of chaos when a concept is being challenged, knowing that it doesn't fit but not knowing how to make it right. (Schifter, 1993, pp. 277–278)

Teachers' Classroom Practice

Knowledge and beliefs become meaningful only in practice; practice in turn shapes knowledge and beliefs. The comments of an elementary school teacher working out a new way of teaching mathematics suggest the way beliefs and practice interact:

> I am so much more aware of what the kids can really do. . . . Before I would never have thought about first grade[rs] trying multiplication and

division. . . . [But] when I gave the children the opportunity, [I] saw how they really [could] . . . solve those problems. Now [that] I realize that they can do them, [I] give them the opportunity. (Fennema et al., 1993, p. 104)

Teaching that facilitates students' construction of mathematical knowledge is largely inquiry (Duckworth, 1991; Richards, 1991; Schifter & Fosnot, 1993). Teachers attend carefully to students' oral and written expressions of ideas and use these to develop conjectures about students' understanding. Teachers offer questions, counterexamples, or activities meant to check the depth, breadth, or robustness of students' ideas; make salient the inconsistencies in their thinking; and help students clarify or extend their understanding. This form of instruction is quite different from conventional mathematics instruction, which emphasizes whole-class instruction, with students listening to a teacher's explanation and watching the teacher work sample problems, followed by students working alone on problems presented in their textbooks or on worksheets, the goal of which is to produce the single, right answer, already known by the teacher (Cohen & Ball, 1990; Porter, 1989; Stodolsky, 1988).

Change toward a teaching practice based on a constructivist view of intellectual development generates substantial dissonance with most teachers' prior ideas about teaching which teachers must work through to extend their knowledge and teaching skills. Reinventing one's practice from within a new epistemology requires much classroom experimentation and the opportunity to share and discuss classroom events with other people—researchers, teacher educators, or other teachers. Teachers may need help initially in looking at their classrooms through new eyes and in thinking through facilitative responses to what they are seeing. Intensive individual consultation during the time that teachers are changing their practice often has provided such support (Fosnot, 1989; Joyce & Showers, 1988; Schifter & Fosnot, 1993; Simon & Schifter, 1991). It also may be socially mediated through teachers' participation in a group of peers working on similar issues in their own teaching practice (Little, 1992; Wiske, undated).

The Culture and Structure of Schools and Teaching

Teachers are part of a complex system, extending from the school and the school district to the society at large. Changes in one part of the system echo throughout the entire system. In describing the experience of three teachers from different school systems, Patricia Wasley (1991) notes:

> Each time the teachers changed something, they found themselves needing
> to educate everyone else in the system with regard to the whys and hows.
> . . . None of them had realized how interconnected and interdependent
> schools are, nor did they realize how complex changing schools really is.
> (pp. 53–54)

Moreover, the current expectation that education will help all students to think well extends beyond what society has previously expected from schools, teachers, and students, with the exception of a relatively small elite (Resnick, 1987). The intellectual culture and administrative structure of most public schools have not yet readjusted in response to this new expectation, nor has the public's view of what schools should be like.

The mismatch between new goals for teaching and both the current structure of schooling and the ideas of the general public puts teachers in the vanguard of a far-reaching social and intellectual movement. However, past experience suggests that if teachers are to succeed in profoundly changing their beliefs and teaching practice, the system must support teachers' change and must change in complementary ways (Elmore & McLaughlin, 1988; Sarason, 1982; Wasley, 1991).

Case studies of teachers undergoing changes in belief and practice have identified specific structural and cultural changes needed to support changes in teaching. Such teachers seek not only larger blocks of time for teaching and greater flexibility in curricular scope and sequence, but also the opportunity to explore an idea beyond the classroom, to integrate the teaching of several subjects, and generally to be able to respond on short notice to the direction of student interest and inquiry. Teachers likewise seek more time for planning, administrative support for collaboration, and decision-making authority to accomplish changes in curriculum, teaching methods, and assessment (Wasley, 1991; Wiske, undated; Wiske & Houde, in press).

Further, teachers who are in the process of changing their practice seek opportunities that amount to changes in the culture of teaching as a profession. Such teachers try to become more reflective—considering what happened in class, diagnosing where particular students have progressed in their thinking, and designing the next day's activities based on such diagnoses (Lampert, 1987; Wasley, 1991). As inquirers into their own and their students' thinking, teachers develop insights about their subjects and about instruction that they wish to pursue. Such teachers want the freedom to express their doubts and uncertainties but often find it difficult to admit that they do not have all the answers, that they are themselves continuing to learn. Finally, teachers truly enjoy working together with colleagues, although many find it difficult to emerge from their traditional isolation (Wasley, 1991). These tendencies imply the need for a new culture of teaching that would encourage reflection, experimentation, ongoing learning, uncertainty, and collegiality.

However, if such changes are to become a permanent part of school life, there will need to be not only a "restructuring" of current school schedules and curricula, but also a "reculturing" of school (Fullan, 1993). That is, not only is it necessary for teachers to reinvent mathematics instruction from within a new conceptual frame, it also is necessary for teachers and administrators together to reinvent school culture from within a new conceptual frame. What is needed is to develop a school culture in which ongoing intellectual curiosity is encouraged for everyone—students, teachers, and administrators; in which teachers and administrators develop working relationships that are more like problem-solving partnerships than like hierarchies; and in which all parties share an understanding of the nature of learning and teaching that will occur there and do their part to make it happen (Fullan, 1993; Nolan & Price, 1992; Senge, 1990).

THE CENTER FOR THE DEVELOPMENT OF TEACHING

The Center's research and development program is built on this emergent body of knowledge and aims to extend it in particular directions. We are currently interested in the impact of teachers' mathematics knowledge on their instructional options, in the role of affect in teacher change, in the nature of the professional culture that supports teaching for understanding, in the role of material resources in the process of teacher change, and in the process of teacher education itself.

Four basic principles underlie the design of the Center's practical work with teachers:

1. Since knowledge is subject specific, studies of teachers in transition and programs to help teachers change are particular to the subjects teachers teach and include opportunities for teachers to explore and deepen their own knowledge of the subject matter.
2. Since teachers build their professional knowledge through their work in classrooms as well as in summer programs and workshops, studies of teachers in transition and programs to help teachers de-

velop their knowledge, beliefs, and practice are designed to take place over time and to include opportunities to reflect on and change classroom practice.
3. Since knowledge is personally constructed, professional development programs support teachers' deep and robust construction of knowledge about their subjects and about learning and teaching.
4. Since doing mathematics, science, history, or writing entails being part of a community of inquirers, communities are created in which teachers are engaged in inquiry into subject matter and pedagogy. When they have become inquirers, teachers are engaged in the same fundamental enterprise as researchers, and a "layered" community of inquiry is created—students inquiring into mathematics and what it means to understand it; teachers inquiring into mathematics, students' mathematical thinking, and teaching practice; teacher educator/researchers inquiring into teachers' mathematical and pedagogical thinking, change in teachers' practice, and their own practice as teacher educators.

The experience of one recent summer workshop illustrates how the Center weaves the several strands of teacher change together in its programs, creates contexts in which teachers can confront the limits of their knowledge, and enacts a pedagogy meant to support teachers' construction of knowledge.[1] During two weeks in July and one week at the end of August, elementary school teachers had the opportunity to reconstruct some of their mathematics, reconsider their beliefs about how children learn mathematics, experience being part of a culture of inquiry, and begin to explore the implications of this work for their classroom practice.

The mathematics work of the summer institute included (1) a variety of explorations into basic arithmetic operations, (2) explorations into the nature of number systems, (3) work on measurement, and (4) explorations of functions and patterns. Teachers had the opportunity to reconsider some of their beliefs about how children learn mathematics through a set of activities in which they viewed and discussed videotapes of clinical interviews with elementary school students, observed and discussed live clinical interviews, and conducted their own clinical interviews with children they knew. By examining how a child who succeeded algorithmically could fail to explain his or her thinking sensibly, or to make connections to related ideas, teachers were challenged to reconsider what it means to understand mathematics.

The institute was conducted in such a way that it, itself, created a culture of inquiry. Mathematical exploration was experiential, using manipulatives, diagrams, and software tools as appropriate. Teachers often did their work in cooperative groups, and the staff used a style of teaching consistent with the vision of the NCTM *Standards*. Because of this modeling, there was regular discussion that analyzed the activities of the institute themselves, both mathematically and pedagogically. Finally, teachers were encouraged to reflect on the implications of the institute for their own instructional practice.

The goal of the work of the summer institute is to provide teachers many opportunities to explore the boundaries of their knowledge of mathematics, the nature of children's mathematical thinking, and the nature of teaching. In particular, in providing teachers with opportunities to deepen their own mathematics, they also have the opportunity to reflect on what it means to learn mathematics—reflections that can inform their ideas about what it means for students, too, to learn mathematics.

The Case of Starfish Math

In what follows, we describe one activity in depth to make clear the intellectual dynamics of the work. This activity, which typically takes place toward the end of the first week of the first-year summer institute, takes several half-days. "Starfish Math" focuses on numeration, number systems, and place value.[2] The context presented to the teachers is a society that has used the numerals "0" for none of something, "A" for one of something, "B" for ** , "C" for ***, and so forth up to "Z" for ************************ and "Lots" for anything more than that. A mathematician has discovered a system using only the numerals "0, A, B, C, D" in which all numbers, even "Lots", can be expressed exactly, but unfortunately, she was in an accident before having had time to explain the system. Fortunately, she left some "artifacts" of her system. In the attempt to re-create her system, teachers use base-5 manipulatives to invent number systems using just these digits, to develop ways to write numerals for different numbers in their systems, and to calculate in their systems.

Understanding place value is essential to working with our number system. Yet teachers often underestimate what is difficult about such a system—that the value of a digit varies depending on its place in a numeral; that this requires the use of a place holder, namely 0, for the instances in which no groups of a certain value are required to build the number; and that the system's very compactness and flexibility are a source of both strength and student difficulties. For example, while teachers may ask students to "pay attention to what place" a numeral is in to understand its value, it is not clear to teachers why this is not a trivial request. Teachers may not understand the confusion students feel between the view that 0 means nothing, no matter where it is, and that somehow it means something different when it's in the tens place than when it's in the hundreds place. Because it is familiar, teachers often assume a place value system is "the obvious" system. They are surprised when they find that their own inventions vary widely.

By asking teachers to invent a numeration system from scratch, we give them a chance to grapple with their own ideas about numbers and how they are represented, as well as to compare different systems. By providing manipulatives that embody a base-5 system, to which the rules from base-10 place-value aren't trivially transferred, we confront teachers with some of their own incomplete thinking about numeration and place value, and we give them a chance to explore these ideas and make them more robust.

The task is, typically, quite difficult. While teachers use manipulatives correctly to show quantity, they usually generate a variety of written systems to describe these quantities, each of which makes sense. These systems often resemble historically constructed systems: the Egyptian or Roman numeral system, the Chinese or Mayan systems, and our Hindu–Arabic place-value system, among others. While other systems are more concrete in their representations of quantity, this is not true of a place-value system. Teachers usually find that the place-value representation, because it is so concise, is also more difficult because it requires more abstract, assumed knowledge—namely, that value depends on a digit's position in a numeral. As teachers struggle to interpret these different representations of quantity, they begin to see some of the difficulties of understanding a place-value system.

After exploring the problem in small groups for a morning, teachers present their systems to one another and we discuss both the specific content of the systems and what was learned about the mathematics and about the process of learning and teaching. Teachers then spend some time exploring one another's systems and working on methods of computing in each. Those who didn't invent a place-value system have a chance to explore it, while those who transferred knowledge about our base-10 system to base-5 get a chance to examine other systems.

Our experience is that this exploration is important both in the opportunities it provides teachers to grapple with differences in the systems and in the affirmation it provides teachers that their inventions are worthy of exploration—thereby modeling what might be important for students. As teachers try to compute using these systems, they discover how important the availability of the manipulatives is in helping them understand processes and how to record them; they find that knowing their "facts" is important to facilitate quick computation, but that seeing where these facts come from is even more critical; and they begin to evaluate the utility and efficiency of different systems from the standpoint of someone learning them for the first time.

They discover that number systems and the algorithms used to work within them are inventable by ordinary humans, that different algorithms work better within different numeration systems, and that they can develop criteria for choosing one system over another, or choosing to use different ones in different circumstances. They also explore the importance of developing new ideas in the context of a community of inquiry—discussing, disputing, supporting, developing, and refining ideas until all members understand them and feel they are robust. As we explore manipulations in base-5, we also examine curriculum materials and resource books to see how these materials develop the important ideas of place value and computation. With the new understanding they've developed about both mathematics and pedagogy, teachers return to these often familiar materials with an eye to how they can be adapted to help students better grapple with important concepts.

The summer's work is followed by biweekly "inquiry groups" that meet throughout the school year to explore ideas and issues that arise out of teachers' classroom practice. Inquiry groups, too, weave together mathematical exploration, changes in beliefs and teaching practice, and opportunities for conceptual dissonance in several dimensions in the context of a new culture of mutual inquiry and support. In these small, school-based groups, teachers learn to reflect together on issues of mathematics learning and practice. They ask one another questions, offer alternative perspectives and suggestions, and generally help one another broaden and deepen the range of ideas available for consideration by each individual participant. By sharing particular personal experiences in the process of change—both struggles and triumphs—teachers remember and affirm for one another that learning can be both arduous and joyous, whether for themselves, their colleagues, or their students.

Teachers bring to the inquiry group issues from their practice that they wish to think about further, with the help of colleagues. Often this involves making sense of students' thinking—an activity that we start in the summer by listening to students on videotapes or in one-on-one interviews but that seems much more salient in the context of the group of children for whom one is responsible throughout the year.

Sometimes teachers bring to the group small "case studies" of children they are worried about for some reason—usually those who either seem bored or lost. By examining the evidence of a child's work and behavior in math class, the group helps the teacher develop both a deeper understanding and alternative hypotheses about what is going on for that child. This analysis can lead to ideas for further work with the child.

Teachers also bring explicitly pedagogical issues to the group—that is, questions about *how* to help students grapple with important mathematical ideas. Late in the first year of inquiry group meetings, one teacher came to the group asking for help designing an activity that would get the children "having a heated debate about the issues." Through some discussion it became clear that "the issues" she wanted them to debate involved understanding the equivalence of multiple ways of representing a number within a place-value framework. By probing deeply into the concepts that the teacher felt were important for students to grapple with, the group was able to come to an informed analysis of what the teacher should do next and together designed an activity. Interestingly, the teacher later reported that the activity hadn't engendered the heated debate she wanted, because the students found the equivalence of these representations much more obvious than she had expected. But while the activity "flopped," since it didn't meet her goals, it gave the teacher valuable information about her students' understanding.

As teachers work together to analyze and understand one another's practice, they begin to see themselves as a community of professionals examining issues of teaching in order to improve it. This is far different from the unreflective and unanalyzed "swapping" among teachers of activities "that work." Teachers start asking questions that challenge assumptions and probe deeper into the nature of the content or the students' understanding. The transformation of teaching from delivery of knowledge to inquiry about students' mathematical thinking and the nature of teaching practice moves teachers into a realm quite like that which teacher educator/researchers inhabit.

Center Education and Research Projects

The Center currently has five teacher education and research projects through which we work with elementary teachers on the teaching of mathematics. All of the Center's work is based on the premise that most teachers need to change their epistemological orientation and reconstruct their practice. Work with teachers uses a pedagogy which assumes that the intellectual development of teachers, too, proceeds according to constructivist principles. Our work treats all four strands of teacher change—change in beliefs about learning, deepening of mathematical knowledge, change in instructional practice, and development of a new professional culture—in an integrated way. Center projects and the central issues they address are described below.

Teaching to the Big Ideas. Directed by Deborah Schifter, funded by the National Science Foundation, Teaching to the Big Ideas (TBI) is a four-year professional development and research project in which teachers and staff collaboratively address the development of elementary teachers' mathematical understanding and how it affects instruction; the interaction of teacher development and curriculum reform; and the central mathematical ideas that emerge in classroom contexts as teachers open up their teaching to students' ideas. During the first two years—through two summer institutes, biweekly after-school meetings, and biweekly classroom visits—participants explore mathematics content and reflect on the nature of mathematics, how it is learned, and the implications of these new insights for their own instruction. During the latter two years, two summer institutes and an academic-year course are geared toward helping participants become teacher leaders.

TBI's research agenda is complex. With regard to teachers' developing mathematical understandings and their effect on instruction, the issue is how to characterize and assess the process by which teachers develop a level of mathematical understanding adequate for facilitating students' construction of significant mathematics. Finally, what *are* the big ideas, or core concepts, of mathematics that emerge as elementary teachers transform their instruction? Teachers and staff developers, both collaboratively and separately, identify big ideas as they arise in the classroom, examining how big ideas shift, change, and grow across grade levels.

Mathematics for Tomorrow. Directed by Barbara Scott Nelson, funded by the National Science Foundation, Mathematics for Tomorrow (MFT) is a four-year, systemically embedded teacher development and research project, in which we explore the individual process of teacher change; the culture of biweekly inquiry groups, through which teachers help one another examine and change instructional practice; and the process by which building principals, district math supervisors, and teachers can work together to "reculture" schools. For teachers, the program consists of two summer institutes, biweekly inquiry group meetings during two academic years, four day-long workshops each academic year, and four classroom consultations each academic year. There is a parallel program for building principals and district administrators. In its work with teachers and with administrators, this project focuses on what is needed to develop a culture—in the classroom, in the inquiry group, in the school—in which ongoing intellectual curiosity is encouraged for everyone—students, teachers, and administrators. Research questions focus on the nature and patterns of teachers' change, the culture of inquiry groups, and implications for administrators' change and practice.

Teachers' Resources Network. Directed by Linda Ruiz Davenport, supported by the DeWitt Wallace–Reader's Digest Fund, Teachers' Resource Network (TRN) seeks to discover the potential role of material resources (books, articles, videotapes and transcripts of clinical interviews, curriculum materials, descriptions by teachers of their own change processes, and so on) in the process of teacher change. Teachers work together in facilitated after-school inquiry groups and participate in a facilitated, multisite electronic network. TRN seeks to identify the characteristics of resources that seem to be particularly powerful in challenging teachers' beliefs and assumptions about mathematics, mathematics teaching, and mathematics learning as well as to explore the ways in which teachers find different kinds of meaning in resources at different points in the process in which their own ideas and beliefs change. Research questions concentrate on issues such as the resources teachers choose at various points in their careers, the role of inquiry groups, and the nature of discourse over the electronic network.

Affective Aspects of Transforming Teaching. Directed by Lynn T. Goldsmith, funded by the National Science Foundation, Affective Aspects of Transforming Teaching (AATT) explores the emotional side of teacher change by investigating the kinds of feelings teachers experience as they work to transform their practice; the conditions that stimulate strong emotional responses in teachers; the ways in which emotions can support or interfere with the process of changing teaching practice; teachers' awareness of their own affect and its influence on their practice; and whether there are "signature" emotional mixes that characterize certain phases of the process of teacher change.

Making fundamental changes in teaching is no easy task, even for teachers who deeply wish to do so. While researchers and teacher educators are aware that making significant changes in teaching practice stimulates strong emotions, there has been little systematic study of the issue. The work being conducted in this project has both practical and theoretical contributions to make—practical in that we will be able to do a better job of helping teachers to develop their practice when we can take into account all the aspects of the process; theoretical in the contribution it makes toward an integrated account of thought and feeling in complex human endeavors.

Network of Affiliated Schools. Directed by Christine Kaplan, supported by the DeWitt Wallace–Reader's Digest Fund, Network of Affiliated Schools (NAS) is a national network of school districts committed to exploring new modes of professional development. Current members include Boston, Arlington, Brookline, and Cambridge, Massachusetts; Decatur, Georgia; Salt Lake City; San Antonio, Texas; Bloomfield, New Mexico; and San Francisco. Together with the Center's staff, these districts comprise a national discourse community on issues of professional development. Affiliated districts collaborate with the Center on its funded projects, participate in an issues-oriented electronic mail system with one another and with Center staff, and meet annually to discuss issues of mutual interest. NAS seeks to identify the issues that districts find problematic as they move toward reformed instruction and the ways in which professional development issues are clustered with other issues—curriculum redefinition, assessment, decentralization of policymaking, and so on—in the process of educational policymaking at the district level.

The Center's teacher education and research program has been underway for about three years. So far, our experience confirms that of colleagues who have provided teachers with the opportunity to change beliefs, deepen subject-matter knowledge, and reconstruct their practice (Fennema et al., 1993; Russell & Corwin, 1993; Schifter, 1996; Schifter & Fosnot, 1993; Wood & Cobb, 1991). Specifically, examining one's conceptions of learning, teaching, and mathematics, as well as reconstructing one's instructional practice, takes time (years, not weeks), requires a small and supportive community in which one's intellectual and practical struggles are sympathetically understood and supported, and consists of an iterative movement between changes in belief and changes in practice.

As our work proceeds, we will come to understand more about individual trajectories of change, the roles of affect and growing mathematical knowledge in the process, the contribution that materials can make, and the nature of teacher and school cultures that legitimate and support intellectual work on the part of students, teachers, and administrators.

CONCLUSION

The current education reform environment, with its expectations for mathematics instruction that build on students' understanding and provide opportunities for students to work together in viable intellectual communities, creates the need for new forms of teacher development. Teachers need the opportunity to examine their fundamental beliefs about learning and teaching, deepen their mathematical knowledge, and reconstruct their practice from within a new conceptual frame.

The process of coming to question and then gradually reconstruct prior beliefs and knowledge is lengthy and difficult. It requires sustained supportive contexts that provide both challenge and help, respectful and affectionate collegiality, and opportunities to examine one's own teaching over time and to explore new modes of seeing and acting in the classroom. This kind of respectful, ongoing, simultaneous support and challenge is a central feature of a pedagogy designed to support the intellectual development that unfolds via dissonance and reconstruction, whether used by teachers with students or by teacher educators with teachers.

There is a modest research literature that examines the constituent processes of teacher change, but much remains to be learned about the process by which teachers reinvent their practice and, indeed, about the very nature of this new form of practice. Further, working with teachers as they reinvent their practice provides the opportunity to develop "layered" communities of inquiry in which students investigate mathematics and what it means to understand it; teachers investigate students' mathematical thinking and the nature of teaching practice; and teacher educator/researchers investigate teachers' mathematical and pedagogical thinking, the process by which they change their practice, the contexts that support change, and their own practice. Such "layered" communities of inquiry imply that all parties inhabit the same epistemological space and learn together.

NOTES

Acknowledgments. The work on which this chapter is based has been supported by grants from the DeWitt Wallace–Reader's Digest Fund and the National Science Foundation—Grant # ESI 9524479. Any opinions, findings, and conclusions or recommendations expressed in this paper are those of the authors and do not necessarily reflect the views of the National Science Foundation. We are indebted to our colleagues Tom Bassarear, Ellen Davidson, Linda Ruiz Davenport, Lynn Goldsmith, Annette Sassi, and Deborah Schifter for many useful discussions, from which the work of the Center has grown. We also are indebted to Ilene Kantrov for her many contributions to an earlier version of this paper.

1. This work was conducted as part of the Mathematics for Tomorrow project and was designed and conducted by Jim Hammerman, Ellen Davidson, and Tom Bassarear.

2. "Starfish Math" is adapted from "X-Mania," designed by Martin A. Simon and used at the SummerMath for Teachers Program, Mt. Holyoke College, South Hadley, Massachusetts, since 1984. A version of "X-Mania" is also described in Fosnot (1989).

Chapter 2

Teaching the Way Children Learn

Beverly Falk

Rooted in the assumption that all human beings have a deep drive to make sense of the world (Carini, 1987), constructivism sees learning as motivated by interest and shaped by individuals' cultural and linguistic backgrounds as well as their different learning styles and strengths (Carini, 1986; Gardner, 1983). In the constructivist view, learning is supported by multiple experiences and social interactions, rather than by solitary drill and rote memorization (Dewey, 1916, 1902/1956; Piaget, 1973; Piaget & Inhelder, 1969; Vygotsky, 1978). It is a nonlinear process that requires extended periods of time in which to visit and revisit ideas until they are organized into coherent, stable, and generalizable understandings (Bruner, 1966; O'Brien, 1987).

Because constructivist principles are based on knowledge of learning, they provide a good starting place for school improvement efforts aimed at supporting students to become better thinkers, creators, and problem solvers. Without such a focus, reform efforts run the risk of merely "reforming again, again, and again" (Cuban, 1990), focusing on the surface structures of schooling but leaving the central problems untouched.

This chapter describes constructivist teaching, highlighting some of its essential elements. It closes by pointing out some of the challenges that constructivist teaching poses for teacher development. It argues that a constructivist approach to teaching calls on teachers to be learners themselves, revealing how embedded within constructivist teaching experiences are continual opportunities for teachers to learn about students, about student learning, and about the very nature of the learning process itself.

CONSTRUCTIVIST TEACHING IN THE CLASSROOM

Constructivist classrooms operate on the premise that learning in school need not, and should not, be different from the many rich natural forms of learning that students have experienced before they ever entered the corridors of a school.

Rich Contexts for Learning

That real-life situations form the basis for learning and teaching is based on the conviction that in the course of trying to solve practical problems, children have continual opportunities to organize and reorganize their understandings and to develop multiple access routes to their knowledge.

Classrooms guided by constructivist understandings often have a workshop-like atmosphere. They provide opportunities for students to actively explore, inquire, discover, and experiment. They offer a variety of learning situations and instructional formats—projects, trips, readings, reports, discussions, fieldwork, and internships. They challenge students to reason, question, draw connections, communicate, evaluate viewpoints, frame problems, acquire and use evidence, and create new knowledge, understandings, relationships, and products.

Social Interaction

Building on the understanding that social interaction is indispensable to the development of thought, constructivist learning environments are organized to include ample opportunities for students to collaborate and to exchange ideas with peers and adults. Classrooms are set up to include cooperative learning and peer teaching situations, so that students can talk together freely as well as question and argue with one another about ideas. These kinds of exchanges enrich, extend, and solidify understandings as well as continually expose students to different perspectives.

Valuing Differences, Valuing Diversity

To enhance this exposure to different ideas and perspectives, constructivist classrooms are structured to include students of different ages and abilities as well as students of different cultural and linguistic backgrounds. The more diverse student groupings are—and the more opportunities that are provided for exchange of ideas among this diversity—the better students are prepared to reach beyond their own frames of reference, to appreciate a range of ideas, and to understand the viewpoints of others.

Heterogeneous and multiage grouping structures provide just this kind of diversity. Classes containing a span of grades take into account students' naturally uneven growth patterns and rates of development. By including students who represent a range of ages and abilities, they provide a flexible environment in which students can find different matches to their varying strengths, interests, learning styles, and paces, allowing each individual student simultaneously to be challenged by some and to excel among others.

Exposure to differences—both cognitive and cultural—can often provide just the impetus needed for a student to make the connection that consolidates understanding of a concept or a skill. A student having difficulty with multiplication, for example, may find that witnessing another student's approach—using repeated addition rather than the conventional algorithm—may turn out to be the way that works for him and helps him learn how to figure it out.

Respect for difference in the multicultural and multilingual world of today requires that teachers make deliberate efforts to be attentive to and respectful of students' linguistic and cultural backgrounds. Teachers need to learn to view such differences not as deficits that need to be overcome but rather as "funds of knowledge" (Greenberg, 1989; Moll, Amanti, Neff, & Gonzalez, 1992) that can be developed to enrich and strengthen student learning. Conscious efforts must be made to incorporate the viewpoints and contributions of the diverse cultures of the students and their communities into the curriculum—to teach about as well as for diversity.

Providing Time for Deep Understanding

Classroom environments in which teacher and students construct knowledge together provide ample time for students to go through the uneven, messy process that is part of arriving at deep understanding—a process that often requires a period of weaving in and out of knowing that is "sometimes forward, sometimes in return, sometimes momentarily intense, sometimes bypassing" (Weber, 1991, p. 11). This kind of learning fosters thinking things out deeply, strategizing and recognizing the complexities of ideas, extending thought in new, unanticipated ways. It values meaning over speed and efficiency. Its goal is to produce that "Aha!" moment—that flash of "Now I get it!" when connections are made to past understandings and are solidified in new ways.

The process of developing such understandings cannot be completed on a schedule; often it progresses unpredictably and takes far longer than originally anticipated. For this reason, constructivist classrooms provide students with flexible schedules and lots of time to explore a variety of issues and topics, allowing them the opportunity, if needed, to temporarily shift their attention and their work to focus on other studies and to return, at later dates, to previously unfinished projects or interests. In this way students are able to work out their own way of piecing together their experiences until personally meaningful understandings take hold.

Integrating the Curriculum Around Big Ideas

Because deep understandings develop in meaningful contexts that transcend disciplines, the curriculum in such classrooms is generally interdisciplinary in nature. It provides opportunities for students to extend the continuity of their thoughts through inquiry into big ideas organized around generative themes. Themes of study match curriculum content with students' developmental abilities. These are large enough to incorporate many perspectives and many levels of participation, taking differences in learning styles and approaches into account by providing multiple entry points for student involvement.

"Changes over Time," "How Things Work," "Motion," and "Beginnings" are some examples of these kinds of curricula. While they develop differently depending on the context and age group of different classroom settings, they are open-ended enough to be responsive to individual interests and questions. They allow students to find their own purposes for learning and to integrate ideas and understandings in their own way.

While the starting point of this curriculum is open-ended individual inquiry, it ties individual students' projects and understandings together through the teacher's deliberate efforts to help them extend and frame their ideas into larger, generalizable themes. This kind of curriculum recognizes the complexity, interconnectedness, and highly personal nature of learning, while it also builds group knowledge and creates shared experiences that help the class develop as a cohesive learning community.

Such a conception of integrated curriculum is quite different from the thematic unit sometimes developed by teachers and textbooks, which parcels out the same set of activities and information to all the students in a class. Even though this kind of curriculum is integrated around a theme and generally consists of more active assignments than paper-and-pencil types of tasks, the ideas in it are developed and organized by someone other than the student. It still transmits information from the teacher or text to the students in a uniform way, without regard for individuals' past understandings or present modes of learning. In contrast, curricula developed through constructivist teaching are not only driven by learners' pursuits of their own questions but also are built to include opportunities for learners themselves to connect, organize, and integrate their understandings from the information they encounter in the course of their various experiences.

Teacher as Facilitator

The role of the teacher in this process is to give the students center stage in the classroom, providing a setting in which the students play an active, inquiring role in their own learning. Teachers act as coaches, or mentors, building bridges between their students' individual interests and understandings and the common skills and knowledge society expects them to acquire. In order to do this, teachers formulate general plans about what they will teach. They avoid fixed recipes and timetables for their lessons and do not feel compelled to have a thorough knowledge of everything that will arise in the course of a study. Rather, they allow themselves to learn along with their students, and they try to maintain enough flexibility to let students' responses shift their teaching, alter the content, drive instructional strategies, and generate new learnings.

Questioning is an important part of the role of the teacher in such a setting. Teachers use questions as a scaffold for learning, asking questions that help their students to become good questioners themselves: Have you seen anything new? What do you think happens if . . . ? Can you find another way? How might we find out? Can you show me where the text supports you? Can you give me an example? How does this relate to our original questions? How does this relate to what we concluded yesterday? Questions like these call for analysis, synthesis, and evaluative judgment. They help students to understand differing perspectives and to differentiate between opinions and facts (Wiggins, 1987). They call attention to the contexts in which other questions arise and suggest still other opportunities to obtain information and to structure experiences in which students can come up against their own thinking so that it is stretched, elaborated, and even contradicted until deeper understandings develop.

Mistakes are greatly valued in this process. They not only reveal information about students' thinking but provide important opportunities for students to rethink their ideas. Because mistakes are viewed in this light, students are therefore less afraid to make errors and more inclined to take the kind of risks that lead to new discoveries and understandings.

Building on Student Interests and Strengths

For the teacher who co-constructs meaning together with the students, no motivator for learning is as powerful as a deep and compelling interest in something (Eisner, 1991; Perrone, 1991). In order for students to be able to play a central role in charting the course of their learning, they need to know what interests and strengths they can draw on to support themselves in their work. Constructivist teachers help students to discover what these strengths and interests are. They then try to incorporate as many as possible of these interests and strengths into their curriculum.

A study discussed on National Public Radio, released a number of years ago, adds credence to this belief and approach. The study followed high school valedictorians for 20 years after their graduation—through college, graduate school, and beyond. It found that these students, the academic stars of their respective schools, did not achieve anywhere near the professional success of their peers who were less successful academically but who nurtured and pursued a single passion as they proceeded through real-life challenges (Goddard, 1994).

Equally important as an ingredient for learning is building on students' individual strengths. Experiencing success and affirmation greatly enhances the learning process. Those who have interests and strengths that are different from those generally provided for in the mainstream of classroom life often feel that because there is no room in school for the activities that they value, there is no room for them, either. By extending the range of what is valued as learning as well as the possibilities for both engaging in and expressing that learning, teachers help students understand that there is a place for everyone in the classroom and the school. They value the builder as well as the writer, the artist as well as the mathematician. They consciously look for what students can do rather than what students cannot do, and they build on these strengths as they develop the learning program for their classrooms.

Assessment That Supports Teaching and Learning

To help them identify students' strengths and interests, teachers consciously engaged in co-constructing meaning with their students use diverse kinds of assessments. These also help them to gain insight into students' different strategies for learning and to determine student progress and achievement. Multiple forms of evidence provide this information. Some teachers keep documented observations of their students as they make things, conduct research, collaborate with others. Some teachers use skills inventories, checklists, and developmental scales that provide them with information about what they can appropriately expect from their students at different ages and stages. Other teachers keep portfolio collections of student work that are compiled over time and that include selected "best works," as well as products and processes that reveal the idiosyncrasies of each individual learner. Still other teachers have students present "exhibitions" of completed studies to others. These demonstrate, in a variety of formats, what students know and are able to do. Many teachers also incorporate students' self-assessment of their own learning. Some even involve the families of the students in commenting on and evaluating student work.

These kinds of assessments provide richer information than traditional paper-and-pencil tests. They are flexible enough to recognize and allow for differences in the ways that students demonstrate knowledge. They drive curriculum in ways that help students better attain skills and information as well as gain deeper understandings of their learnings.

TEACHER LEARNING FOR CONSTRUCTIVIST TEACHING

Just as students learn through active inquiry, social interaction, and personal reflection, teachers learn to teach in a constructivist manner by experiencing constructivist learning themselves. As they apply these learnings with their students, they learn even more about teaching because the very process of constructivist teaching provides numerous opportunities to gain new knowledge—about students, their learning, and the nature of learning.

If our schools are to provide experiences for students that fire their spirits, identify and nurture their capacities as learners, and enable them to be independent thinkers, then new forms of teaching need to be developed that are solidly based on emerging understandings of how human beings engage in learning. These understandings call for changes in the processes, contexts, and content of teacher education and professional development programs—changes guided by a constructivist pedagogy that educates teachers to be learners themselves and that model for teachers the same kind of learning they are being asked to provide for their students. Teacher learning for this form of teaching needs to include many opportunities to engage directly in the struggles of learning, the risk-taking and the thrill of generating new ideas; continually investigate the learning process so that teachers gain ever deeper understandings of how disciplines connect and involve different modes of inquiry; become ever more conscious and responsive to the ways in which differences impact on the learning process; and communicate clearly what teachers know and how they teach to support student growth and development.

Changes such as these in teacher education will support teachers in becoming powerful thinkers. Powerful thinkers make powerful teachers, and it is this kind of educator that is required to provide the students of our nation with an education that supports them to be powerful themselves, developing the skills and capacities they need to take charge of their own thinking and their own lives.

Chapter 3

Constructivism and School Reform

Martin G. Brooks and Jacqueline Grennon Brooks

When schools attempt to impart one truth to all students, to standardize experiences, to control contexts, and to ignore relevance, they are operating in opposition to central principles of human learning. They are organizing around issues of administration, not issues of education. Prawat (1992) discusses four basic sets of beliefs about teaching and learning that, in his view and in ours, perpetuate this deeply rooted, misguided model of education. These beliefs are held by many teachers and administrators, as well as parents, and they interfere with attempts at reform that promote a constructivist approach to education.

Becoming a constructivist teacher for many people requires a major shift in the assumptions about teaching and learning. For example, most teachers assume that students learn most effectively when they are taught part to whole, largely because this is how most teachers have been trained. Think, for example, of the teaching of reading. It was not so long ago that "forward-thinking" educators viewed reading in school as a combination of decoding, practice with the sound/symbol relationship, and exposure to visual and auditory discrimination activities, while less "forward-thinking" educators viewed reading in school as detailed lists of skills to be mastered, skills such as initial consonant blends and the schwa sound.

The whole-language movement has, for many teachers, called both of these sets of assumptions about learning to read into question. Some teachers who now advocate a holistic approach to the teaching of reading work in school systems that encouraged them to reflect on new teaching practices. This required them to confront their current beliefs.

Other teachers who now advocate a holistic approach to the teaching of reading work in school systems that required them to change their practices with little or no institutional time for reflection. What both groups share in common, however, is a sense of disequilibrium (either internally constructed or externally provoked) that caused them to rethink and change their practices. There are other teachers in both types of school systems, however, who participated in the same inservice opportunities and/or were given the same dictates who did not experience disequilibrium, did not reflect on their practices, and did not change. Learning for teachers, just like learning for students, is invitational.

CONSTRUCTIVIST ASSUMPTIONS

In our view, constructivist education is underpinned by a set of assumptions about teaching and learning that contravene many of the normative assumptions about education in this nation. The following is a brief discussion of some of these assumptions.

Assumption 1: Students construct deeper meaning when teachers present curriculum whole to part with emphasis on broad concepts. This is how we learn, and curricula need to be organized accordingly. When the learner is presented with broad concepts—large "wholes" to be explored—narrower concepts and discrete skills become more focused and understandable. In fact, students often seek to construct the parts themselves once they have "seen" the wholes.

A lesson about electricity can provide an example. Some teachers give students information about batteries, wires, bulbs, and switches, then distribute the materials to them with a step-by-step explanation of how to build a circuit. Other teachers place batteries, bulbs, wires, and switches on the students' desks at the onset of the lesson and say, "Can you find some ways to make these bulbs light up?" The student "products" that emerge from these two approaches are usually different. Through the former approach, most students become concerned with following directions; they construct the type of circuit instructed by the teacher and then wait for further instructions. Through the latter approach, students usually focus on the materials, often fashion a variety of circuits, and ask one another and the teacher many questions. In the sequence of events for the learner, the construction of deep understanding is usually triggered more by a good question or problem and access to appropriate materials than by a carefully sequenced lesson that purports to introduce concepts piece by piece.

Assumption 2: Students construct deeper meaning when their questions are highly valued. Where adherence to a fixed curriculum is the standard practice, coverage of the material overwhelms most other considerations in the classroom. Lessons have fixed time boundaries; students are viewed as absorbers of information and teachers, as disseminators. Student questions that do not pertain directly to lessons are often seen as distractions.

In constructivist classrooms, however, student questions are an essential component of the curriculum. Students' questions help to guide the evolution of lessons. For example, in an elementary school class studying the history of Long Island, several students asked questions about the lives of Native Americans on Long Island. Among the questions asked by students were "What did the Native Americans eat long ago, and how did they get it?" and "How did they travel?" The teacher suggested that they make a topological model of Long Island. The model the class built—after much discussion about size, proportions, material, how to read the physical map, and so on—led to inferences that Long Island would be a good area for farming and raising animals. But did the Native Americans do that back then? More information was needed, and the research continued. The unit grew into a lengthy and exciting experience for these students, with different groups of students working on different aspects of Native American life, as initiated by their own questions. Together with the students, the teacher co-investigates.

Assumption 3: Students construct deeper meaning when they engage in curriculum activities that rely on primary sources of data and manipulative materials. Imagine a group of middle school students studying cell growth. Or a group of high school students learning about the habits of different populations. Or a group of first graders exploring the life cycles of insects. The teachers are confronted with a fundamental option in each of these classes. Their students can gather information about these topics through the use of lectures, textbooks, and workbooks, or their students can construct their own understandings of these concepts through exposure to primary sources of data and the use of interactive materials.

Through the use of textbooks and workbooks, students in these classes seek and receive information passively and expect that they can trust that the information is correct. Through the culturing of bacteria, or the tracing of family life patterns in various cultures, or the tracking of praying mantis egg case development, students in these classes can do more than simply find and collect information about their topics. Through primary data and hands-on experiences, students construct understandings—some rudimentary and others quite sophisticated—about phenomena in their worlds. The learning that occurs through these experiences is lasting.

RESPONDING TO CRITICISMS OF CONSTRUCTIVIST TEACHING

Prawat (1992) discusses the amount of time involved in teaching in a constructivist manner and touches on some of the difficulties involved in teaching this way. Proponents of traditional, behavioral approaches to education assert, in brief, that constructivism ignores the central role of curriculum in education and that teaching in a constructivist manner is very complex, difficult, and time-consuming. We'd like to address these criticisms.

In terms of content, the most common criticism of constructivism is that, in contructivist classrooms, anything goes: If the students are not interested in the topic, it isn't introduced or it isn't completed. This is not what happens in constructivist classrooms. The key issue here is not *what* is taught but rather *how* the "what" is taught. Many students do not find a good deal of the school curriculum initially relevant. They do not spend much out-of-school time thinking about recombinant DNA, or Kipling, or the political tensions between Greece and Macedonia, or computing square roots. The teacher's challenge is to help students find relevance in these topics, and this ability is a function not so much of the inherent properties of the topics themselves, but of the approaches used in introducing and exploring them. Constructivist teachers do not eliminate curriculum; they help to make it meaningful for their students through the posing of important questions. Solving a socially contextual problem often necessitates specific information. Once students have a good problem into which to sink their teeth, information has both a context and a purpose. The construction of knowledge reaps many more rewards than does the acquisition of specific facts in and of themselves.

A second critique of constructivism is that it is very time-consuming and therefore interferes with coverage of the curriculum. If coverage of the curriculum implies that a textbook must be read and an endless list of discrete facts must be taught so that students can correctly answer multiple-choice questions on tests, then any in-depth approach to topics and concepts interferes with coverage. If, however, coverage implies the identification of major concepts and topics, then coverage is not a concern in the constructivist paradigm. Time spent on the construction of understanding is time well spent for the student, and it usually piques the student's interest in learning more about the topic. Virtually all of the major reports on educational reform call for greater conceptual understanding. How do we do this? By recognizing that less is more. By encouraging students to construct meaning. By acknowledging the student's present conceptual understandings and valuing what the student knows rather than bemoaning what the student doesn't yet know.

The third critique has to do with complexity: Constructivist teaching is hard to do. But then, any task for which an individual lacks the necessary skills or dispositions is hard to do! Tasks for which an individual has developed the necessary skills and dispositions can be joyful, invigorating, and productive. What does it take to be a constructivist teacher? Constructivist teaching requires negotiating skills, insights into human behavior, sensitivity to human emotions, integrated subject knowledge, self-confidence, the disposition to handle risk, and the ability to say, "I don't know," "Let's find out," and "What do you think?" It requires inherent trust in students' abilities to pose meaningful questions and to answer them. It requires teachers to subordinate slavish adherence to sequential curricula to the abilities and interests of their students. It requires the willingness to withhold one's own answers so that students may discover answers for themselves, so that students will be able to fully explore important issues in their worlds, so that students will want to engage in an exploration. This list of skills and dispositions is not unreasonable, certainly no less reasonable than the skills required to teach in a mastery learning paradigm, or the Hunter model, or the effective schools movement.

THE CHALLENGE OF CONSTRUCTIVIST TEACHING FOR TEACHER DEVELOPMENT

What does constructivism tell us about teacher education? How can the criticisms of compromised subject content and ill-invested student and teacher time be avoided? How can cognitive research provide support and direction for more than 2.5 million public school teachers today? Professional development in today's context poses a dual question of both will and capacity.

Learning constructivist teaching practices means "disequilibration and reconstruction" (Scott Nelson & Hammerman, Chapter 1, this volume). For the individual, such a process emerges from a sense that existing practices are not satisfactory, that there exist alternative practices that are intelligible and useful, and that there is a reasonable path from the old to the new (Prawat, 1992). This process describes how people learn. Teachers teach in the ways in which they have learned. Thus teachers need to experience what learning is like in constructivist classrooms and need to learn pedagogy and practice in constructivist-based professional development classrooms.

As Prawat says: "In moving toward a constructivist approach to teaching, teachers will need to attend to their own conceptual change at least as much as they attend to this process in their students. This will not be easy" (p. 389). No change that is truly meaningful is easy. "Easy" and "hard" are concepts that emerge from one's perspective. But whether or not the change is easy or hard doesn't matter. The change is necessary. Without it, efforts at reforming America's schools may alter school governance structures, the scope and manner of assessment, and maybe even the professionalization of teaching. Who knows: We might even have a set of national curriculum standards. But when all is said and done, the quality of education for students—that which occurs daily in classrooms throughout the nation—will not have been altered. Constructivism, as an epistemological paradigm, provides a radical point of departure from present thought and practice, and it offers real promise for the improvement of education in America.

PART II

A NEW LENS ON
TRADITIONAL ROLES

When practice is designed together by fellow teachers and students, usual institutional lines melt and traditional roles are reinvented. Part II considers how the usual practices of institutional arrangements can be recast as valuable conduits of information and occasions for teachers' learning and growth. As the authors of this section illustrate, everyday aspects of the school environment can be rethought to provide new meaning for those who hold and shape them.

High School Departments. Departments are a fact of life and often an isolating element in the secondary school workplace. In Chapter 4, Pamela Grossman takes an up-close look at a number of high schools in the process of restructuring and examines the role of traditional high school structures. Grossman uses this framework to analyze how the emergent shape of high school departments present occasions for professional growth.

Student-Teacher Supervision. Based on a wide range of conversations with supervising teachers, Edith S. Tatel, in Chapter 5, explores the traditional relationship of supervising teacher and student teacher. Tatel shows the value of reframing student–teacher supervision from responsibility for "imparting of what's known to the novice" to an opportunity for experienced teachers to critically consider their own practice and take advantage of the new research and ideas student teachers bring to their classrooms.

Student Assessment. Assessment traditionally refers to the measure of meaning and substance. In Chapter 6, Kate Jamentz reflects on the lessons garnered at the California Assessment Collaborative and provides a report on the emergence of a reconceptualized form of assessment, one which becomes visible when assessment is examined under the lens of construction rather than as mere measure of meaning. Jamentz shows how the mission of assessment itself can be reconsidered to render assessment an agent of cultural change and professional development.

Chapter 4

Of Regularities and Reform

Navigating the Subject-Specific Territory of High Schools

Pamela Grossman

The regularities of high school life are well known (Boyer, 1983; Sizer, 1984). Teachers work, mostly on their own, to teach the content prescribed by states, districts, or departments, within a finite amount of time. Teachers encounter as many as 180 students a day, day in and day out, for approximately 50-minute classes. Unlike elementary teachers, secondary teachers are prepared as subject specialists. Organized traditionally into subject-matter departments, they are responsible for teaching classes in one or perhaps two school subjects. How can we rethink these regularities so that they can ease steps toward reform, rather than hobble them? What opportunities for rethinking and redesigning classroom practice exist within these very regularities of school life? And how can policies help create and sustain professional communities that will support reform efforts?

Making the taken-for-granted aspects of schooling open for negotiation can spark the process of reform. Sizer's (1992) recommendations for the Coalition of Essential Schools, for example, represent a dismantling of the regularities regarding the organization of time, of content, and of teachers and students. However, as Sizer's work suggests, only by using the examination of any one structure to look critically at the range of regularities and how they impact teaching and learning can reform efforts gain a solid foothold. One underlying regularity explored in this chapter is the subject-specific organization of most high schools and how it affects professional development and reform efforts. As reformers attempt to change other regularities of schooling, such as the organization of time or content, they will need to reckon with the stubbornly subject-specific aspects of high schools.

THE ORGANIZATION OF TIME

Time is both one of the most common and the most serious barriers to reform voiced by teachers and administrators. As many teachers and reformers have observed, a schedule of 50-minute periods hardly allows for the sustained interaction among students and teachers with problems, materials, or texts that enable all individuals to construct and test new understandings of content. Lack of common planning time for teachers limits their own opportunities to learn from one another or to plan for integration across courses or subject matters. Most recently, national reports have urged high schools to increase substantially the amount of time spent on the core academic subjects (National Commission on Time and Learning, 1994).

A number of high schools have begun experimenting with new schedules that provide longer class periods and limit the number of classes a student takes each day. For example, high schools around Washington state have begun to emulate the example of Gig Harbor High School by changing the school schedule to 100-minute classes that alternate by day of the week, with most classes meeting for 100 minutes twice a week and for 50 minutes once a week. This change does more than simply provide longer class periods for science experiments or social studies debates. Almost inevitably, this change will lead to a rethinking of other regularities of schooling, such as what gets taught, how it gets taught, how students learn a subject, and how learning is assessed. For example, changing the schedule so that classes meet only two or three times a week may be opposed by some math and foreign language teachers who worry about issues of coverage and the need for daily practice to achieve mastery. A change in schedule, coupled with a change in emphasis from skill-building to developing conceptual understanding, may create difficulties for teachers who believe strongly in the need for students to master discrete skills before tackling complex problems.

Changing the schedule also opens up for teachers the issue of instructional strategies. Students who may sit still for a 45- or 50-minute lecture are unlikely to remain docile if the lecture extends for 100 minutes. While some teachers will welcome the extended time period to do, in more depth, the kinds of activities in which they have always engaged students, other teachers will find the prospect of longer class periods intimidating or perhaps even contrary to their beliefs about how students best learn.

A natural opportunity for professional development unfolds as schools deliberate proposals to reform the use of time. As changes in schedule are proposed, opportunities must be created for teachers to explore what changes in the organization of time will mean for their curriculum and instruction. Teachers who worry about how an extended class period might affect the way they organize instruction can visit one another's classes and experiment with extended class periods prior to the change. Teachers who feel most comfortable with the change can share ideas for how to use longer time blocks; one school has had teachers take turns trying out 100-minute classes in the year before the change of schedule was to take place. Differences between subject-matter departments will almost inevitably arise in these discussions. Professional development should help teachers address their implicit assumptions about how students learn particular subject matter and how these assumptions fit, or do not fit, proposed reforms. Building time for departments to explore what schedule changes will mean for their particular subject, while encouraging cross-subject-matter discussions to share approaches and perspectives, will allow teachers to reflect on their assumptions about teaching and learning within a particular school subject. If schools simply move to a different schedule, without allowing for these discussions, the reform is unlikely to succeed.

THE ORGANIZATION OF CONTENT

The organization of student learning represents yet another regularity of schools that is being challenged by current reform efforts. Reformers argue that packaging student learning into school subjects may not allow students to make connections across subjects or to understand how to apply disciplinary knowledge to real-life problems. Efforts to create interdisciplinary or multidisciplinary curricula represent a rethinking of this regularity. Reformers urge teachers to develop humanities curricula or environmental studies classes that include the study of science, social science, and technology, or to focus on a common theme across several academic classes.

The chance for teachers to rethink how they organize content for student learning represents another natural opportunity for professional development. Teachers can explore their own subjects in new ways, as they consider how best to help students make connections with other subjects. Working with teachers from other disciplines may also require teachers to make explicit their assumptions about their own subjects and how students learn them. Creating interdisciplinary curricula can also help teachers explore in greater depth what it means to understand their own subject, as well as providing opportunities to develop understandings of new fields.

These efforts to rethink the organization of content, however, fly in the face of both the subject-specific preparation of secondary teachers and the organization of teachers into subject-matter departments (Grossman & Stodolsky, 1994). Assumptions about the inherent sequentiality of subjects such as math or foreign language may make it difficult for teachers of those subjects to accept a curriculum that is organized thematically rather than sequentially (Stodolsky, 1993). The organization of teachers into subject-matter departments also means that schools may lack the intradepartmental leadership required to create interdisciplinary curriculum (Ladwig & King, 1992).

THE ORGANIZATION OF TEACHERS

While elementary teachers often identify themselves with a grade level rather than with a specific aspect of the curriculum—"I teach second grade"—high school teachers identify themselves by subject matter—"I teach math." Subject-matter affiliations and departmentalization are a fact of life in secondary schools, one that pervades the lives of teachers from their initial preparation through their involvement in professional organizations (Grossman & Stodolsky, 1994). In order for reforms such as curriculum integration to take root, policymakers and practitioners alike will need to unearth the implications of this feature of secondary schools for reform efforts.

Current reforms reflect a paradoxical attitude toward traditional school subjects and their centrality to teaching and learning. On one hand, policies regarding teacher certification have turned the tide against teachers as generalists, requiring elementary and secondary teachers alike to major in a discipline other than pedagogy. During pedagogical coursework, students are now more likely to encounter subject-specific methods courses than the general teaching methods courses found in earlier decades (Edmundson, 1989). These changes reflect a belief in the importance of teachers' subject-matter knowledge to curriculum reform efforts. The kinds of curricular and instructional reforms advocated by states such as California clearly assume depth of subject-matter knowledge in traditional academic disciplines such as mathematics, literature, and history (e.g., Cohen, 1990; Shulman, 1987). And the National Board for Professional Teaching Standards (1991) is developing assessments for master teachers built around subject-matter understandings and pedagogical content knowledge (Shulman, 1987). All of these efforts seem to reflect a belief in the deep entanglement of content and teaching.

At the same time, some reforms aimed at the middle and high school urge teachers to move beyond their affiliations to a specific subject. One of the key principles of the Coalition of Essential Schools is "teacher as generalist" (Sizer, 1992). As middle schools move toward a more integrated curriculum, middle school administrators would prefer to hire teachers who are certified to teach across a number of content areas in order to staff these newly emerging courses. And studies of high schools that have attempted to restructure identify the departmental organization of high schools as a barrier to cross-disciplinary curriculum development (Ladwig & King, 1992). In either case, the organization of high school teachers into subject-matter departments becomes a regularity of schooling well worth investigating for the pitfalls and potential it promises reformers.

THE ROLE OF DEPARTMENTS IN REFORM EFFORTS

Although subject-matter departmentalization is the default organization of most larger high schools, policies pay far too little attention to departmental structures as they affect reform efforts. Departments can often play a key role in determining policies that affect teachers' and students' lives. Teaching assignments are often negotiated within the department setting, as are decisions about student placement in particular courses (Little, 1993a; Siskin, 1994). By helping determine the courses a teacher will teach and those a student will take, departments play a strategic role in the "tracking" of both teachers and students (Talbert & Ennis, 1990). Departments also help construct the curriculum within a subject area at a specific high school, recommending courses to be added or eliminated and overseeing the coordination of content across courses. If departments in most schools are indeed responsible for making strategic decisions about teaching assignment, student placement, and curriculum (and more research would need to confirm this pattern), then departments represent a strategic target at which to focus reform efforts.

If departments are to work for reform, the role of department chair may assume a new importance. The role of department chair represents an administrative anomaly in high school life. In some schools the chair is a voluntary, unpaid position, while in others it represents a career ladder of sorts, allowing an experienced teacher to remain in the classroom while also assuming administrative responsibilities (Siskin, 1994). Chairs both retain the credibility of a classroom teacher and represent a subject-specific perspective to teachers and administrators. The power of a department chair to control teacher assignment and other aspects of scheduling may vary widely from school to school. However, to whatever extent decisions about the curriculum, or about student and teacher assignment, are moved through department chairs, they can either support or foil reform efforts. For example, in a recent effort to create a professional development partnership between a local high school and the University of Washington, the chair of the history/social studies department represented the critical link between the university and school. Professionally active nationwide and involved with other professional development activities at the university, the chair was able to broker the proposed partnership. Not all department chairs can function in this way. However, many could, if given appropriate support and professional development opportunities aimed at leadership. Investing in chairs as instructional leaders and providing them with the skills to work with colleagues both within and across departmental lines may help support professional development efforts in high schools.

Despite the superficial similarity across high school departments, recent studies have demonstrated that departments within a school can differ dramatically (McLaughlin & Talbert, 1993; Siskin, 1994; Stodolsky & Grossman, 1992). Departmental differences across subject matters may include differing beliefs about the negotiability of the content to be taught or about the importance of sequence in learning a subject, as well as differing norms about the autonomy granted to teachers of different sections of the same course. These differences in subject subculture can mediate the effects of reform. As Stephen Ball (1981) illustrated in his study of one British comprehensive school, Beachside Comprehensive, efforts to create multiability classrooms at the school were received very differently by different departments, with English teachers strongly supporting the effort and math and foreign language teachers arguing vehemently against such a reform. Finally, the math and foreign language departments were able to argue for an exception to the reform, on the grounds that their "subjects wouldn't allow" for multiability teaching. Recent research demonstrates that math teachers hold a much more sequential view of subject matter than do English teachers (Grossman & Stodolsky, 1993), a difference that may help explain the stance of the math and foreign language departments at Beachside Comprehensive.

Departmental norms and cultures within a specific subject area also matter to teachers. Department members can build a consensus concerning the teaching and learning of a subject that permeates department policies and is communicated to new members. One study demonstrates how math departments at two different schools within the same district responded very differently to a changing student population and to state reform efforts (Grossman & Stodolsky, 1993). In each case, responses to reform were mediated by shared departmental beliefs about teaching and learning.

Departments also differ in their norms of collegiality and collaboration. These departmental differences are of critical import to reform efforts. As the initial discussion of how changes in scheduling may be received by teachers suggests, teachers of different subjects may respond entirely differently to the same reform. Departments will also mediate reforms made at school, district, state, or even national levels (Ball & Bowe, 1992). This suggests that a significant part of the professional development enterprise at the high school level should be subject-specific. Allowing teachers to work through their objections to specific reforms with others who share a subject subculture may be an appropriate starting point. Those who engage in professional development must be more knowledgeable about school subjects and much more sensitive to subject-matter differences as they arise in discussion. However, allowing discussions to take place only within subject subcultures may thwart reform efforts. Structures for cross-departmental collaboration and conversation must be created if interdisciplinary forms of curriculum or instruction are to survive.

Departments therefore represent a strategic starting point for reform efforts. Focusing initially on departments while simultaneously creating opportunities for teachers of different subject matters to talk together might represent one route for professional development. Selecting and investing in department chairs as teacher leaders who have credibility both within and outside their departments represents another avenue. Using already existing subject-specific organizations as part of an overall reform strategy represents a third path.

SUBJECT-AREA NETWORKS AND PROFESSIONAL ORGANIZATIONS

In addition to departments, another subject-specific structure already exists in the form of subject-matter networks, such as the Urban

Math Collaborative (Lieberman & McLaughlin, Chapter 7, this volume; Little & McLaughlin, 1991), or professional organizations, such as the National Council for Teachers of English.

Through publications aimed at classroom teachers and annual meetings, these organizations are able to reach a large number of teachers and represent a valuable avenue for professional development. Subject-matter organizations offer a natural forum for discussions of the subject-specific implications of reform efforts. Policies aimed at reform could consider using these networks and subject-matter organizations more intentionally in designing reform strategies. However, we also need to know more about who belongs to these organizations and what distinguishes teachers who affiliate with subject-matter networks from those who do not.

CONCLUSION

The persistence of regularities regarding the organization of time, content, and teachers in high schools suggests that these will not be easy to change. In addition, changing any one of these regularities will inevitably call into question any other. For example, altering the time schedule will open for scrutiny the organization of curriculum and variety of instructional strategies. The creation of interdisciplinary curricula will run into the departmental organization of high schools. For this reason, opening up possibilities for change in one area may offer opportunities for professional development in other areas as well.

The challenge for professional development consists of understanding the subject subcultures within high schools well enough to know what aspects of reform are likely to be most troublesome for teachers of different subjects and to address those concerns within a subject-specific context. Professional development activities at the high school level that treat teaching and learning as generic may fail to convince teachers of the value of reform efforts in their particular subject area. To the extent that subject matter serves as a filter through which high school teachers evaluate and respond to various reform proposals, professional development will need to identify and address potential subject-specific concerns explicitly.

From this perspective, departments provide a natural locus for professional development activities. Departments already serve organizational functions in high school that directly impact teaching and learning. They also can serve as a local professional community for teachers. As departments are unlikely to vanish overnight from the high school landscape, reformers should consider using this existing organizational structure intentionally to further reform efforts. Strengthening and rewarding the role of the department chair to include more responsibility for professional development can build on subject-specific leadership already available at many schools. Expanding the role of the department chair would also provide a natural career path for expert teachers who wish to move beyond the classroom.

At the same time, efforts to build on subject-matter structures within high schools should be coupled with the creation of new structures that encourage greater communication across department boundaries. The current interest in interdisciplinary curriculum and team-teaching across departments might provide an impetus for creating such structures.

The departmentalized organization of high schools may make them even more resistant to change than elementary schools. If subject subcultures exist within high schools, then reforms that focus on teachers as generalists risk running aground on the shoals of subject matter. At the same time, allowing high school teachers to remain sequestered within these subcultures may forestall progress toward reform. Successful reform efforts will need to navigate between these two extremes. Identifying preexisting subject-specific structures, such as departments and professional organizations, and using them strategically in reform efforts represent a promising middle channel for reformers.

Chapter 5

Improving Classroom Practice

Ways Experienced Teachers Change After Supervising Student Teachers

Edith S. Tatel

Opportunities to learn are often hidden. Under the pressure of daily responsibilities, they become "sunken in what seems given" (Greene, 1986, p. 78). One such hidden opportunity for active development of practice is supervising student teachers.

Many people see supervising as a burden. Teachers largely ignore the potential personal benefits of supervising a student teacher. The very familiarity of the role and the meanings traditionally associated with supervision work against teachers' use of this role as a route to professional development (Grossman, 1992). However, viewed through the constructivist lens, the role of cooperating teacher provides a unique opportunity for up-close learning.

LEARNING FROM STUDENT TEACHERS

In this chapter we listen to the voices of senior teachers who, as a result of their work with novice teachers, made changes in their professional practice. The study is based on testimonials of experienced secondary school teachers.[1] The 30 teachers interviewed for this study remarked that it was unusual for them to consider student teaching from the point of view of their personal professional practice. These were experienced teachers who had usually viewed student teaching as an opportunity for the novice, a time to concentrate on the growth and development of the student teacher, and a time to support the student's induction into "the real world of teaching." But when asked to reflect on how they as supervisors had become learners, they offered myriad specific examples. What are the ways in which the presence of the student teacher opens up professional development opportunities for the senior teacher? I found that the kinds of growth senior teachers described fell into three broad areas.

New Perspectives on Old Content and Method

The student teacher's visit allows the experienced teacher to reevaluate "same old" and incorporate new ideas about content and process of teaching. Many teachers reported that supervision had expanded their curricular repertoires. The practice teachers bring new material, fueled by their enthusiastic approach, to the lesson. One teacher reported on the impact his student teacher's lesson on the beauty of the Northwest Coastal Indians had on him. A band teacher learned from a student teacher who had extensive jazz experience how to teach tongue use, or articulation, in a new way. He learned to articulate sounds for the students that the students then did on their instruments. The new lessons teachers were able to observe up close become grist for the mill of the teacher's own future teaching.

It is indicative of how we construct meaning that, through collaboration with student teachers, the senior teachers often see possibilities for applying methods they already knew about but recognize as meaningful to themselves for the first time. Student teachers offer senior teachers the opportunity to move away from "hearing about" to "being involved with" new curricula and methods (cf. Lieberman, Chapter 15, this volume). New lesson units can be taught in inservice workshops. Finding appropriate context-specific application for one's own classroom presents a challenge. The student teacher can function as key catalyst to implement something new.

One teacher reported that he had been aware of cooperative learning for quite some time. He knew that many of his colleagues had incorporated cooperative learning practices into their classrooms, but he had "never been too big on it." The example set by the student teacher allowed this teacher to discover that the students in the lower level of his math class were highly responsive to cooperative learning activities. By the senior teacher's account, this experience changed his practice. When another teacher saw that her students began to write with enthusiasm with her practice teacher, this experienced teacher changed her practice to include the student teacher's new material and methodology of reading poetry and of bringing related news articles to the readings. Yet another senior teacher spoke of the pedagogical power the presence of the practice teacher had on him. He changed his practice once he saw how his student teacher was able to help the students learn difficult concepts through a collaborative learning exercise. When teaching the concept "nuclear war," he learned to have students set up comparison lists of Hiroshima and Berlin, elicit related fact, compile them under each heading, and eventually let the students deduce the bigger concepts. Remembering how the student teacher drew out students through this exercise, the social studies teacher observed: "Sometimes I need to be forced to change, I must admit. And this forced me to change." Veteran teachers who pride themselves on remaining current with research see student teachers doing familiar things in their very familiar context, but in different ways; and because of this experience, they incorporate new approaches.

Recasting Images and Expectations of Students

Student teachers can remind veteran teachers of the high expectations they should hold for all their students. When student teachers boldly or naively expect every student to recite poems or state capitals or formulae by memory, experienced teachers are amazed at the nearly unanimous compliance. When enthusiastic student teachers surrender chalk and responsibility to students for listing assignments and displaying material, classroom teachers recognize that efficiency can be worthily sacrificed for increased response and participation.

Senior teachers can learn to rethink test construction and discover new modes of assessment through the work with their novice colleagues. One teacher reported how the work with his student teacher brought him to rediscover the significance of assessment. "I guess I had lost touch with the importance of having different types of assessment," he recalled. Having watched his student teacher spend hours designing assessment, the senior teacher moved from the multiple-choice format and other standardized tests he had grown accustomed to, to a variety of laboratory tests.

Classroom dynamics can change when a second adult enters the classroom and when the second adult leaves. Arrival and departure of the student teacher offer the senior teacher opportunities to take a fresh look at the class as a social unit and at individual student needs in this unit. If the student teacher leaves before the year's end—as often happens—teachers must reconsider the classroom dynamic. After the student teacher leaves, many teachers rearrange their rooms physically in order to "shake the kids loose of one pattern." The senior teacher might choose to rearrange the class, and moving students to create new pairs or break up groups.

The arrival of the student teacher can dissolve firm distinctions within the class between teacher and student, actor and audience. It can challenge the classroom's social hierarchy. This change in class hierarchy is partly due to the role the student teacher plays as both student and audience and partly due to the need to teach children to be cooperative and responsible with the novice teacher rather than challenging and discouraging. The change means that the relationship shifts a bit between the senior teacher and the pupils, as the teacher introduces the student teacher, then increasingly includes the student teacher in classroom activity, and then ultimately recedes from the room.

Senior teachers often react to these changes by incorporating thoughtful improvements in their classroom practice. As one teacher put it: "I have to work with the kids, sometimes outside of class, to help the new teacher. This means that I am turning the kids into teachers, getting them to help the student teacher as well as themselves."

Self-Discovery as Solo Teacher, Team Teacher, and Fellow Learner

The visit from the practice teacher allows the senior teacher to rethink his or her own role in the classroom's changed context of learning. One way senior teachers rethink their role is through team-teaching. Many experienced classroom teachers welcome the chance to team-teach with the student teacher, even though "teaming" might mean different things to different teachers. Some teachers share responsibility for a class period or a unit; some share responsibility for different students or groups within the class. Depending on the skills of both the cooperating and student teachers, and on whether the collaboration occurs early or late in the experience, teaming can mean that the student teacher acts as an aide or as a collegial equal. In either case, the senior teacher is invited to stretch and reexamine where he or she "sits" in the class's social hierarchy.

Another way teachers reshape their self-image is on-screen. Because teacher-training programs frequently stress self-evaluation as a pedagogical tool, many student teachers are required, as part of their university program, to videotape themselves in action. Several cooperating teachers, challenged to submit themselves to the same kind of celluloid scrutiny, learned an enormous amount in their private viewing of themselves teaching. "The videotaping let me see myself. One year I saw how the discussion, which I had thought was proceeding quite well, had concentrated on a single student," one teacher remembered. Another reported, "Until I saw myself on the videotape, I had no idea how my facial expressions looked. I learned that I conducted with my mouth open in a funny way. I also realized I needed to pay attention to moving on to a new piece sooner."

The classroom culture will change when a second adult joins. Experienced teachers will take note of that change. Several senior teachers reported that the presence and needs of the student teacher required them to teach with deliberate purpose, clarity, and invention, taking into account changes in class dynamics. Most profoundly, through supervision, experienced teachers have the opportunity to share the joys, challenges, pressures, and responsibilities of their classroom.

CONCLUSION

"Probably nothing within a school has more impact on students in terms of skill development, self-confidence, or classroom behavior than the personal and professional growth of the teacher" (Barth, 1990). The research presented here identified changes that experienced classroom teachers make in their actual classroom practice—changes that improve their effectiveness—as a result of the new perspectives they gain on material and methods and above all on their students and on themselves by supervising a student teacher.

Studying the student teaching experience from the perspective of the senior teacher yields information relevant to education schools, regarding their roles and goals in student teaching situations; to schools and school systems, regarding their assignments of cooperating teachers and their attitudes toward participating in student teaching efforts; and—most of all—to practicing teachers who are looking for ways to enhance their own professional development within the regular working day and the context of their own classrooms.

NOTE

1. This is significant, for most research on the relationship of student teacher and cooperating teacher has concentrated on the elementary grades, which differ from secondary contexts in many ways, ranging from departmentalization by subject-matter expertise to student–teacher relationships and professional collegiality (Brophy & Evertson, 1976; Johnson, 1990; Little & Bird, 1987; McLaughlin, Talbert, & Bascia, 1990).

Chapter 6

Assessment as a Heuristic for Professional Practice

Kate Jamentz

Assessment has taken center stage in school reform as a guide to the teaching of the knowledge and skills necessary to productive life in the 21st century. Long recognized as a potent influence on instructional practice, assessments are being redesigned throughout the educational system to do more than measure student "outcomes," narrowly conceived. Teachers have initiated grassroots projects to develop performance-based strategies, such as portfolios, which can assess the full range of what is considered important for students to know and be able to do. Several states, and the national-level New Standards Project, have announced initiatives to use performance tasks in large-scale assessments that tap students' higher-order thinking skills. Even major commercial test publishers have begun work on products that use more complex tasks based on conceptual understanding.

Reformers envision assessments that will not only measure but also enhance meaningful student achievement. Assessments that require students to tackle complex tasks involving many possible solutions, as well as collaborate on challenges similar to those they might experience outside school, signal to both students and teachers the value placed on this kind of work. By making clear the standards on which student work will be judged, these assessments empower both teachers and students to reflect on and take increased responsibility for improving their own work. When these kinds of assessments are widespread, schools are challenged to provide congruent instructional programs that give students numerous opportunities to prepare to do well.

The promise of performance-based technologies has ignited the imagination of many policymakers, community leaders, school administrators, teachers, and students. However, the key to fulfilling this promise lies in recognizing new assessment strategies as both a challenge to and a vehicle for the professional development of teachers.

THE CENTRAL ROLE OF CLASSROOM TEACHERS

The classroom teacher is central to a vision of assessment systems that aim to improve student performance. Unlike the teacher-proof and decontextualized features of tests designed only to measure student performance, assessments with the potential to improve student performance are embedded in day-to-day classroom practice. The utility of these assessment tools turns on teachers' ability to use them effectively. New assessment strategies have profound implications both for what teachers need to know and be able to do and for the context in which they learn. Teachers' effectiveness in using these new forms of assessment to improve teaching and learning depends on both their expertise in their content area and their ability to develop effective instructional strategies to teach that content. Teachers need a deep understanding of accepted standards of what students should know and be able to do in their content area, the ability to communicate these expectations clearly to students, and the capacity to plan instruction and assessment tasks to enable students to learn it. This deep understanding of content and pedagogy requires that teachers operationalize the standards for quality performances by identifying a variety of behaviors that indicate achievement or progress toward those standards and be able to plan learning experiences that provide opportunities to demonstrate progress.

In addition, teachers who use assessment to improve instruction must have the capacity to develop instructional plans based on the analysis of student work. Performance assessments offer opportunities to examine what students actually understand or have failed to learn. However, these new assessment tools can only improve the quality of student performance if teachers have the ability to use the data they find there to effectively plan what happens next. Portfolios of student work are little more than work folders if teachers do not have the skill or time to find out what students most need and are ready to learn.

COLLEGIAL ASSESSMENT WORK:
INCITING QUESTIONS OF PROFESSIONAL PRACTICE

School-based performance assessment projects provide a unique opportunity to understand how teachers develop the capacity to use assessment to improve instruction. In 1991 the California Department of Education established the Alternative Assessment Pilot Project. Known as the California Assessment Collaborative, the project supported and studied a variety of school- and district-based alternative assessment development and implementation efforts.

At their best, these projects are collaborative, grassroots efforts in which teacher participants draft tasks or make collective decisions about the contents of a portfolio, try them out with students, and make numerous revisions based on the data from student responses. The recursive nature of the inquiry process was described by one teacher: "Developing the prototypes has been an experience for us all. The writers have revised and revised, rubrics have been made and revised and revised, and scorers have scored and argued and scored again." The assessment work becomes an action-research project through which teachers explore questions central to their work.

**What Do We Really Want Students
to Know and Be Able to Do?**

The task of developing meaningful performance assessments challenges teachers' understanding of the scope and essential elements of the content they teach. An illustration is provided by a group of U.S. history teachers who set out to assess student understanding of the controversy in 18th-century colonial America over taxation without representation. The initial draft of the task required students to produce two political posters, or "broadsides" as they were known at the time, illustrating the position of both the English colonial government and the opposing colonists. When the task was shared with other teachers, it generated a conversation about the very purpose of teaching history. The conversation challenged the original task writers to acknowledge the importance of helping students to make connections between historical events and their own lives. The teachers agreed that the task would be revised to require students to investigate cases within their own community where citizens were taxed with little or no input into the decision-making process. Students were then challenged to propose a strategy for an initiative to draw public attention to the situation. As one teacher remarked: "[The project] made me think more about what I am teaching. Do kids really need to know this? Am I covering little facts or am I giving the big picture?"

Similarly, decisions about what should be required of students in a portfolio can expand understanding of curriculum content. Many portfolios designed to assess writing skills require students to include a collection of assigned writings. The assigned writings usually cover a variety of genres and thereby communicate to students the expectation that they should be able to write effectively for different purposes. Yet it is not at all uncommon for the contents of these portfolios to be revised after teachers have opportunities to read and consider the work they generate. One teacher explained:

> After years of reading portfolios written in response to assignments the writing became predictable. We wondered whether kids ever found reasons to write in their own lives and realized we had to change the portfolio to find this out.

The decision to revise the portfolio format was inspired by a newly articulated understanding on the part of teachers about what it means to write well.

Collegial efforts to articulate scoring criteria are also opportunities to expand understanding of curriculum standards and content. Said one teacher after a session in which he and his colleagues developed a rubric for a task in which students were asked to conduct a science experiment:

> I guess I really hadn't thought about how important it was to know if kids could come up with their own experimental design. Before this, I would have given a student who followed my directions well the highest score. This has expanded my thinking. My teaching is going to have to change.

A science teacher in another project suggested the ways in which participation in assessment work can guide teachers to learn more about the content they are responsible for teaching and to give focus to professional growth:

> [This project] has made me realize what I don't know about science. Elementary teachers don't major in science. It forced me to do my own inservice, my own reading, and take classes. Now I've found that the more you know, the less you know.

How Will I Know When My Students Have Learned
What They Need to Know?

Performance assessments are complicated to interpret. Portfolios, performance tasks, and anecdotal records provide a great deal of information about individual students over time. Interpretation requires sophisticated knowledge of how skills are likely to be revealed in student discourse and products, as well as the ability to focus data collection on the most informative evidence and to efficiently recognize its significance.

Teachers in collegial assessment projects discover the rich evidence of student progress available in careful analysis of student work. While overreliance on answer keys may have dulled the abilities of some teachers to see detail in student work, collegial analysis of rich performance assessments creates opportunities to sharpen those skills. In contrast to counting right answers, teachers looking at student work over time learn to ask questions such as: What skills does this student have control over? With what skills is this student beginning to experiment? What successes does the work display that I can build on when I present new material? As one teacher explains, analysis of student work gives direction to future instruction: "When you ask students to write about their learning you find out about your teaching. . . . You get it right away if your students have got the concept."

The development of scoring frameworks provide similarly rich learning opportunities for teachers. A rubric that informs instruction and learning makes use of precise descriptors to illustrate various levels of achievement. Using a close analysis of samples of student work to guide their efforts, teachers learn to replace vague terminology such as "well-organized writing" with precise descriptors of what well-organized writing looks like, such as "states problem and follows with supporting evidence," "has distinct beginning and closure," "uses headings and subheadings to label ideas." Phrases such as "solves problems creatively" become more clearly illustrated by "did not rely solely on models provided by others" or "considered more than one possible solution." The precise descriptors help teachers to determine exactly what needs to be taught in order to help students improve their work.

PROVIDING ADEQUATE OPPORTUNITIES TO LEARN

Participation in performance assessment projects inspires and guides increased use of performance-based instructional strategies designed to help students prepare to perform well. After analyzing numerous samples, teachers have access to graphic evidence that students are able to perform at a high level and must confront their own responsibility to provide opportunities for all students to do so. A teacher comments on the value of these analyses to her professional growth:

When I looked at this prompt, I said "get real, kids can't do that." [But] the scoring session was really revealing. We really saw some

great work. It made you want to find out what those teachers were
doing!

The conversation that naturally follows from scoring opportunities
causes teachers to consider their own instructional strategies and tailor
them to individual students. One teacher illustrated:

> We used the results to target students who would normally slip
> through the cracks. We had data to proceed to work with individ-
> ual students. I realized some students were doing better than I
> thought. I now set higher expectations.

A colleague concurred:

> I've had to wrestle with what exactly I teach and how it can be mea-
> sured. I've found I need to use all kinds of approaches. I tailor in-
> struction to fit students and use different materials to meet differ-
> ent needs.

FULFILLING THE PROMISE OF PERFORMANCE ASSESSMENT

The promise of performance assessment cannot be realized by the
simple production of new assessment tools. When teachers talk about
what they learn from assessment work, they refer to the discussions,
debates, and negotiations that are a part of an ongoing process of collegial inquiry. They refer to the opportunities they have had to operationalize standards, construct and revise tasks, interpret student work, and
analyze what it will take to help students perform better.

Assessment systems with the power to improve student performance need to be embedded into school practice structures in which
administrators and teachers regularly have opportunities to collaborate
on analysis of student performance, to conduct investigations on questions of common concern, and to determine the implications of the
results for instructional and program planning.

There is a danger in times of shrinking resources to think of assessment reform as simply a costly innovation, "one more thing" to challenge a profession already stretched thin. Assessment development
work is often done in isolation from the context of school life and exists
at the behest of special program funds or grants, vulnerable to the
whims of budget makers or competition from the next "innovation of
the year."

But the real challenge of assessment reform is not about what to put into a portfolio, how to score it, or even what professional development is necessary to help teachers use it effectively. Assessment development and implementation is a vehicle for exploring questions at the very heart of the purposes and processes of schooling: What do we want students to know and be able to do? How will we know they can do it? What resources and opportunities must be available to all students to assure that they succeed?

These questions are central to the work of every classroom teacher, school administrator, and education policymaker, and they must be answered by those most directly responsible for making schools work. They will not be answered by the ad hoc "Alternative Assessment Task Force" or by using the latest testmaker's product in schools as we know them today.

Site-level alternative assessment development efforts are most valuable as a heuristic for teacher learning and school restructuring when the task is defined not as making performance assessments but as inciting all those connected with schools today to examine and, as necessary, restructure the work they do.

PART III

NEW STRUCTURES FOR LEARNING AND CHANGE

Within daily contexts reported on in the preceding chapters, traditional structures are in the process of being redefined and reconsidered by all participants. Outside school, new structures and institutional forms have emerged to support this reform of daily practice and foster teachers' learning communities. Reformers' call for fundamental change in teaching and learning requires new opportunities for teachers' professional development. The chapters included in Part III examine the role of new agencies for change located in the broader environment.

Networks. In Chapter 7, Ann Lieberman and Milbrey W. McLaughlin probe the new landscape of outside-school teacher communies of practice; they analyze possibilities and challenges of teacher networks.

Restructuring Centers. Margaret Szabo, in Chapter 8, reports on one emergent external support agent for whole-school change efforts: the California Center for School Restructuring. From this perspective, Szabo looks across school sites that strive to provide an environment shaped through ongoing professional development and elaborates lessons for building communities to promote learning and change.

Action Research. Teachers in the reform era are asked to be both conscious and communicative regarding dynamics of context within a department or school, as well as with students they assess. Demand for reflective practice presumes opportunity for ongoing inquiry and exchange of findings. As teachers' professional development has become central to reform, teachers' research is now central to professional development. In Chapter 9, Marilyn Cochran-Smith and Susan L. Lytle report about their work with action-research networks and collaboratives. They explore the pervasive presence, the possibilities and challenges, and the novel framework and novel centrality of the person of two worlds: the practitioner/researcher.

Chapter 7

Networks for Educational Change

Powerful and Problematic

Ann Lieberman and Milbrey W. McLaughlin

Why would teachers elect to belong to yet another organization or volunteer to attend yet another meeting? What is it about networks that inspires teachers to put in extra hours and to struggle with educational change? Teachers' aversion to inservice education activities—workshops, special skills sessions, generic staff development programs—is legendary (Lieberman & Miller, 1992a; Little, 1987a). Yet the popularity of networks suggests that teachers stay away from conventional staff development activities—or attend only if required—not because of a lack of interest in professional growth but because the inservice training formats fail to meet their needs.

Despite the significant claims that networks make on their time and energy, teachers are as vocally enthusiastic about networks as they are critical of conventional staff development ventures (Lichtenstein, McLaughlin, & Knudsen, 1992; Little & McLaughlin, 1991). Teachers choose to become active in collegial networks because they afford occasion for professional development and collegiality and reward participants with a renewed sense of purpose and efficacy. Networks offer a way for teachers to experience growth in their careers through deepened and expanded classroom expertise and new leadership roles (Bascia, 1991; Carter, 1991; Fine, 1991; Lord, 1991; Smith & Wigginton, 1991).

This piece is reprinted with permission from the 1992 *Phi Delta Kappan, Vol. 73*, No. 9, pp. 673–677.

THE POWER OF NETWORKS

The concept of "network" embraces diverse activities and participants. For example, teachers in the Foxfire Teacher Outreach Network
are introduced to the Foxfire philosophy in a one-week summer workshop. During this workshop teachers become active learners, participating the way students do: choosing a project, planning, doing the work,
assessing the outcomes. These shared activities and experience not only
encourage teacher learning but also serve as organizing tools to keep
teachers working together, sharing, and learning from one another over
time. Teachers who identify with the Foxfire approach to learning try it
out in their classrooms and then seek professional affiliation with the
network. Thus teachers model the kinds of learning and involvement
they hope to elicit from their students. During the periods between
their formal regional meetings, Foxfire teachers keep in touch with one
another and with the mission of their educational collaboration through
publications, correspondence, and electronic communication.

The Puget Sound Educational Consortium, a school–university partnership between the University of Washington and 12 Seattle-area
school districts, began with a group of teachers working on an action-
research project to investigate dimensions of teacher leadership (Puget
Sound Educational Consortium, 1988, 1989). This undertaking eventually led to other teacher-directed activities, including a series of publications reporting the group's work and the submission of proposals for
grants to support future initiatives. The consortium stimulated critical
reflection on practice and made possible the collaborative construction
of new roles for teachers.

Subject-matter collaboratives, such as the Urban Mathematics Collaboratives and the National Writing Project, were created to support
teaching and learning in a particular domain. The math collaboratives
focus on building a mathematics community by bringing together mathematicians from the schools, the universities, and the private sector.
The National Writing Project enables teachers of writing from the
K–12 and the post-secondary education systems to join in collaborative
ventures.

Subject-area collaboratives focus specifically on the critical examination of practice in a particular discipline, evaluating and developing
new pedagogies and deepening teachers' content knowledge. Participants find themselves involved in a professional community in which
they help shape their own learning—a privilege historically denied in
staff development programs (Lieberman & Miller, 1992a). Teachers
work with others who are struggling in similar ways to learn new mate-

rial and to try out different approaches for reaching students. Many become more enthusiastic about their subject matter:

> Geometry was the thing that really turned me on to mathematics. . . . It was so logical and so obvious, I thought God had given me the answer to the universe, in a sense. . . . It's kind of like listening to a Beethoven symphony in a way—this is the way it's supposed to be. (Little & McLaughlin, 1991, p. 4)

Whether organized around subject matter, teaching methods, school improvement, or restructuring efforts, successful networks share common features.

Focus

Unlike the all-purpose teacher centers begun during the 1970s, effective teacher networks are not "generic." Networks select a clear focus of activity and thus target a specific component of the professional community. Those who join the network establish a sense of identity through the pursuit of activities relating to their common interests and objectives.

Variety

Networks provide opportunities for collegiality and professional growth by engaging members in varied activities, such as curriculum workshops, leadership institutes, internships, conferences, and work on reform policies. Network participants stay in touch informally through electronic bulletin boards or by telephone. This "Chinese menu" approach to professional development gives participating teachers an important measure of flexibility and self-determination. It departs radically from forums in which some outside "experts" offer a set of workshops on topics selected for their appeal to the broadest possible audience.

Networks that engage and sustain teachers' interest and commitment blend, rather than differentiate between, personal and professional, social and work-related activities. Most network functions include some social time in which teachers can relax and get to know one another outside the school setting. Indeed, some network functions are purely social, serving to reward participants for jobs well done, to mark special occasions, or to provide a ceremonial affirmation of the network and its purpose. This social aspect of networks is an important ingredient in establishing a climate of trust and support because it enables members to know and appreciate one another as people, not just as math teachers or science specialists.

Discourse Communities

Traditional staff development often exacerbates the already strong feeling on the part of many teachers that their own views and voices are not important—those of the "experts" are. But networks, committed as they are to addressing the tough and enduring problems of teaching, deliberately create a discourse community that encourages exchange among the members. Being a part of the discourse community assures teachers that their knowledge of their students and of schooling is respected. Once they know this, they become committed to change, willing to take risks, and dedicated to self-improvement.

Participation in networks also gives teachers firsthand experience of the constructivist notion of teaching and learning that is central to conceptions of higher-order thinking and problem solving. When they construct ideas about practice with their colleagues, teachers act as both experts and apprentices, teachers and learners. Members of networks report an intellectual and emotional stimulation that gives them the courage to engage students differently in the classroom—an opportunity especially valued by teachers working in urban schools (Lichtenstein et al., 1992; Little & McLaughlin, 1991).

Leadership Opportunities

Networks have made a substantial contribution to the professional lives of all teachers by expanding the pool of teachers who are capable of providing leadership in diverse spheres. Those who participate in networks return to their schools with new ideas and practices and a willingness to experiment. They also display leadership by teaching other teachers or by becoming active in local, state, or national education reform efforts. A teacher from Durham, North Carolina, explains: "The workshops and other Urban Mathematics Collaborative activities have helped me use active listening and negotiation with my students and colleagues. I am now more willing to take a leadership role when decisions have to be made, even though I do not have an official title" (Madzimoyo, 1992, p. 5).

If reformers can't mandate teacher commitment, motivation, and willingness to change, then they must find the means to engender these attitudes. Networks provide teachers with the motivation to challenge existing practices and to grow professionally (cf. Shedd & Bacharach, 1991).

But while networks provide the support, knowledge, and encouragement necessary for teachers to implement innovative ideas, their greatest strengths may turn out to cause their greatest difficulties. Creating an essentially new structure for teacher involvement and learning outside of teachers' workplaces results in new norms of collegiality, a broadened view of leadership, enhanced teacher perspectives on students' needs, opportunities for teachers to be both learners and partners in the construction of knowledge, and an authentic professional voice for teachers. But the new structure is also the source of problems.

THE PROBLEMS OF NETWORKS

Creating a new network, unencumbered by bureaucratic restrictions and free of traditional forms of inspection, is exciting because there is no old political or social baggage to carry and because teachers play a leading role in the venture. Unfortunately, this autonomy is no guarantee against other nagging problems.

Quality

Networks inspire teachers to construct and try out new ideas, but how can the quality of these innovations be continuously evaluated and improved? Close monitoring has not been effective in traditional staff development offerings; in the case of these new arrangements, traditional forms of oversight or evaluation are destructive of the trust, the sense of safety, and the supportive professional collegiality that are crucial to a strong network for teachers. Yet networks need to reflect on and modify their own practices and to obtain useful feedback. Without procedures for ongoing outside review, networks can fall prey to the myopia of familiar practices and the misdirection of unchallenged assumptions.

Application

The practices and perspectives created within a network must eventually make their way into the schools if meaningful change is to occur. Ironically, the existence of a strong, vibrant network can in some cases actually impede that transfer. Networks constitute professional communities that transcend particular workplaces and draw teachers from many sites. The danger is that these extra-school involvements may also draw teachers' loyalty and interest away from the school to the network itself, especially when the workplace setting is a difficult one.

The corollary to this problem is the sometimes chilly reception that network teachers encounter in their schools or departments. Teachers who belong to or are sent to join a network, even if they have legitimate credentials within their school, still have the problem of gaining support for new ideas brought in from the outside. Past reform efforts have taught us that, in order to become part of the school culture, new practices must be seen as credible and legitimate by administrators and by a critical mass of teachers. How can networks both support teacher participants in their efforts to bring new ideas and practices into their schools and protect them from potential ostracism (cf. Clark, 1988)?

The Los Angeles Urban Math Collaborative responded to this dilemma by requiring that whole departments elect to participate in the network, thereby ensuring that teacher participants would have at least a moderately receptive workplace in which to try out new ideas. Yet this strategy is not always successful. If the entire department is not willing to participate, then even those teachers who want to learn and change will be deprived of support for their professional growth.

Stability

Maintaining the stability of networks is a daunting prospect. Networks provide resources for teachers, giving them access to researchers, reformers, and subject-matter specialists and introducing them to new structures or projects that provide the basis for learning. But whatever their benefits, these resources eventually become the focus of new uncertainties. How can the resources be sustained? Who will pay for them? Whose priorities do they represent? If teachers learn new ways of working with students, how can their efforts continue to be supported? Given the slow pace of change in schools, there must be some assurance that the necessary resources will be available for an extended period of time.

Foundations that fund networks see their role as providing seed money or risk capital—not indefinite maintenance. The eventual withdrawal of such support threatens a network's survival—as has been the case even with some of the successful networks associated with the Urban Mathematics Collaboratives, whose funding from the Ford Foundation was phased out. The withdrawal of foundation support typically puts a network in the position of having to request assistance from the very entity from which it sought independence—the district. And the district, pressed by its own budget demands, is at best an insecure source of support, especially if it had no previous role in constructing or defining the network. Yet requiring the district to buy in at the outset is not always a good strategy either, since it risks the independence of the collaborative (Little & McLaughlin, 1991).

Overextension

Ideas that can be transformed into activities are attractive to teachers, as are the networks that generate them. But the success of such ideas and activities in itself creates problems: The more popular the network, collaborative, or coalition, the greater the demand on its limited resources and the lower the amount of time, money, and energy it has for understanding what is being learned and how to apply it. As more and more people join, the networks soon find themselves overextended. Like a business that is successful and expands too fast, a network can expand too rapidly and risk falling into a kind of intellectual bankruptcy. But to limit membership to a level commensurate with the available material and human resources risks creating or aggravating a "them/us" divisiveness among teachers. Managing success is a fundamental problem for networks and their sponsors.

Ownership

The independence of many networks from districts or other "official" structures has been a source of strength because it has fostered teachers' sense of ownership and professional safety—perceptions that are essential to the difficult process of unlearning old practices and acquiring new ones. For most teachers, becoming a learner means giving up some appearances of professional authority—admitting uncertainty, admitting incomplete knowledge. Not surprisingly, teachers are hesitant to assume this vulnerable role unless they feel secure in doing so.

Many networks that are initiated by foundations, by school–university partnerships, or by national or local reform efforts come with an agenda of their own, even though they do not have a prescribed strategy, form, or duration. The success of such networks is frequently the result of strong input from teachers in the shaping of programs and practices. But as these networks develop, a consistent problem surfaces: Who controls the agenda? This question is especially pertinent when a foundation or university is paying the bill and specific goals have been determined. Since the power of these networks lies in their flexibility, the agendas are in a constant state of refinement, rather than irrevocably fixed in time and place. Sometimes, the partners with the money and/or the status become uncomfortable as teachers are emboldened to take more control.

Expanding Objectives

Most networks, while conceived with specific goals in mind, such as changing the writing process or involving teachers in learning new teaching methods, call on teachers to play roles to which they are unaccustomed. Political strategies, negotiation, policymaking, and conflict are all unavoidable elements of organizational change. Subject-matter specialists or others in leadership positions in networks are not usually knowledgeable about the processes of change. Yet without this knowledge, systemic changes may be difficult to achieve and reform efforts will be derailed. How can this kind of knowledge be made accessible, and who will teach it? How can the process of creating, implementing, and sustaining change become part of the focus of networks?

Leadership

Network failures are usually linking failures. Effective networks require the clear assignment of responsibility for managing the network, orchestrating its activities, brokering resources from diverse segments of the community, and promoting and sustaining the involvement of teachers and possible partners from the private sector, from the university, and from the community. To remain effective, networks must tread a fine line between the explicit assignment of organizational responsibility and the temptation to create hierarchical structures to manage the network's growth or to respond to mandates or constraints imposed by outside funders or governmental bodies. In and of itself, hierarchical organization is not a problem. It becomes one when hierarchical structures reproduce the differences in status and authority that squelch teachers' willingness to engage seriously in educational change, when they are used to control members, or when they corrode the links between network leadership and membership.

What makes an effective network leader is also of extreme importance, and we know precious little about it. One does not normally associate bureaucrats with such qualities as being visionary, multicultural (comfortable in school and university, private sector, and general community settings), at ease with ambiguity and flexibility, knowledgeable about alternative forms of organization, action-oriented, and able to nurture emergent talent. Yet this is the stuff of capable network leaders. Without leadership of this kind, networks soon become very much like the bureaucracies they are trying to change. If we do not learn more about the life histories of these leaders and the contexts within which they are learning to lead differently from managers in conventional bureaucracies, we will be unable to find and develop more of them.

Evaluation

Models of accountability or evaluation need to reflect and support the nature and power of networks. As teachers become more involved and their vision continues to grow and change as a result of learning more and doing more in real schools and classrooms, evaluation based solely on student outcomes and classroom-focused goals will fail to illuminate the total context within which teacher and student learning takes place. Traditional evaluation models that measure teachers' success by student outcomes make it more difficult for teachers to be learners as well as dispensers of knowledge. Classical measures, such as standardized tests, do not assess or take account of changes in adult and student behavior, attitudes, and learning. Funders or governmental bodies that insist on such measures inhibit the very kinds of problem solving and risk-taking that impart power to teacher networks.

Goals

The success of networks turns to a significant extent on teachers' perceptions that the groups to which they belong serve their own goals—not goals specified by some outside agent, even a friendly funding source. For example, while the Ford Foundation gave its support to local collaboratives of mathematics teachers, it did not detail specific objectives or strategies. As a result, each of the 15 Urban Mathematics Collaboratives has different priorities, different programmatic characteristics, and different relations with its district, with institutions of higher education, and with its community.

Funders or education policymakers must be aware that goals that are articulated outside of the network, worthy though they may be, could jeopardize the strength of the network. This observation doesn't mean that "teachers rule" or that outsiders should just write checks. But it does suggest that administrators and others outside the network must restrain the urge to use the network to further purposes other than those specified by its members.

IMPLICATIONS FOR POLICY

A number of lessons can be learned from examining the conditions that generate the power of networks and from recognizing the problems that can arise in terms of policy and practice. A most important lesson is that, contrary to cynical generalizations about teachers' lack of enthusiasm for staff development efforts, teachers are willing and eager to be involved in activities that challenge them and that promote their professional growth. A related lesson is that, given this opportunity, teachers can and will make significant changes in their practices and perspectives on teaching and learning. And nowhere have these changes been more profound than in urban classrooms in which teachers are challenged by the demands of differences among today's students (McLaughlin, Talbert, & Phelan, 1990).

The networks that promoted these changes in practice and in conceptions of professionalism illuminate a fundamental lesson for policymakers: The context in which educational change is pursued is everything. Many policies are based on assumptions about contexts for reform that do not take into account the alternatives that networks offer. Instead of targeting individuals and attempting to provide them with new skills or perspectives, networks concentrate on building communities of teacher/learners. It is thus critical that policymakers and others approach teacher networks not from the standpoint of management and control, but from that of the norms and agreements of communal relations.

Furthermore, teacher networks should be viewed through an occupational rather than an organizational lens. Organizational perspectives focus on questions of administration, reporting, incentives, "delivery," and outcomes. Switching to an occupational lens moves the policy focus from a concentration on "what works," framed solely in terms of student outcomes, to an examination of the meaning of teaching for those who do it. What are the challenges of teaching? The rewards? The frustrations? The power of networks is that, by focusing on the meaning of work for teachers, networks can affect student learning—the overarching goal of reform.

The experience of diverse networks suggests that a policy can lever change more effectively if it takes an indirect approach—concentrating on the environments available to support and stimulate teachers' professional growth—than if it directly tackles concerns about teachers' knowledge base and classroom competencies. In this period of intensive school reform, when traditional inservice training and staff development have been shown to be inadequate, networks can provide fresh ways of thinking about teacher learning.

Chapter 8

Rethinking Restructuring

Building Habits of Effective Inquiry

Margaret Szabo

Recent calls for reform set forth a dramatically new purpose for schooling—developing all children—as well as a more ambitious definition of the kind of learning that schools must foster—problem-solving, constructivist, active learning. The call to restructure schools attempts to create the conditions to accomplish these challenging goals. The logic animating school restructuring efforts can be summarized as follows: New purposes (articulated, for example, by the California curriculum frameworks or by Goals 2000) necessitate new structures and practices of teaching and learning.

In January 1993, 144 California schools and their districts embarked on a five-year restructuring effort funded under Senate Bill 1274, "A Demonstration of Restructuring in Public Education." Supported by a broad spectrum of stakeholders and professional organizations, California's restructuring initiative earmarks $25 million per year for five years for selected K–12 schools and districts to engage in comprehensive restructuring. SB 1274 schools and districts are rethinking and creating new structures and practices around six major elements: curriculum and student assessment, accountability systems, professional collaboration, decision making and the change process, technology, and program evaluation. The schools engaged in California's restructuring effort are diverse in many respects: configuration (K–12), geography (urban, suburban, rural), performance level (low, moderate, high), capacity and knowledge base relevant to restructuring, and location along the "change path."

To guide and support the five-year efforts of SB 1274 schools and districts, the California Department of Education established the California Center for School Restructuring (CCSR). From the outset, the work of the CCSR was intended to model a different kind of technical assistance and support—one grounded in the belief that support strategies must be co-created with participating schools and districts. Proceeding from this assumption, the CCSR's work and strategies rely on creating learning opportunities—for schools, districts, stakeholders, diverse regional support providers, and itself—that respond to the challenges faced by restructuring schools and districts. The Center's mission is to create the climate, incentive, and impetus to act on that learning. Together with participating schools and districts, we are devising ways to press forward with ambitious, purposeful change; to learn from our experiences; and to share that learning with others.

WHY RETHINK RESTRUCTURING?

Observations and experiences to date in California reveal many strengths and accomplishments: Schools are using restructuring seriously as a central organizing activity to foster thought, discussion, and action; they are beginning to address major core issues related to student outcomes, curriculum, and governance; they are seeking and grappling with new ideas about curriculum, assessment, and processes for focusing the change effort on the work and learning of students; and among principals and teachers, new leadership patterns are developing that help to broaden inclusion in and ownership of the change process (Inverness Associates, 1994). However, we need to do more than celebrate these important accomplishments. We must also look for troubling patterns, seek to understand them, and help the system build strategies for deeper and smarter work. This chapter is offered in such a spirit.

In addition to successes, the CCSR's own observations and data reveal some sobering trends and issues—ones echoed in reviews of restructuring efforts around the country (Fullan, 1993): Many schools implement programs, structures, or practices in a compliance-oriented manner rather than in outcome-based, intentful ways; "many are more invested in 'doing it' than in 'thinking about it'" (Inverness Associates, 1994); ideas like advisory, thematic instruction, or houses are treated as a given goal of restructuring without agreement about purpose or content; turbulence in the system (e.g., personnel changes) often overwhelms the school change effort; actions to address equal access and diversity tend not to be central or primary in the design of many restructuring efforts; and the majority of innovations are not bringing about fundamental change in classrooms, teaching, and learning—instead, the changes are often supplemental in nature, leaving basic policies and practices unchanged (Wehlage, Smith, & Lipman, 1992).

While it is yet early in the change effort (year two of five years in California), it is time to rethink restructuring and ask some hard questions. Why are core teaching and learning practices so difficult to change in meaningful ways? Why, in ambitious, hardworking schools and districts do structural changes—time patterns, grouping strategies, advisories, more inclusive governance, and so forth—so rarely lead to whole-school change or to dramatic improvement in learning and teaching for all students? What is missing in the restructuring equation?

A Tale of Two Advisory Structures

As a starting point for these queries, witness brief accounts by two teachers about the purpose and use of a new advisory structure in two restructuring high schools (the names are pseudonyms):

Columbia High School. We lose our students in droves. Half fail one or more academic classes each semester. The hope is advisory will help, but we didn't have much choice about it; it was pretty much rammed down our throats. I have 25 junior students in my advisory, and I'll have a different group of juniors next year. It meets once a week for 40 minutes. I'm supposed to help them stay connected to school. Yesterday we got a summary of the semester grades for each of our advisory students with phone numbers for each family. But what can I do now that will make a difference? There's no sense of realistic goals or objectives for advisory; we're not clear on its purposes. We should have had an inservice on advisory to help us. Some teachers use it to teach skills, like filling out job applications; others use it to talk about personal or social problems. It's so new—we just started it last semester—we have no way to evaluate which approaches work. We'll think about that later.

Intrepid High School. Our staff decided every student needs to establish close contact with an adult over their four years here. They also need a way to participate in decisions and governing the school. So advisory is a way for every kid to have an adult they can talk to nearly every day—to get information, to talk about teachers, grades, future plans, school decisions and activities. To do all this, we need both quantity and continuity of time. So every adult in the school has an advisory group of 20 students who meet four times a week and stay together for four years. All advisories do academic and career planning, health issues, issues of concern to individuals or the group. Next year we're strengthening the academic guidance aspect. All freshmen and their parents will develop an individual education plan and monitor and revise it each year. We're also considering the role advisory teachers may play in our evolving student portfolios for graduation. When we asked students to evaluate advisory, they liked the chance each mid-morning to be reflective, discuss issues, and just have an adult to chat with and get practical information from.

Clearly, both schools are "doing advisory"; but Intrepid High's structural innovation has a much higher probability of deep impact on students' learning than does Columbia's. What accounts for these very different ways of thinking about and deploying a new structure?

What's Missing from the Restructuring Equation?

Experience observing the work of diverse restructuring schools suggests that the missing link in the restructuring equation is a robust "culture of inquiry" within both the school and the district. The two advisory tales tell how promising structures lose impact for lack of carefully constructed purposes, design features, and adjustment mechanisms. If the culture of the school (and its district) is one in which thinking and action are isolated, fragmented, reactive, and rule-bound, there is little opportunity for members of the school community to build understanding and commitment to new purposes and thus to use new structures in intentful and powerful ways. Sooner or later, the inertia of old, implicit, and unquestioned practices overwhelms the new structures. In schools with such a "culture of inertia," the more things change, the more they stay the same.

In schools and districts with a culture of inquiry, thinking and action are coordinated, systemic, generative, and self-reflective. Members of the school community build shared understandings that allow them purposefully to design, deploy, evaluate, and revise new structures. The differences evident in the advisory vignettes reflect the differences in these two cultures—Columbia shows a culture of inertia, Intrepid a culture of inquiry.

Restructuring must be equally and simultaneously about reculturing (Fullan, 1993). Structures are tools to accomplish a purpose, but structures per se are purpose-neutral. Cooperative learning and project-based curricula, for example, can be used for drill and skill teaching as easily as for problem-solving and higher-level thinking. New structures and practices alone, without mechanisms for building clarity and commitment to the new purposes and goals of reform, will result in little impact on improving learning. It is what is done *within* new structures, not the structures themselves, that matters most. Further, it is the culture of a school—the beliefs, habits, understandings, and norms about appropriate behavior—that guides everyday actions and determines whether structures will be used intentfully. The culture of the school surrounding learning is the "hardest core to crack. . . . Changing formal structures is not the same as changing norms, habits, skills and beliefs" (Fullan, 1993, p. 49).

Many restructuring schools are "doing things," usually potentially powerful things; fewer, however, are simultaneously reculturing: building the kind of robust habits of inquiry that imbue new structures with purpose and with the energy for continuous adjustment and improvement. We have learned a great deal about cultures of inquiry from observing and working with schools and districts participating in California's restructuring initiative. The remainder of this chapter summarizes and illustrates these lessons.

HABITS SUPPORTING A CULTURE OF INQUIRY

Shifting cultural patterns involves leaving behind old habits, beliefs, and assumptions and building new, more functional ones. The culture of inertia that needs to be supplanted through reculturing is well documented (see, e.g., Boyer, 1983; Goodlad, 1984; Lortie, 1975; Sizer, 1984). Senge (1990) refers to such cultures as "learning disabled"; Argyris (1993) identifies "organizational defensive routines"; Rosenholtz (1991) contrasts "learning impoverished" school organizations with those that are "learning enriched."

Conversely, other studies describe qualities of a more functional cultural pattern in schools and districts—one suited to the new purposes and goals of the reform agenda. Robert Schaefer painted an early vision of such a culture in *The School as a Center of Inquiry* (1967). The work of researchers such as Rosenholtz, Barth, Little, McLaughlin, Lieberman, and Miller builds a rich picture of school and district communities that break the pattern of inertia to think and act in more collaborative, growth-oriented ways. Table 8.1 illustrates the most prominent differences in the overall thinking and action patterns of these contrasting cultures.

But how is a transformation from inertia to inquiry accomplished?

TABLE 8.1. Inertia Versus Inquiry: Qualities of Thinking and Action in Two Contrasting Cultural Patterns

Culture of Inertia	*Culture of Inquiry*
• Isolated	• Coordinated
• Fragmented	• Holistic & systemic
• Reactive & defensive	• Generative
• Rule-bound & inflexible	• Self-reflective

What set of habits—norms, behaviors, processes—support building a culture of inquiry and leaving behind the forces of inertia? How do people in such cultures think, and what do they do? Observation of emerging patterns in California's restructuring schools and districts surfaces a set of habits of effective inquiry, summarized in Table 8.2.

The habits in Table 8.2 are ways of thinking and acting. They are expressed as things school and district people can do—individually, collectively, and organizationally. Importantly, these habits are overlapping and contain one another. Often they are mutually reinforcing; the more one is present, the easier it usually is to practice another. Together, these habits express a vision of a powerful inquiry culture supporting continuous individual and collective learning, experimentation, and improvement.

Such a vision—coupled with concrete examples of ordinary people and ordinary school and district communities carrying out this vision—is a change force, helping people break old habits and choose more effective forms of action. Now we turn to some concrete and specific examples of habits of inquiry in two California restructuring schools and their districts.

HABITS OF INQUIRY INCARNATE: TWO COLLAGES

The actions and thinking patterns outlined in Table 8.2 emerge in varied forms and textures in particular school and district contexts. Offered here are two collages—assemblages of self-descriptions—of pieces of work undertaken on behalf of restructuring in one elementary school (and its district) and in one high school (and its district). The collages illustrate how the habits comprising a culture of inquiry look and feel as expressed in the perspectives and action choices of these two schools and their districts. Ambitious structural change and innovation

TABLE 8.2. Habits of Effective Cultures of Inquiry

1. **Shared Leadership**
   - seeing everyone as a leader
   - embracing "servant leadership"—serving one another and a higher purpose
   - leading from a vision translated into usable criteria to guide actions
   - practicing *kaizen*—responsibility for supporting yourself and others in continuous learning and improvement
   - modeling, coaching, and designing learning opportunities for others

2. **Visioning and Holistic Thinking**
   - developing clarity of vision, purposes, ideas—continuously
   - using vision, purposes, ideas as a change force
   - identifying and working from criteria that express the vision in action
   - seeing and working with the flow and potential power of a whole system

3. **Inquiry-Action Cycles**
   - inviting problem finding and defining
   - examining actions and practices rigorously
   - generating feedback, findings, meanings
   - formulating and carrying out strategies for improvement
   - using coaching relationships and critical dialogue

4. **Generative Discourse**
   - developing informed, defensible, and shared understandings
   - including diverse stakeholders
   - questioning deep beliefs and assumptions
   - viewing perspectives and actions as provisional and always open to revision
   - valuing questions more than answers
   - creating time and interaction formats to support such discourse

5. **Valuing Diversity**
   - using racial, cultural, and linguistic diversity as an asset that makes us smarter
   - continuously broadening and deepening inclusion of diverse stakeholders
   - seeking, including, and responding to divergent perspectives
   - honoring multiple learning styles

6. **Inclusion and Community Building**
   - sharing power; sharing responsibility
   - creating structures and processes for doing so
   - building relationships and mutual trust through collaborative work
   - acting with regard for people

7. **Capacity Building**
   - focusing on self- and locally identified questions of great interest
   - linking to outside perspectives and expertise in ways adapted to local needs
   - experimenting, practicing, and taking risks
   - recognizing that meaningful learning involves personal change; all are willing to change

Sources: CCSR, 1992, 1993; Fullan & Miles, 1992; Kofman & Senge, 1993; Sergiovanni, 1992

are givens in these schools; of interest here are the habits and attitudes that guide how people think about the structures they are inventing and how they decide what to do within these structures.

The comments are drawn from my conversations with various participants and their responses to a central question: What activities or processes help guide your restructuring efforts? The overall thinking and action of each school and district illustrate many—though not all—of the habits of an effective culture of inquiry. The purpose here is to make manifest some of the habits in a brief sketch. The role in parentheses in the title of each segment of the collage identifies whose views are represented therein. The numbers in parentheses at the end of each segment correspond to the seven habits in Table 8.2.

Will Rogers Elementary School
Santa Monica–Malibu Unified School District

Philosophy and Learning Outcomes (Teachers). Will Rogers serves an extremely diverse student population. In our attempt to ensure that every child be a success, we have to work hard at developing a shared philosophy among everyone in our school community. At Rogers we spend lots of time developing, arguing, and clarifying our philosophy, beliefs, and learning outcomes. Over many years and many hours, we developed a philosophy of teaching and learning that is held by all the adults who work in the school. We can all pretty much recite our belief and outcome statements, now. But it's one thing to have outcomes and another to agree on what they look like in student work. It takes continuous work to develop our beliefs and outcomes and then plan backwards, but it's worth it. Our belief statements and our six learner outcomes for exiting fifth graders help us as grade-level teams, houses, and families to plan more coherent learning for kids. They also help us collaborate to a common purpose and keep us from getting lost in just doing things. (Habits 2,4,5,6)

Mid-Year Institute (Teachers). Mid-Year Institute is five straight pupil-free days each winter for us to design and lead our own staff development. We plan in-depth studies of what we've tried, what's working and what's not. We plan roles for everyone—and everyone comes: teachers, aides, noncredentialed staff, nurses, parent classroom volunteers. We all learn and we all lead something. We discuss, argue, and build our belief statements. We also look at our major actions and strategies and check how it's going. (Habits 1,3,4,5)

Pilot Report Card (Teachers and Principal). The report card we have now doesn't work; even parents agree it isn't helpful. We want to pilot a new one next year. We're looking for a format that allows us to set standards in language arts and math, and on our holistic student outcomes, and show the student's progress toward meeting those standards. We've looked at examples from Kentucky that use benchmarks. We want a way to communicate to parents about how kids are doing academically and how parents can help. We hope it will be more thematic and narrative, and allow for some individual goal setting for students in collaboration with parents. (Habits 2,5,6,7)

District Restructuring (District Administrator). The district is engaged in its own restructuring to redefine relationships with schools to allow maximum flexibility for schools to respond to the needs of their community. We're asking: What is "districtness," given more autonomy at the site? We're developing some tentative answers: a joining together of values around criteria and frameworks; working with sites in interpreting and using these frameworks; brokering learning across sites as they experiment and change. Another role that's emerging is supporting schools in building agreements with their parent communities about new forms of assessment, like Rogers's new report card. We need to gain and keep the public trust as we move toward performance assessment. That's a good role for the district: structuring continuous conversations about traditional and nontraditional forms of assessment. Another role for us is coaching schools—helping them focus and refocus on the big purposes and issues and not get bogged down in the nitty-gritty; helping them ask the what-ifs and the hard questions that sometimes create discomfort. Coaching is a trust relationship, not a hierarchical one; within it you are able to say the hard things. (Habits 1,2,3,7)

District Curriculum Committees (District Administrator). District curriculum leadership and decisions are made in subject-area committees that are teacher-led and comprised of volunteers from each school. They have control of their own budget. Each committee poses and explores several critical questions each year. I participate on two committees as a co-equal with the teachers. We really get into it and open up. We don't have answers, but we struggle together and agree to experiment and try new strategies. When our experiments aren't perfect, we adjust or try something different to get where we want. As the district liaison to my committees, I also coach the committee or the teacher co-leaders. As a liaison, I support the committee's inquiry processes, especially by helping define good, deep, focusing questions—ones central to improving teaching, learning, and curriculum. (Habits 3,4,6,7)

Santa Monica Alliance (District Administrator). Santa Monica–Malibu Unified has strong links with the community—for example, the city pledges $2 million annually for support of at-risk youth that otherwise would have been cut from the budget. Recently the district has taken the lead in a new concept of melding school and community social services. Traditionally there are separate pots of money for different kinds of student services; for example, gang prevention, mediator training, jobs, parent education. Instead of viewing these as separate pots, we're pulling together the Santa Monica Alliance so we can impact whole kids, not parts of kids. It will be centered at the high school and guided by holistic, multiyear strategies. The focus shifts from agency-centered work to student- and school-centered services that pull everything together. (Habits 2,5,6)

Staff Development (Teachers and Principal). We've become critical consumers of staff development. We won't let people waste our time. We paid a supposed expert lots of money this winter to help us with deploying our family groupings. He just sat on the stage and pontificated. We're at a point where it's hard to use outsiders because it's too hard to bring them up to speed with where we are. The district now gives every school eight pupil-free days to do their own staff development. At first, the district planned and led all of the inservice on these days. Over time, the district built the capacity of every school to identify its own learning needs and build plans for addressing them. Now we are all weaned. Each school has a committee that plans the days. The district coaches us, if needed, to concentrate on a few things each year or over several years rather than have a potpourri. (Habits 1,3,7)

Professional Practice School (Teachers). Rogers is a professional practice school working with UCLA in a collaborative model for teacher education. We learn so much from having student teachers who work in several classrooms over the year. They're always asking, why did you do that? It makes us think and grow along with them—and it gives us a wonderful source of new hires, people we've seen teach and who have begun to build a shared philosophy with us. It also gives us two kinds of teacher-leader opportunities—master teacher and clinical consultant. Now everyone in the school shares responsibility for helping student teachers learn; we have a sense of being a community of teachers all continuously honing our practice. (Habits 1,6,7)

House Structure (Principal). The house structure and grade-level teamwork have built leadership and common commitments. When I first became principal here, I gave every grade level release time for teachers, and the teachers said: What are we supposed to be doing with all this free time? Now we have eight pupil-free days, nearly two hours every week on late-start Fridays, and teachers use every minute—and want more—for looking at student work, examining portfolios, unit planning, adjusting our strategies based on what we see in student's work and progress. (Habits 3,4,7)

Principal's Role (Principal). I'm the kind of person who wants things done yesterday. But I've learned that everyone in the school community needs time to crystallize what it is we're really trying to do. Everyone, especially the loyal opposition, needs to be involved in discussion, arguing, and the diversity of thinking it takes to plan really well. Our work is not dependent on any one person or a few people. The way we work with adults—inquiry, discussion, problem solving— is the way we want to work with kids. We're always modeling strategies and involving teachers and parents in personal learning of the kind we hope will be true for the students. The quality of interaction and discussion that happens among adults translates directly into the classroom. (Habits 1,2,4,5)

Oceana High School
Jefferson Union High School District

District Restructuring Committee (District Administrators). Restructuring the four high schools in the Jefferson Union High School District is a districtwide commitment. Several members of the teachers' union attended a national conference with Al Shanker. They returned with ideas and readings that they brought to the teacher center and to the district Effective Schools Committee [ESC]. The ESC had a tradition of research—looking at test scores, surveys, brainstorming sessions. But we finally admitted that we'd done all this research, and nothing was changing. Together, the district and union decided to replace the ESC with a Restructuring Committee [RC]. By contractual agreement, the RC brings together a school board member, the superintendent, a district administrator, all four high school principals, the union president, and two elected staff members from each site. The charge to the RC was to research various approaches to restructuring—by reading, investigating national restructuring efforts, and discussion—and to shape our own definition and approach based on our students' needs. From early on the RC was a safe place where together we could raise critical questions about why our students are not achieving as we'd like them to and why we continue to do the same things in our high schools when we know it doesn't work. (Habits 1,3,4,5,6,7)

The "New" Oceana (Principal). When the decision was made to reconstitute Oceana as a restructuring school, a new faculty and principal were selected and charged with developing a new vision of the school. We wanted a school that was more personalized and engaging, one that encouraged active involvement by students in their own education. We wanted to respond to the needs of today's kids and to the new demands of society. The more we change, the more we see how many new directions, possibilities, and challenges open up before us. We are a work-in-progress. (Habits 2,3,4)

New Roles and Decision Structures (District Administrators). We have extraordinary teachers in our district. So we've created opportunities for them to decide and lead. Through the old ESC, the RC, and the Academic Councils [ACs] at each site, we've redefined and expanded roles for everyone—board, district, principals, teachers. We've flattened the organization, distributing leadership for what would typically be district roles to people in the schools. For example, curriculum leadership comes entirely from the ACs at each school. From all of this working together has come a greater respect among us for the problems teachers deal with and for the issues the district and board deal with. We now have a new mentality among teachers and the union. The bottom line with the teachers when it comes to salary negotiations and budget issues is: What effect will it have on the students? The teachers went without raises in the last round because they did not want cuts to impact kids. Also, the teachers are now saying that administrators are overworked! Lines of power and of separate roles are becoming blurred. (Habits 1,4,5,6)

Academic Council (Teachers). Each site now has an AC made up of the principal, four teachers, the site union representative, a student, and a staff member. The power that used to be vested in the principal is now shared with the AC. At Oceana, the AC is the steering and leadership committee for our restructuring effort. We stay focused on curriculum and student issues because AC works from our school-wide learning outcomes, the restructuring grant proposal we developed, and the principles of the Coalition of Essential Schools [CES]. (Habits 1,2,5,6)

Flexible Board and District Policies (Teachers and Principal). When Oceana became a CES school and developed student outcomes and a state restructuring proposal, the board and district felt they needed to give us room to decide and invent for ourselves. We now have our own graduation requirements linked to portfolios and performance assessments; we utilize staff any way we want within an overall allotment; we organize time and the curriculum as we see best; we do all our own hiring. The board and district give us all this flexibility because we are clear on the learning outcomes we developed to guide our restructuring decisions and because they understand and support the CES principles that also help guide our work. The bottom line in this district is a willingness to let schools take a risk and organize differently, provided there is a rational basis for it. (Habits 1,2,7)

District Leadership (District Administrators). It's easier to manage something than it is to lead. As a district, we stress with our principals that we value leadership rather than management. District administrators visit each site at least four times each week. We help schools stay focused on students by modeling that focus ourselves in our daily relationships with principals: by the questions we ask, by visiting classrooms and staying for the entire 90 minutes. Also, we provide learning and development for our principals; each has gone through the three-year Bay Area School Leadership Center experience. (Habits 1,2,7)

Staff Development (Teachers). There is no one who can give us any answers as we try to reorganize Oceana. There are resources for us, but, in the end, we must come up with our own answers. And we feel capable of doing just that. Before we began to reorganize, staff development happened to us; people came in with charts, jokes, and lectures. And we listened, but nothing actually changed as a result. Now when we identify problems, we look toward each other to solve them; we draw on our teachers who have gone to outside sources to build expertise. We have people who are experts on student-centered pedagogy, exhibitions, performance assessment, portfolios, critical dialogue, examining student work, Socratic seminar, planning backwards from student outcomes, literature-based and multicultural curricula. When we work as a whole faculty on one thing, it happens because we've decided at faculty meetings or at AC that it's a common need. We've used grant money to pay ourselves for extra time, like two extra days before school opens and two days after the close just to learn, discuss, and problem-solve together. This year we used our time to work on portfolios as proof of graduation competencies, exhibitions, our staff accountability plan, and reviewing the learning outcomes. We have a short student day every Wednesday, and we use these 90 minutes each week for learning together in various formats: teaching houses, full faculty, grade level, subject area. (Habits 3,4,7)

Teacher Evaluation Plan (Teachers and Principal). We all agreed—the union, the board, the district, the teachers—that the old system of teacher evaluation did not work. At Oceana, we came up with a new self-evaluation system; the board approved a pilot. All teachers develop their own written self-evaluations based on reflections of issues in their own teaching. In every class, each teacher asks students to evaluate the curriculum and the teaching. One part of each teacher's self-evaluation must be a reflection on how students evaluate us as teachers. Collectively, we're also working on how to link and build greater student accountability for learning with corresponding staff accountability. If we insist that students be more accountable, we must also hold ourselves more accountable. On our after-school planning days, we identified five student behaviors that are critical to the kind of learning we're after; then we identified teacher behaviors that are likely to elicit and support the five student behaviors. We agreed to use our peer coaching teams to hold ourselves more accountable to these teacher behaviors. (Habits 2,3,4)

Principal's Role (Teachers). Our principal was willing and eager to give up the traditional role of a principal and work with the AC. She's a practical leader and a people-person who centers things on kids. She's both a pragmatist and a visionary, and she uses her role flexibly. She has her own personal vision, but she sees her role as brokering a shared vision for the whole school; Oceana is not going to depend on the principal's personal vision; what we're developing is an Oceana vision. (Habits 1,2,6)

District Network Committee (District Administrators). We're in the process of disbanding the district Restructuring Committee because its charge has been met; we've defined a learner-centered approach to restructuring and said that every one of the four schools will, through its Academic Council, develop a restructuring plan. The next issue is to determine how schools learn from each other so that all this decentralization doesn't result in five disjointed entities. For that, we've created the District Networking Committee; it's charged with helping schools communicate with, learn from, and support one another as they restructure, rather than compete. (Habits 2,4,5)

ENABLERS AND CONSTRAINTS

What factors enable or constrain the development of the habits of inquiry evident in these two schools and districts? Observation and conversations with Oceana and Rogers and at the larger set of California's restructuring schools reveal several enabling factors that support the development and practice of habits of inquiry.

Enablers

Learning and Coaching Relationships. These two schools have a variety of rich and stable learning relationships: with the district, with their communities, with selected support providers, with networks, and with professional organizations. The relationships include two-way sharing of information, ideas, examples, coaching, and critique; they involve individuals, subgroups such as teams or houses, and, importantly, whole-school commitments and affiliations—for example, the California Restructuring Support Network and the Coalition of Essential Schools. The learning and coaching relationships are supported by various financial sources: the school's core budget and its categorical funds, grant money such as state restructuring or professional development funds, district-generated grants, and district staff development funds.

Process and Discourse Tools. Rogers and Oceana frequently use specific processes and discourse tools that facilitate discussion and generate agreements among diverse stakeholders. Raising fundamental questions by necessity generates uncertainty, ambiguity, confusion, passion, and sometimes anger. Schools undertaking deep, intentful change use specific, agreed-upon tools and processes that facilitate the unearthing and airing of deeply held beliefs and feelings. Examples include the development and use of ground rules to guide meetings and structured discussion, such as about the five learner behaviors and corresponding five teacher behaviors described above at Oceana. These tools and processes also serve as symbols for "what's important here" and as mechanisms for generating common criteria that guide the thinking and actions of diverse individuals. Staff at Oceana and Rogers frequently referred to critical understandings, insights, and improvement strategies that arose in the course of employing these kinds of tools and processes.

Modeling and Public Practice. A few learn by hearing, more by seeing, and most by doing. As the Rogers principal said, "With something new and risky like the collaborative examination of student work, you can show people, you can tell them, but sometimes you just have to make them do it." The norms of individualism and unexamined practice are deeply ingrained. To make the transition to the new, unfamiliar territory of collaboration and inquiry, teachers need structured opportunities to practice and develop these new habits. The 1994 Symposium of California's Restructuring Schools is an example of such a "practice field" (Kofman & Senge, 1993). The yearly spring symposium is purposefully analogous to an end-of-year authentic assessment and a vehicle for reculturing. Members of the restructuring network—guided and supported by the CCSR—created the task of engaging in a public, interactive, co-critique session at year's end. Every aspect of its design, content, and structure models and elicits habits of effective inquiry. More important, however, is the in-depth, long-term inquiry that everyone at the school must do to prepare for the spring symposium. This ongoing, deep preparation is the real practice field, calling forth several habits among individuals and the whole school community: focusing change efforts on the work and learning of students; creating the need to develop and use a set of commonly held learning outcomes for all students; giving and receiving critiques on teaching, curriculum, and the standards teachers hold for judging the quality of student work.

Flexibility Accompanied by Accountability. The work of restructuring schools is the invention of entirely new learning environments and systems that support all students in achieving rigorous learning outcomes. Such work requires freedom from detailed rules and policies (for example, instructional time, credentialing, curriculum structures). Rogers and Oceana enjoy considerable permission to innovate. Their districts—and, on occasion, the state—have given them leeway to carry out their own hiring processes; reorganize time for both students and adults; have and use pupil-free days at their own discretion; develop their own grading policies and performance-based graduation requirements; and deploy new curriculum structures. A concomitant condition for these freedoms and flexibilities, however, is accountability to monitor and show improvement for agreed-upon indicators of student learning. Oceana, for example, sought and received from the state board of education permission to reduce instructional time for a trial period. The principal cited the coaching and collaboration received from the state department as enabling her staff to sharpen their thinking and use the time they gained in ways directly related to improving teaching and learning.

Constraints

Detailed State or District Requirements. Such requirements hold schools accountable for inputs as opposed to outcomes. Many inventive schools and districts feel severely hampered by the multitude of detailed, specific requirements surrounding curriculum, instructional time, credentialing, and use of categorical funds. Their net effect is to cast cold water on the flames of inventive thinking and action in restructuring schools. A powerful example is the sway that college entrance requirements—expressed in terms of seat time in discrete subject areas—hold over the curriculum structures of high schools. The fear of sacrificing college entrance competitiveness makes rethinking and restructuring curricula and the nature of learning extremely difficult.

Scale. Building communication, coherence, and inquiry is easier in smaller and simpler systems than in large and complex ones. Cultures of inquiry depend on collective processes for generating both personal and shared meanings about (1) what is true now—based on data patterns and findings—and (2) what we want to be true—purposes and visions. A major challenge to leaders and policymakers is how to create, within nested units and subunits, the kind of personal, interactive relationships and dialogue crucial to fundamental rethinking and reform.

Turbulence and Instabilities Within the System. Restructuring ecosystems are very fragile. A single change or instability within the school, district, or state context can kill or seriously disable the restructuring effort. Of primary concern is the instability of funding streams. Changes in personnel are an additional threat. For example, some 40% of the 144 funded restructuring schools in California have changed principals in two years' time. In many of these cases, new principals were assigned with little regard for their desire or capacity to sustain the school's restructuring effort. Another potential source of turbulence is relations between local unions and innovative schools and districts. Schools and districts such as Rogers and Oceana are defining new and expanded roles for teachers, often including greater visibility and mutual accountability to fellow teachers. When union leaders are not involved in the generative conversations that give rise to innovative roles for teachers, they may feel more responsible for safeguarding "freedom from" rather than "freedom to." Union, school board, and district leaders need to develop policies that institutionalize both the pressure and the permission to pursue restructuring.

Conflicting or Mixed Messages from Authorities Within the System. Schools and districts garner funds, ideas, incentives, and support from diverse sources. When these sources emit conflicting or mixed messages regarding the purpose or importance of restructuring and improvement efforts, schools rightfully feel confused and storm-tossed. Within the state department of education, the community of educational grant-making foundations, and the varied support providers throughout the state, there accumulates a cacophony of voices, each advocating particular brands or flavors of reform work—many of which are incompatible or directly contradictory with one another. One school, for example, described the year as a siege of compliance checks and inspection visits due to the coincidence of several different grant sources, curriculum initiatives, and directives from the district office. In order to secure continued funding and access to assistance connected with each initiative, the school was required to mount five separate, and qualitatively different, accountability processes.

PROVOCATIONS FOR POLICY

Seeing meaningful restructuring and reform as dependent on reculturing means framing a new role for policy. The traditional role of policy as mandating new structures and practices does little to support reculturing. The efforts of California's restructuring schools reveal that promising new structures and practices per se are not the answer. In the absence of a rich culture of inquiry, the most promising new practices lose their potential to transform learning for every child. Rethinking restructuring in this way means reframing policy as a problem of enabling the development of cultures of inquiry within schools and districts. The activities that follow may help policymakers move away from policy as solution-giving and toward policy as culture-building:

• *Publish a "habits-of-inquiry impact report."* A new role for policymakers and leaders is to use an understanding of the habits of inquiry to frame policies that enhance the enablers and remove the constraints on a culture of inquiry at the school site. Every new policy should be accompanied by a report addressing how the policy will effect the habits of effective cultures of inquiry.

- *Use the seven habits of effective cultures of inquiry as design features for professional development and grant-making decisions.* In this view, designers of capacity-building, support, and training would create strategies involving long-term, inquiry-based learning and coaching relationships. Strategies would be pursued to the degree that they model, elicit, and support the development of the habits of inquiry among individuals and across whole schools. Reform networks would establish norms and processes of interaction that encompass the seven habits of inquiry. Network meetings and conferences would feature critical dialogue and the sharing and critique of works-in-progress as opposed to presentations of successful programs. Grant makers, both public and private, would use the habits as criteria for seeking and selecting school reform plans for funding.

- *View accountability as learning and change agency.* Most schools and districts experience accountability as judgments imposed from outside. Such accountability creates little commitment and energy for self-reflection and improvement. A more sensible means of quality assurance involves viewing the "targets" of accountability as learners who must participate in designing the means by which they will hold themselves publicly accountable. California's 1994 Symposium of Restructuring Schools, and the "Protocol" practiced within it, is a first draft attempt to design a public accountability system that honors and promotes self-reflection and learning.

- *Think systemically; act locally.* Reform is about reculturing the system, not just schools. We've made a great deal of progress in envisioning more functional school organizations. We know far less about—and pay less attention to—creating cultures of inquiry within districts, support organizations, state departments of education, and legislatures. Achieving the goals of reform will require personal and collective learning and change at every level. Each of us within the system must begin to heed the age-old advice: Physician, heal thyself.

Chapter 9

Communities for Teacher Research

Fringe or Forefront?

Marilyn Cochran-Smith and Susan L. Lytle

There is growing support for the notion that research by teachers about their own classroom and school practices can function as a powerful means of professional development and also contribute to the knowledge base in education (Erickson, 1986; Goswami & Stillman, 1987; Stenhouse, cited in Rudduck & Hopkins, 1985). We have been positing the stronger position that research by teachers represents a distinctive way of knowing about teaching and learning that will alter, not just add to, what we know in the field (Cochran-Smith & Lytle, 1990; Lytle & Cochran-Smith, 1991). Furthermore, we have argued that, as it accumulates and is more widely disseminated, research by teachers will represent a radical challenge to our current assumptions about the relationships of theory and practice, schools and universities, and inquiry and reform (Cochran-Smith & Lytle, 1993). Despite its potential, however, there is also widespread agreement that there are no obvious and simple ways to create the conditions that support teacher research, and, in fact, there are major obstacles that constrain this activity in schools and make it difficult to redefine teaching as a form of inquiry. While many current proposals for school reform involve innovative arrangements of time, space, and resources intended to enhance teachers' autonomy and their opportunities for collaboration and inquiry, structural rearrangements

This chapter is adapted from M. Cochran-Smith & S. L. Lytle, "Communities for teacher research: Fringe or forefront?" In *Inside/Outside: Teacher Research and Knowledge* (pp. 85–103). New York: Teachers College Press, 1993.

alone are not sufficient for teacher research to contribute fully to the burgeoning national movement for the professionalization of teaching. Innovative structures are necessary but not sufficient to realize the potential of teacher research as both a legitimate and unique form of knowledge generation and a profound means of professional growth that can radically alter teaching and learning.

This chapter begins by stating the rationale for teacher research and then considers some of the obstacles to teacher research in schools, teacher groups, school–university partnerships, and regional and national forums. We argue that overcoming these obstacles requires the building and sustaining of intellectual communities of teacher/researchers, or networks of individuals who enter with other teachers into "a common search" for meaning in their work lives (Westerhoff, 1987, p. 193) and who regard their research as part of larger efforts to transform teaching, learning, and schooling. Drawing on examples from a number of teacher and student teacher groups in the greater Philadelphia area, we develop a framework for analyzing and evaluating the work of communities for teacher research according to four perspectives: the ways in which communities organize time, use talk, construct texts, and interpret the tasks of teaching and schooling. A framework based on time, talk, text, and task provides a way to critique systematically the various structures and strategies intended to foster teacher inquiry that are currently in place or being developed in teacher organizations, partnerships, and schools. It may be used as a heuristic to help existing and prospective teacher groups plan their collaborative work and raise questions about the cultures of school and university organizations as sites of inquiry.

TEACHER RESEARCH: A RATIONALE

What is missing from the knowledge base for teaching are the voices of teachers themselves, the questions teachers ask, the ways teachers use writing and intentional talk in their work lives, and the interpretive frames teachers use to understand and improve their own classroom practices. Limiting the official knowledge base for teaching to what academics have chosen to study and write about has contributed to a number of problems, including discontinuity between what is taught in universities and what is taught in classrooms, teachers' ambivalence about the claims of academic research, and a general lack of information among academics about classroom life from a truly endemic perspective.

While teacher research has the potential to provide this perspective on teaching and learning, several critical issues related to institutionalization and methodological rigor divide teacher research from research on teaching and make it difficult for the university-based community to acknowledge its potential. As we have shown (Cochran-Smith & Lytle, 1990), comparing teacher research with university-based research involves a complicated set of assumptions and relationships that act as barriers to enhancing our knowledge base about teaching. Researchers in the academy equate "knowledge about teaching" with the high-status information attained through traditional modes of inquiry. They fault teachers for not reading or not implementing the findings of such research, even though teachers often find it irrelevant and counterintuitive. Yet teacher research, which by definition has special potential to address issues that teachers themselves identify as significant, does not have a legitimate place.[1]

Although its roots are in the action research of the 1950s, the current teacher research movement remains in many ways on the margins of both the teaching and research communities. Furthermore, there has been debate about its methods and its status as research. In its recent iterations, teacher research has been thought of primarily as classroom-based studies conducted by teachers of their own practice and resembling university-based research in methods, forms, and reporting conventions. Equating teacher research with classroom studies puts limits on what we can learn from teachers about their work. A broader perspective (Lytle & Cochran-Smith, 1990) helps to legitimate teacher inquiry as a critical dimension of the activity of teaching: It allows us to reclaim and reexamine more of the existing literature on teaching written by teachers themselves and enables us to make distinctions about a variety of teacher-research texts and the contexts in which they are produced.[2]

There is little disagreement that teachers who engage in self-directed inquiry about their own work in classrooms find the process intellectually satisfying. However, the value of teacher research is not limited to teachers. Just as teachers read and use the research of university-based researchers, many academics committed to teacher education and/or the study of teaching and learning find the research of teachers a rich and unique source of knowledge. Teacher research provides rich data about classroom life, reveals what teachers regard as seminal issues about learning and the cultures of teaching, and provides rich classroom cases that are often more powerful and memorable influences on teachers' decision making than are conventional research findings in the form of rules and generalizations (Nisbett & Ross, 1980; Shulman, 1986). But despite its potential, teacher research remains on the margins of both school and university communities. In the following section, we discuss some of the reasons for this situation.

ON THE FRINGE: SOME OBSTACLES TO TEACHER RESEARCH

The various commission reports on the state of schools and teachers have chronicled a now-familiar list of reasons why teaching has failed to become a major profession, including poor preservice preparation, absence of clearly articulated standards for performance, lack of public confidence, flatness of the career ladder, and failure of teachers to remain current in the theory and research on teaching. The obstacles to teacher research are more subtle than the items on this familiar list. They are deeply embedded in the cultures of school and university organizations, in pervasive assumptions about the nature of teaching and learning, and in the traditions involved in the generation of new knowledge. In the following section, we briefly describe four of the most important obstacles to teacher research.

Teacher Isolation

As a profession, teaching is primarily defined by what teachers do when they are not with other teachers. When teachers are evaluated, it is individual classroom performance that is scrutinized. When contracts are negotiated, it is amount of instructional time that is often a key issue. In fact, when teachers are out of their classrooms or talking to other teachers, they are often perceived by administrators, parents, and sometimes even by teachers themselves as not working. The isolation of teachers at all stages of their careers is well documented (Goodlad, 1984; Lieberman & Miller, 1992b; Lortie, 1975), and it is clear that the daily rhythms of schools typically provide little time for teachers to talk, reflect, and share ideas with colleagues (Little, 1989; Lytle & Fecho, 1991). Yet teacher research is by definition a collaborative and social activity that requires opportunities for sustained and substantive intellectual exchange among colleagues (Cazden, Diamondstone, & Naso, 1989; Goswami & Stillman, 1987). It also requires time within the school day to perform the fundamental tasks that researchers in all other professions take for granted—observing and documenting phenomena, conducting interviews, and gathering artifacts and supporting data.

Tacit images of teaching as a solo performance carried out on the class-room stage militate against the institutionalization of inquiry (Myers, 1985) both as an integral part of teaching (Britton, 1987) and as a way for teachers to interact professionally (Schaefer, 1967).

However, isolation from other teachers is not a condition that is simply imposed on teachers by outside forces, nor is it necessarily always perceived by them as a problem. Rather, isolation has two sides: It makes for privacy as well as loneliness, autonomy as well as separation. As Little (1989) points out, isolation often safeguards teachers from the scrutiny of others: They may "forfeit the opportunity to display their successes, [but they also] reserve the right to conceal their failures" (p. 60). We are suggesting, then, that, even when teachers have opportunities to collaborate with one another to conduct teacher research, they may be hesitant to do so. Isolation acts as a deterrent by secluding teachers from one another and creating a cycle in which teachers may view teacher research as hazardous—a high-stakes game in which collaboration may come at the price of exposure and loss of autonomy (Lytle & Fecho, 1991).

Occupational Socialization

In many schools, the competent teacher is assumed to be self-sufficient, certain, and independent (Lortie, 1975). Asking questions and being uncertain are inappropriate behaviors for all but the most inexperienced teachers, and even they have only brief periods of grace during which they may ask limited numbers of questions (Richardson-Koehler, 1988). Teachers are not encouraged to talk about classroom failures, ask critical questions, or openly express frustrations. In short, the occupational culture perpetuates the myth that good teachers rarely have questions they cannot answer about their own practices or about the larger issues of schools and schooling (Lortie, 1975).

Researching teachers, on the other hand, are noted for their questions (Berthoff, 1987; Knoblauch & Brannon, 1988). They may indeed be self-sufficient, competent, and, sometimes, certain. But they also pose problems, identify discrepancies between their theories and their practices, challenge common routines, and attempt to make visible much of that which is taken for granted about teaching and learning. They often count on other teachers for alternative perspectives on their work (Cochran-Smith, 1991). They seek help not because they are failing, but because they are learning (Traugh et al., 1986). And they regard struggle and self-critical questioning as integral parts of their intellectual lives (Lather, 1986; Miller, 1987).

The Knowledge Base for Teaching

A third obstacle to the creation of communities for teacher research, closely related to the second, is the push to make teaching a legitimate profession by the generation of what Pellegrin (1976) calls "a systematic codified technology that is universally known to practitioners" (p. 348). The question here is not whether we need a knowledge base for teaching, but rather what kind of knowledge base is needed, who constructs it, and what roles teachers play in its formation (Cochran-Smith & Lytle, 1990). If the generation of a knowledge base is primarily associated with a technical view of teaching (Apple, 1986), and if it is constructed only by university-based researchers, then the teacher's role is clear. He or she is expected to learn the skills of effective teaching and also learn how to apply them in practice. When the professionalization of teaching is linked to this technical view, staff development is regarded as a vehicle for transmitting skills to teachers rather than as a process for collaborative inquiry (Lambert, 1989), and the teacher has no role to play in the generation of a knowledge base.

In contrast to the technical model of professionalization, wherein the teacher is an increasingly sophisticated consumer of other people's knowledge, the teacher/researcher movement is based on the notion that a professional plays a participatory role in the creation and use of knowledge in the field. This relationship involves ways of knowing about teaching in which teachers themselves develop theories in order to "interpret, understand, and eventually transform the social life of schools" (Smyth, 1987, p. 12).

The Reputation of Educational Research

Finally and somewhat ironically, the reputation of educational research itself tends to function as an obstacle to promoting teacher research. Teachers' suspicions and even contempt for educational research are hardly surprising, given that research has been used to blame teachers for the failings of the larger educational and sociopolitical systems. Research is often called on as the rationale for school systems to train and retrain their teachers in a wide variety of areas and is used as the grist for countless checklists, scripts for teaching, and evaluation schemes (Zumwalt, 1982), which have deskilled teachers (Apple, 1986) by regarding them as replaceable and fixable parts in the larger educational machinery.

Unfortunately, even when educational researchers have addressed problems that are of interest to teachers, their findings have frequently been reported in ways that are generally inaccessible, seemingly unrelated to the everyday realities of teaching, and counterintuitive to lessons learned from hard-earned experience. Furthermore, educational research has frequently been presented to teachers as "uncovered truths" about the most effective ways to teach and "definitive procedures" for assessing students' learning. As Howe and Eisenhart (1990) have recently pointed out, there is an emerging consensus even in the scientific community that no research can be accurately regarded as value-neutral or completely objective. Our point here is that, because educational research is rarely presented to teachers as value-laden and socially constructed, teachers are not encouraged to interrogate its premises and relevance for their own situations. The fact that most educational research is perceived by teachers as irrelevant to their daily work lives spills into and contaminates their willingness to believe both that teacher research has the potential to be relevant and that they themselves might want to be researchers. To many teachers, then, research (more or less by definition) is something that is distant, uninteresting, and impenetrable. Furthermore, since few teachers have had the opportunity in their own graduate and professional training to become acquainted with alternative conventions and paradigms of research, they have little reason to identify with a professionalization movement that is based on the notion of teachers as researchers (Fecho, 1993; Pincus, 1993).

In order to encourage wider involvement of teachers in research, it will be necessary to overcome the serious obstacles caused by teacher isolation, a school culture that works against raising questions, a technical view of knowledge for teaching, and the negative reputation of educational research. In the remainder of this chapter, we propose that overcoming these obstacles requires the building of communities for teacher research.

TO THE FOREFRONT: COMMUNITIES THAT SUPPORT TEACHER RESEARCH

There has been a growing effort over the past decade to provide organizational structures that enable groups of teachers to come together to talk about their work, learn from one another, and address curricular and instructional issues. Innovative arrangements include in-school and school–university structures such as cross-visitation, teacher study groups, schools within schools, writing projects, student teacher–cooperating teacher discussion groups, and on-site courses and seminars that focus on teacher inquiry. These arrangements include schools, schools within schools, teacher groups that meet outside the auspices of schools or school systems, projects or programs that are based on school–university collaborations, and local, regional, or national networks that provide forums for teachers to exchange ideas with colleagues from across the country. All these structures have in common the purpose of enabling teachers to reflect on their work, and some of them are intended explicitly to encourage teacher or action research.

Using examples from a number of teacher groups, we provide an analytic framework describing the qualities of such communities, which can be used to raise questions about current school and university efforts to promote teachers' participation in research. Represented in Figure 9.1, our framework provides four perspectives on teacher-research communities: the ways in which communities organize time, use talk, construct texts, and interpret the tasks of teaching and schooling. Although the interrelationships of these four perspectives will vary in particular communities, the framework can be used as a heuristic to help existing and prospective teacher groups plan their collaborative work and raise questions about the cultures of school and university organizations as sites of inquiry.

FIGURE 9.1. **Communities for Teacher Research: A Framework for Analysis**

Organizing time	Using talk
Constructing texts	Interpreting the tasks of teaching and schooling

Organizing Time

It is no accident that one of the most common characteristics of fantasy literature for both children and adults is the manipulation of time. In novels we can wrinkle in and out of time; make time fly, drag, and stand still; shift back and forth between time spheres; and ultimately surpass its boundaries altogether. Unfortunately, some of the harshest contrasts to literary images of unbounded time are real-life images of the factory and the schoolroom. In schools, teachers and students are organized according to whether they are on time, behind time, out of time, killing time, saving time, serving time, watching their time, or moving at double-time. Teachers are often evaluated according to how they manage transition time, allocated time, academic time, and time-on-task. Clearly time is a central dimension in the work lives of teachers. It is also one of the most critical factors in the formation and maintenance of learning communities for teacher research.

As mentioned above, unlike other professions, which are organized to support research activities, teaching is a profession in which it is extraordinarily difficult to find enough time even to collect data and almost impossible to find time to reflect, reread, or share with colleagues (Goodlad, 1984; Griffin, 1986; Zeichner, 1986). When groups of teachers come together as researchers, they need sufficient chunks of time in which to work, and they also need sufficient longevity as a group over time (Little, 1987b). When the pace of a community's work is unhurried and when members of the group make a commitment to work through complicated issues over time, then ideas have a chance to incubate and develop, trust builds in the group, and participants feel comfortable raising sensitive issues and risking self-revelation. These ways of organizing time are frequently identified in the feminist literature as critical for fostering collaborative ways of knowing and constructing knowledge (Belenky, Clinchy, Goldberger, & Tarule, 1986). Over time, communities that support teacher research develop their own histories and, in a certain sense, their own culture—a common discourse, shared experiences that function as touchstones, and a set of procedures that provide structure and form for continued experience. Longevity makes it possible for teacher/researchers to engage in inquiry that is both systematic and spontaneous.

However, maintaining teacher-research communities over relatively long periods of time also presents a number of challenges. How can a group meet the needs of both new and experienced members? Can a group become too large or too small? What happens to a group as members come and go? How can a group avoid becoming locked into procedures and continue to be receptive to critique and change, even when many members feel satisfied with the status quo? What are the ways in which teacher/researcher groups can be increasingly responsive to special interests without fragmenting the organization? If teacher/ researcher groups are to be more than the latest educational fad or the newest theme for staff development programs, they need to be analyzed and reconceptualized as enduring structures subject to many of the same problems as other voluntary organizations that exist over time. For example, in the Network of New and Experienced Urban Teachers (NNEUT) (Cochran-Smith, Larkin, & Lytle, 1990), which combines inservice and preservice teacher education, longevity is a mixed blessing. In contrast to more typical student teaching terms, which range from 10 to 14 weeks, NNEUT's full-year student teaching period allows supervisors, cooperating teachers, and student teachers to work together in a variety of stable groups to reflect on their work and write about their practices. On the other hand, each year student teachers who are by definition new to the group have many of the same needs. New and returning cooperating teacher mentors bring more diverse backgrounds and differing prior experiences with the notions of reflective practice, teacher research, and urban education. This means that project activities need to be redesigned continuously in order to meet the needs of preservice and inservice teachers with varying degrees of readiness to be teacher/researchers. Some have been teacher/researchers in their own classrooms and published their work in local and national publications, while others need to be introduced to the notion of critique and analysis of their own practice. Finding activities that are intellectually exciting and useful to all members of the community is a tricky balancing act. However, unlike more typical modes of staff development, teacher research both generates and is generated by individual and collective questions about practices and theories that evolve over time. The activities of teacher/researchers, therefore, change qualitatively over time even though inquiry structures remain the same.

One of the most salient issues regarding time and teacher-research communities is how much control teachers have over their time. Forming and maintaining communities that support teacher research in schools requires attending to the constraints and conflicts around the construction and interpretation of time by both teachers and administrators. Hargreaves (1989), for example, argues that control of teachers' time is a highly contested arena in the school as a workplace. Three of the dimensions of time that Hargreaves identifies help us understand how little control teachers actually have. "Micropolitical" time refers to the way time is distributed according to power and status relationships.

While all teachers' work is defined by time spent in the classroom, high school teachers have more time allotted for planning outside the classroom than their elementary and middle school colleagues. This suggests that it might be easier to form teacher-research communities in secondary schools or that secondary teachers might have more discretionary time to allot to research activities.

Hargreaves's category of "phenomenological" time refers to the way time is lived or experienced by different members of the school. Using Hall's categories, Hargreaves argues that operating within a "monochronic" view of time means working on one task at a time, complying with a schedule, and giving priority to procedures rather than relationships. Operating within a "polychronic" perspective on time, on the other hand, means doing several tasks at once, being highly sensitive to context, and being oriented primarily to people and relationships rather than procedures. Hargreaves argues that a polychronic conception of time is more common among women than men and is more likely in smaller organizations with a personal, rather than an official, style of leadership. Many of the activities of teacher/researchers working in schools require pursuing several tasks simultaneously, attending to complex relationships between and among teachers and students, and recognizing the multiple layers of context in which learning and teaching are embedded. Monochronic time frames dominate education because they are, as Hargreaves argues, the "prerogative of the powerful" (1989, p. 19) and not necessarily because they are effective administratively or pedagogically. The issue here is whether a teacher-research community can exist within a monochronic time frame or whether it is necessary to examine and attempt to alter the way time is constructed in school settings.

"Sociopolitical" time refers to the way teachers' time is allocated and used in schools. Sometimes, as Hargreaves points out, administrators "colonize" teachers' time by claiming more and more of it for formal purposes and leaving teachers with less and less discretionary or flexible time. In relation to teacher-research communities, the issue of control of teachers' time involves redistributing some of the time during the school day already allotted for other purposes, adding to the contracted amounts of time for research purposes, and enabling teachers to make different arrangements of class, preparation, and meeting times. For example, in Crossroads, a charter school within a school at Gratz High School in Philadelphia, eight teachers have reorganized the school day so that they share students and planning periods in order to construct an integrated interdisciplinary curriculum. By redistributing time across the school day, they have reframed and reconstructed their own teaching lives and significantly altered the learning opportunities of their students. As part of the continuous cycle of inventing, enacting, and evaluating the curriculum, they collect, share, and interpret data about the effects of these innovations (Fecho, 1993).

Doing teacher research cannot simply be an additional task added to the already crowded teachers' day. Building communities requires that teachers have more discretion over how they spend in-classroom and out-of-classroom time. Increased control over time enables teachers to engage in research by analyzing data gathered in their own classrooms as well as by documenting learning in one another's classrooms and schools, team-teaching, and scheduling classes to accommodate informal and formal group meetings. If teacher groups are to become communities, participants will have to integrate research more fully into the ongoing activities of the school day and work out some of the difficult issues associated with the politics of time.

Using Talk

A second critical factor in the formation and maintenance of learning communities for teacher research is talk—particular ways of describing, discussing, and debating teaching. In communities that support teacher research, groups of teachers engage in joint construction of knowledge through conversation. Through talk they make their tacit knowledge more visible (Polanyi, 1958), call into question assumptions about common practice (Giroux, 1984), and generate data that make possible the consideration of alternatives. We have pointed out previously that teacher research is not limited to classroom studies carried out by teachers but also includes essays, journals, and oral inquiries. Oral inquiry, which we define as teachers' self-conscious and often self-critical attempts to make sense of their daily work by talking about it in planned and formally structured ways (Lytle & Cochran-Smith, 1990), then, is one type of teacher research and one that is only beginning to be recognized as a research process. Some teacher-research groups regularly conduct oral inquiries, such as reflections on practice or descriptive reviews of students (Carini, 1986), literature studies (Edelsky, 1988), and doubting/believing discussions (Elbow, 1973). Other communities do not use formal oral inquiry formats, but they do talk in distinctive ways about their teaching.

In communities that support teacher research, all talk does not contribute directly to the joint construction of knowledge about teaching. Rather, teachers swap classroom stories, share specific ideas, seek one another's advice, and trade opinions about issues and problems in their own schools and the larger educational arena. In most professional contexts, these exchanges are typically considered "small talk," which implies that they are pleasant but unimportant in comparison to the "big talk" or more serious purposes for which the group has convened. In communities that support teacher research these smaller conversations have an important function: They create and sustain the interpersonal relationships necessary for the larger project of the joint construction of knowledge.

Two interrelated ways of talking about teaching are central to building communities for teacher research both in and out of school. The first way is similar to Geertz's (1973) notion of thick description, whereby he emphasizes that what researchers often call data are really their own constructions of what others are saying, doing, and meaning. Thick description is a process of "grasping" and "rendering" the multiple and complicated "webs of significance man himself has spun" (p. 5). In teachers' communities, this kind of rich descriptive talk helps make visible and accessible the day-to-day events, norms, and practices of teaching and learning and the ways different teachers, students, administrators, and families understand them. Talk of this kind transforms what is ordinarily regarded as "just teaching" (Little, 1989, p. 23) into multilayered portraits of school life that depend on diverse and sometimes conflicting interpretations. Structured formats such as Prospect School's Documentary Processes (Carini, 1986) are particularly powerful ways for teachers to make explicit what is often implicit, to remember by drawing on past experiences, to formulate analogies between seemingly unrelated concepts and experiences, and to construct, from disparate data, patterns in students' learning. When teachers' conversations build thick description, they conjointly uncover relationships between concrete cases and more general issues and constructs.

During one session of the year-long Seminar in Teaching and Learning of the Philadelphia Schools Collaborative, for example, a group of black and white urban high school teachers talked about "tracking," inquiring into the many ways students are typically grouped within and across classes. Together they raised questions about race, class, and gender and the short- and long-term impacts of tracking on educational opportunities, including access to courses, programs, and higher education. Using the format of a "reflective conversation" (Carini, 1986) in which participants explore the range of meanings and experiences associated with key educational terms, teachers wrote and then shared their individual images, which they analyzed through integrative summaries from several perspectives. Notes from the session convey some of the images participants shared as they explored their understandings (Philadelphia Schools Collaborative, 1989):

- Tracks which leave a trace or mark, as do animal or needle tracks
- Tracking down those who could excel and making them mediocre
- Running on a track, around and around without a goal—just stuck there only being able to ride one track at a time
- The tracks on 69th Street and what it would take to switch tracks—the early railroads, using cars on tracks to carry coal; everything had to be standardized to make it easier
- Tracks as having known destinations, placing limits on where you can go

Through this talk, teachers shared poignant and even painful memories of being tracked themselves. Some expressed personal sadness and anger at being labeled. Others were outraged as they recounted the very apparent connection they perceived between race and tracking on first walking into the school as beginning teachers some 20 years earlier. The personal and collective experiences of the group helped uncover ways their expectations for students in their own classrooms might be reinforcing rather than interrupting differences. While the individual and collective experiences of teachers always figure significantly in the ongoing construction and interpretation of knowledge about teaching and school culture, these experiences are rarely questioned and then used to generate plans for further inquiry and action. Further, the joint construction of knowledge in teacher-research communities is not a neat or bounded process that leads to consensus (Cochran-Smith, 1991). When teachers are working together to construct greater understandings about teaching, their conversations are recursive, reflecting a fluid, changing view of knowledge.

Closely related to the first, the second way of talking about teaching that is central to building communities for teacher research is broadly termed "critique." In using this term to describe teacher/researchers' talk, we call attention to conversations in which teachers' question common practice, deliberate about what is regarded as expert knowledge, examine underlying assumptions, interrogate educational categories, and attempt to uncover the values and interests served by the common arrangements and structures of schooling (Beyer, 1986; Carr & Kemmis, 1986; Smyth, 1987; Zeichner, 1986). This way of talking makes problematic much of what is usually taken for granted about teaching and learning. According to Giroux (1984), problematics refer "not only to

what is included in a world view but also what is left out and silenced,"
highlighting not only what is said but also what is not said (p. 35).

In teacher-research communities, making teaching problematic
means calling into question labels, practices, and processes that are so
ingrained in our language and metaphors for teaching and learning that
they have become reified. The "givens" of schooling make up a long
list, including reading groups, rostering, inservicing, tracking, abilities,
disabilities, mastery, retention, promotion, giftedness, disadvantage,
special needs, departmentalization, 47-minute periods, coverage, standards, Carnegie units, detention, teacher-proof instructional materials,
and homework. Making the givens of education problematic requires
asking interpretive questions, which rarely take the form "What is the
best way to teach reading to first graders?" or "Is this child reading on
grade level?" but instead are phrased "What do reading and learning to
read mean in this classroom?" or "Under what circumstances does this
particular child ask for which kinds of help?" Talking like this is a way
for teacher-research communities to "learn to struggle collectively"
(Lieberman, 1986c), a process that rarely is aimed at, or ends in, conclusions.

The following excerpt from the discussion of a small group of preservice and inservice teacher/researchers in Project START (Student
Teachers as Research Teachers, 1989) reveals the ways they struggled
together to uncover and call into question some of their assumptions
about race and class. A cooperating teacher, who was white and female,
began the conversation:

Cooperating teacher (white, female): [One thing we've been trying to learn at
  our school is how] the qualities we use to describe ourselves are often the
  qualities we recognize [most] easily in kids. But it's children who have
  opposite qualities or different qualities that we have the most to learn
  from. . . . And often [it turns out that] they are children of a different race
  or a different class or a different social background. And we try to look
  closely at those children, really describe them as carefully as we can, to see
  what they [can] teach us about learning and about us as people.

Student teacher (black, male): I was thinking of a black girl [in my kindergarten
  class] who is very intelligent, but she has a tendency to be very quiet at
  times. And she uses a lot of slang and says, "Jesus" and words like that.
  And then I think of another little boy, a white boy, who's also very intelligent, who sometimes is a management problem. But in terms of the whole
  issue of culture and power—I realize that even when he's difficult, he's
  coming from a whole environment where I assume that they're extremely
  bright. . . . It's almost as if when I see him, I see a child who will probably
  be all right. But when I see this black girl, I always say she's as intelligent,

but I don't assume the same things. . . . I feel some confusion because [when] I think of this little boy, I figure that he'll get a [high] score on tests, and that will just smooth [over] any of the behavior problems.

Student teacher (white, male): I think class differences are related to some of the cultural differences which cause the problems [in the ways we look differently at kids]. But what [he] was [just] saying about things being smoothed out for a white middle-class male, that's, you know, [something] that could go on forever—definitely. Some things in my life I don't think I could have gotten away with as a black male.

Student teacher (black, male): I guess what I mean is that it's almost as if the little [white] boy is already on the track—to an Ivy League university [or something].

Through conversations such as these, beginning and experienced teachers had opportunities to articulate and then to question their own assumptions about children's abilities and prospects based on variables of race, class, and gender. Describing classroom experiences and analyzing their own responses depended on the evolving trust of the group and individual participants' willingness to disclose their previously unexamined ways of categorizing and interpreting their observations.

The co-construction of knowledge through talk is a public process. In spontaneous conversation participants build on one another's ideas in ways that are not possible in solitary situations. Teacher-research communities are often composed of teachers from different schools and school systems, grade levels, and subject-matter areas. When teachers meet at regional or national conferences, these differences provoke analyses of commonalities and contrasts across dramatically different contexts. Their varying experiences make it impossible for teacher/researchers to rely on habituated ways of talking, seeing, and thinking about teaching. Instead they have to work consciously to make their frames of reference clear as they describe and interpret their practices and theories to others in the community.

Constructing Texts

A third factor relates to the critical role of texts in forming and maintaining communities for teacher research. Communities use a wide range of texts, not all of which are published or disseminated but all of which are essential to teachers' individual and collective gathering, recording, and analyzing of data. Texts include teacher/researcher reports in the form of journals, essays, and studies, as well as selections from the extensive theoretical and research literatures in the fields related to teaching and learning. Texts used by teachers in their communities also include the written records of teachers' deliberations, informal writing used to facilitate the talk of teacher groups, transcripts of classroom interactions and interviews, notes made of classroom observations, and drafts of teachers' plans and work-in-progress. In addition, teachers have access to students' work, including writing, drawing, and other materials; school forms, documents, and records; demographic data; and curriculum guidelines and materials. While some schools and districts collect some of these texts for management and research purposes, teachers in research communities regard all of these texts as potential data and attempt to examine their interrelationships from the perspective of the classroom teacher.

Communities play a critical role in making texts accessible and usable by teachers. The Philadelphia Writing Project community, for example, made accessible Philadelphia teacher Lynne Strieb's published journal (Strieb, 1985) to another teacher, Mickey Harris. After reading and discussing Strieb's journal with a group of Philadelphia Writing Project teachers, Harris was prompted to reclassify and thus reclaim her own private teaching journal of some 20 years as a "text" that might be of interest to other teachers. In writing about her journal and revisiting her own experiences over time, Harris punctuated her text with references to James Britton, Eudora Welty, Alexander Pope, and Lynne Strieb—the "tacit tradition" of her field (Emig, 1983)—and in doing so located her own work in relation to a longer history of writers and scholars. This incident makes it clear that teacher research need not be a loose collation of individual efforts. Each separate piece of teacher research can not only inform subsequent activities in an individual teacher's classroom but can also potentially inform and be informed by all teacher research past and present. As the number and modes of communication among teacher-research communities increase, it is more likely that the full potential of teacher research to inform the profession will be realized.

When a wide range of texts are used over time, teacher-research communities function as discourse communities. From his perspective in the field of composition, Harris (1989) has suggested that the concept of discourse community draws on the everyday meaning of community as "a group with common goals and interests" (Harris, 1989, p. 19) as well as the literary idea of interpretive community and the sociolinguistic notion of speech community. "Interpretive community," as used by literary theorists Fish (1980) and others, refers to a network of people with similar meaning perspectives, while "speech community," as used by Hymes (1974), Gumperz (1982), and other linguistic anthropologists, refers to a group of people who engage in face-to-face interaction within a specific context. Teacher-research communities often function as discourse communities in all three of the ways suggested by Harris: They are "real groupings of writers and readers," they share a kind of larger mission, and they become networks of "citations and allusions" that refer to texts both within the speech community and outside it.

Participants in teacher-researcher communities are often part of several of the discourses of their profession—the school, the school system, the union, the university. Thus they are "always committed to a number of conflicting beliefs and practices" (Harris, 1989, p. 19).

Interpreting the Tasks of Teaching and Schooling

Communities for teacher research have particular ways of spending time, talking, and using text. Some research communities are also committed to a common task, which is, ultimately, the radical reform of schooling. Underlying this task is a set of assumptions about teaching, learning, and organizations. One critical assumption of participants in communities for teacher research is that teaching is primarily an intellectual activity that hinges on what Zumwalt (1982) calls the "deliberative" ability to reflect on, and make wise decisions about, practice. Teaching is regarded as a complicated and intentional activity requiring a great breadth and depth of professional knowledge and judgment in conditions that are inherently uncertain (Shulman, 1986, 1987, 1989). In contrast to the more technical view that teaching hinges on the use of particular techniques applied in various situations, a deliberative view of teaching regards teachers as professionals who use their knowledge to construct perspectives, choose actions, manage dilemmas, interpret and create curricula, make strategic choices, and, to a large extent, define their own teaching responsibilities (Cochran-Smith, 1991; Lampert, 1985). Teacher/researchers regard these tasks as opportunities for systematic intentional inquiry and regard the inquiries of others in the communities as opportunities for rethinking their own assumptions and practices. When teachers redefine their own relationships to knowledge about teaching and learning, they reconstruct their classrooms and begin to offer different invitations to their students to learn and know (Tatel, Chapter 5, this volume). A view of teaching as research is connected to a view of learning as constructive, meaning-centered, and social.

What we are emphasizing here is the reciprocal relationship between theories about teaching and theories about learning. Teachers who are actively researching their own practices provide opportunities for their students to become similarly engaged (Johnston, 1990; Schwartz, 1988). This means that what goes on in the classrooms of teacher/researchers is qualitatively different from what typically happens in other classrooms (Goodlad, 1984). Researching teachers create classroom environments in which there are researching students (Branscombe, Goswami, & Schwartz, 1992)—students ask, not just answer questions, pose, not just solve problems, and help to construct curriculum out of their own linguistic and cultural resources, not just receive preselected and predigested information. Britton (1987) reminds us that "every lesson should be for the teacher an inquiry, some further discovery, a quiet form of research" (p. 13). Our point here is that in every classroom where teachers are learners and all learners are teachers, there is a radical, but quiet, kind of school reform in process.

It is well documented that instruction is the most difficult aspect of schooling to control or change within the normal bureaucratic procedures. In fact, despite numerous efforts to govern classroom instruction from the outside—by prescriptive materials, training and inservicing programs, and elaborate schemes for evaluation—these strategies ultimately fail and teachers retain relative autonomy over what goes on in their own classrooms (Joyce, Showers, & Rolheiser-Bennett, 1987). To bring about instructional reform, teachers' potential to be thoughtful and deliberate architects of teaching and learning in their own classroom must be tapped and supported. We are not suggesting that complete independence for teachers is the answer to radical school reform, but that true reform depends on members of the teaching profession developing their own systematic and intentional ways of scrutinizing and improving their practices.

In teacher-research communities, the task of teachers is not simply to produce research, as some have argued is true in the academic research community (Jackson, 1990). Rather, the commitment of teacher/researchers is change—in their own classrooms, schools, districts, and professional organizations. At the base of this commitment is a deep and often passionately enacted responsibility to students' learning and life chances. The Philadelphia Teachers Learning Cooperative, for example, has met weekly for more than a decade in order to raise questions about its members' work and improve their practices with the students in their classrooms. Outsiders regard the work of the cooperative as teacher research and its activities as testimony to a longstanding commitment to systematic, intentional oral inquiry. But until recently members of the group did not refer to their work together as research, and their central purpose was and still is not to produce publications. Rather, teachers in the cooperative referred to their inquiry activities simply as teaching. And, as the following excerpt from a collaboratively written article about their work makes clear, their aim was to meet the needs of their students (Philadelphia Teachers Learning Cooperative, 1984):

> Teachers' Learning Cooperative helps teachers look for a way to accept and work with a diversity of learners, often suggesting that they wait for a year or more to see how the "slow learner" might develop. We do have a luxury of time to ask and wonder what will happen to a child. Last September Barbara asked us for ways to help Billie control her outbursts. What has happened to Billie since then? We often schedule a review of a review. Somehow it makes yesterday's temper tantrums and tomorrow's fight less anxious for us as teachers if we can look at Billie again. Billie is on her way toward greater awareness and control. (p. 733)

Groups like the Philadelphia Teachers Learning Cooperative see a very clear connection between inquiry and making a difference in the lives of their children. When teachers work together to construct knowledge about children's patterns of growth and development and generate teaching strategies, they are involved in an ongoing process of altering the social and intellectual life of their classrooms. In our discussion of the task of communities for teacher research, we have been suggesting that there can be powerful connections between teacher research and school reform. As we have indicated above, the activities of teacher research provide the grist for ongoing instructional revision and improvement. Further, teacher/researchers identify and help to establish priorities for the critical areas of school policy and practice that need to be reexamined. Teacher research will insure that the agenda for school change is informed by teachers' emic perspectives on everyday school life as well as by the perspectives of academic researchers, policymakers and funders, and the media (Cochran-Smith & Lytle, 1993). When teachers play an active role in shaping the agenda and the implementation of school reform efforts, it is inevitable that reform itself will become a contested notion. As teachers are called on to play increasingly important roles in school-based and district-level decision making, their research provides systematic evidence for, and raises serious questions about, what goes on in schools. When teachers themselves accumulate data and share them across school and community contexts, they not only change their relationships to knowledge about teaching but also dramatically realign their relationships to the brokers of knowledge and power in their schools, in the university, and even in the corporate community.

The most fundamental issue is whether teacher research will remain on the fringe of educational reform or be at the forefront. Our argument is that communities for teacher research—communities with particular ways of organizing time, using talk, constructing texts, and interpreting the tasks of teaching and schooling—have the potential to move teacher research from fringe to forefront by fostering reforms that amount to more than tinkering with or reinforcing existing structures. Communities of teacher/researchers can play an essential role in school reform. Not only will their work add to the knowledge base on teaching, but their collective power as knowledge-generating communities is likely to influence broader school policies regarding curriculum, assessment, school organization, and home–school linkages. Through teacher-research communities, teachers' voices can play a more prominent part in the dialogue of school reform.

NOTES

1. We have found it useful to take the following as a working definition for teacher research: *systematic, intentional inquiry by teachers about their own school and classroom work*. We base this definition in part on the work of Lawrence Stenhouse (Rudduck & Hopkins, 1985), who defines research in general as systematic, self-critical inquiry. In part we base it on an ongoing survey of the literature of teacher writing. This literature includes articles written by teachers, in-house collections of teachers' work-in-progress, monographs about teachers' classroom experiences, and published and unpublished teachers' journals and essays. With this definition we emphasize that there already exists a wide array of writing by teachers that is appropriately regarded as research (Lytle & Cochran-Smith, 1990).

2. Many teachers have written about their work in forms that can, we have argued, be appropriately regarded as research. We have proposed four categories as a tentative typology of teacher research that acknowledges a wider range of teachers' writing. In the first we include teachers' journals, published and unpublished. In the second category we place both brief and book-length essays in which teachers analyze their own classrooms or schools and consider issues related to learners, curricula, and school organization. The third category includes accounts of teachers' oral inquiries and discussions brought together specifically for reflection and questioning. These are usually preserved in the form of written transcriptions or notes. Our final category includes small and larger-scale classroom studies based on documentation and analysis procedures similar to those of university-based classroom research (Lytle & Cochran-Smith, 1990).

PART IV

NEW ROLES FOR TRADITIONAL STRUCTURES

If the changes that contour the landscape of teachers' professional practice are to be systemic in fact, then change in teachers' practice alone is not enough. Traditional institutional roles must be redrawn with new visions of practice and professional development in view. Part IV looks at reform from the perspective of two pillars in teachers' professional context—unions and higher education.

Unions. In Chapter 10, Charles Taylor Kerchner offers an analysis of new roles for teachers' organizations as agents and agencies for teachers' professional development. Teacher unions traditionally have focused on teachers' working conditions and have been little involved in their professional development. As Kerchner elaborates, this changed role prompts changes in traditional relationships among teachers, administrators, district trustees, and the union itself.

Teachers' Preservice Programs. The reformers' challenge reaches deep into the design structure and practices of preservice training. Stephanie Dalton and Ellen Moir, in Chapter 11, and Kip Téllez and Myrna D. Cohen, in Chapter 12, describe new teacher preparation programs launched in an effort to better prepare teachers for the contemporary classroom. The diverse languages, cultures, and everyday circumstances today's students bring to school present a challenge most teachers are unprepared to meet. The innovative teacher education programs underway at the University of California, Santa Cruz, and the University of Houston model institutional arrangements and curricula to equip new teachers with the skills and perspectives they need to succeed in today's classroom.

Preservice for Principals. If the redefined role of preservice as training for changing realities is taken seriously, then principals' jobs also must be rethought. Being a principal can no longer simply involve effective management of school affairs, as conveyed through traditional "Ed Admin" courses. The skills of an effective principal must grow out of practice and highlight creating and supporting an effective learning environment for all in the school workplace. In Chapter 13, Edwin Bridges and Philip Hallinger describe the salient features of a new form of preservice professional development for administrators that can meet that demand: problem-based learning.

District–University Partnerships. Systemic creation of a community of practice means constructing a conversation between preservice and inservice educators. Two essential voices in the dialogue—that of a University of Southern Maine faculty member, Lynne Miller, and an involved district principal, Cynthia O'Shea—reflect together, in Chapter 14, on the lessons learned from the first nine years of the Southern Maine Partnership, which ranks among the nation's most successful district–university collaborations.

Chapter 10

The Role of Teachers' Organizations

Reflections on Educational Policy Trust Agreements

Charles Taylor Kerchner

The idea of bread-and-butter unionism is well understood in America: unions as negotiators of salaries and protectors of jobs. Less well understood, but in many respects more at the core, is the potential, and sometimes realized, role of unions in creating professional communities. The transition from industrial to professional modes of unionism is not simply an advancement up the psychological hierarchy from sustenance to self-actualization. Rather, it is the realization that the substance of work permeates everything: how teachers spend time; how the rewards of teaching flow from children and classrooms; the relationships formed with colleagues, children, and parents. Pay and working conditions are not a separate agenda, severed from teaching's substance and relationships. They are a single whole.

The emerging professional unionism is in stark contrast to the established ideology surrounding industrial unionism (Kerchner & Koppich, 1993). Despite the headlines about breakthrough contracts and the academic interest in new labor–management arrangements, the *institution* of labor relations has changed little in the past decade. Most unions and most school districts still negotiate over a relatively narrow package of items. Most act as if the consequences of collective bargaining are somehow divorced from problems of school operation and student achievement. Most simply follow patterns established by state union organizations on the one hand and management associations on the other.

Professional unionism departs from three of industrial unionism's most cherished assumptions and central organizing concepts, and gradually replaces them with an emerging set of beliefs about what unions should do and be:

- Unions and management are discarding beliefs about the inherent separateness of their domains. Emphasis is moving toward a collective mode of operation exemplified by on-site decision making, team-teaching, and district-level councils and committees.
- Unions and management are seeing the limits to adversariness as an organizing strategy. They have come to believe that organizing teaching work depends on flexibility and commitment as well as the observance of rules and the execution of preplanned policies.
- Unions and management are rethinking ideas about the rights and responsibilities of teachers. Unions are beginning to recognize that the integrity of teaching, as well as the due-process rights of individual teachers, need protection. Management sees that unions have a legitimate role to play in the protection of teaching and that evaluation and assessment are not their exclusive prerogative.

One experiment in turning the force of unionism toward the power of professionalism took place in California in the 1980s, and its effects still linger. The Educational Policy Trust Agreement project has its origins in research that Douglas Mitchell and I carried out in the late 1970s and early 1980s (Kerchner & Mitchell, 1988). Looking at schools that had what most agreed to be "good labor relations," we noticed that much of the relationship between union and management occurred in settings away from contract negotiations and that the relationship was either part of the organizational culture or strongly interpersonal. When aspects of this larger relationship were written down, it was usually in documents other than the labor contract. When asked, the parties often said that they chose not to use the labor contract because the problems that they were trying to solve were ambiguous. Both parties understood that there was a problem, both parties were sure that they wanted to work toward a solution, but neither party was confident of the exact dimensions of the solution. Sidebar agreements, memoranda, or unwritten understandings provided the flexibility both parties wanted.

At the same time, we realized that only a few unions had been able to successfully switch focus from wages, benefits, and employment conditions to the substance of teaching. For unions, as for management, the transition is highly ideological and fraught with difficulty. We concluded that if teachers could have an agreement parallel to the contract—one that left their existing relationship in place while allowing an expanded relationship to grow alongside—then the pathway from industrial unionism to professional unionism might be smoothed.

The concept of Educational Policy Trust Agreements was first presented in testimony to the California Commission for the Teaching Professions. The Trust Agreement name embodies its essential logic:

- *Educational policy:* Agreements are intended to focus on the teaching–learning process, the central function of schools. Entering into a Trust Agreement mode of labor relations involves recognizing that policy and practice intertwine and that teachers, through the hundreds of decisions they make daily, are already involved in educational policy. Furthermore, through collective bargaining, teachers already distribute most of the schools' operating funds and dramatically affect the culture of schools.
- *Trust:* The word *trust*, as we use it, has two meanings. The first involves the reliability and truthfulness of the other party. The second involves *entrusting resources to a person or group for the benefit of others*. These are the kinds of trusts that parents establish for their offspring, that philanthropists create for the benefit of society, and that governments found to protect national treasures.

A suggestion for a pilot program was made to both the California Teachers Association and the California Federation of Teachers (CFT). Miles Myers, then president of the CFT, responded favorably to the idea of a trial, and work began in two school districts. The Petaluma City Schools responded to the Trust Agreement idea with great enthusiasm, and after a series of informal meetings, the Petaluma Federation of Teachers and the school administration began to negotiate what would be the first Trust Agreement. Meanwhile, the leadership of the Poway Federation of Teachers began to explore the process.

The California Department of Education supported legislation, and an appropriations bill passed the legislature only to be vetoed by Governor George Deukmejian. In the wake of this defeat, the Stuart Foundations in San Francisco agreed to entertain a proposal. Over a period of five years, the foundations granted the project some $500,000. Julia Koppich agreed to direct the project, which was lodged at Policy Analysis for California Education at the University of California, Berkeley.

With funding secured, the project expanded to 12 districts ranging in enrollment from 2,500 to more than 60,000 students. The project began in 1987 and foundation funding ended in 1991. Five of the twelve districts have continued their projects, and some have expanded them substantially.

AGREEMENTS FOR AMBIGUOUS SITUATIONS

Trust Agreements are designed to do what contracts can't—or don't. Collective bargaining contracts are intended to govern behavior, not to express the concepts, plans, or intentions of those who negotiate them. They are formulated with the express intent of reducing flexibility and uncertainty so that there will be fewer opportunities for mistreatment or abuse of workers. From the standpoint of organizational policy and planning, labor contracts are viewed as restrictions on the practices that can be used. They specify the conditions under which workers are expected to toil, but they do not define the goals or programmatic frameworks for organizing their efforts. And there are good reasons why this is so.

In contrast, a good Trust Agreement requires managing ambiguity: allocating authority so basic goals can be pursued under circumstances unimagined by the document's creators. This is a primary problem in educational reform, where it is seldom possible to predetermine details of successful reform. Knowledge about "what works" is nearly always heuristic, and thus, agreements about educational policy need to work within an inherently uncertain environment.

One of the values of Trust Agreements was to be their individuality: Each agreement was to be crafted by its creators for a particular use in a specific setting. There was no "boilerplate" or prepackaged text that could be transferred from one school district to another. Part of the experiment was to see to what uses the new form of agreement would be put. Three topics predominated: peer review and assistance, organizational development, and staff development.

Peer Review and Assistance

Three Trust Agreement districts built on the experience of the Toledo, Ohio, peer review plan. The Poway Unified School District (23,000 students in suburban San Diego) and the Poway Federation of Teachers (PFT) have developed the largest and most substantive peer assistance and evaluation program. The Lompoc Unified School district

(10,000 students in Santa Barbara County) and the Lompoc Federation of Teachers have developed and implemented a plan for novice teachers. San Diego has a program for staff assistance, but without an evaluation component. The Santa Cruz schools and unions also developed a peer review plan but fell victim to personnel changes and budget cutbacks.

The Poway Agreement was particularly interesting because it came in the wake of antagonistic labor relations. Never in 20 years had the school district and the PFT achieved a contract agreement before school opened in the fall, and in several years, negotiators barely finished negotiating one contract before it was time to start on the next. The superintendent sought a broader dialogue with teachers as a way of making the union less necessary. The union president sought to make the superintendent less credible. Yet out of this situation has come what is arguably the country's most fully developed peer review program, a vastly improved labor relations climate marked by two expeditiously negotiated settlements, a stronger union, and better interpersonal relationships.

The Poway and Lompoc peer review systems are concerned with providing both formative assistance and a substantive recommendation about contract renewal of novice teachers. In each district, teacher consultants are released (either full- or part-time) from other duties to assist new teachers. Interaction between consultants and novices begins with simple survival assistance. Consultants help teachers set up rooms, plan lessons, establish discipline. Sometimes they take over classes so that the novice can visit another school or confer with a teacher who is considered an expert in particular subject or method of teaching.

The consultants report to a governing board composed of union-appointed teachers and superintendent-appointed administrators. In March they make formal recommendations concerning contract continuation. In the first five years of the Poway program, 297 first-year teachers passed through the program, of whom 14 were released; 7 additional teachers were released during or at the end of their second year.

The governing board has yet to have a split vote, and the dialogue among the members clearly shows administrators and unionists alike taking on new roles. Administrators learned to listen and respect teacher judgments; the unionists learned to demand more than minimal standards from teachers. In the process, the standards for teaching in the district changed. During the observation of one governing board session (Kerchner & Koppich, 1993), one teacher said, "This teacher meets district standards . . . but something bothers me. This [24-year-old] teacher is like fine white wine that has begun to go to vinegar. She teaches like someone over 60" (p. 170).

A remarkable discussion followed. The district's evaluation form, modeled after a Madeline Hunter lesson plan, did not mention joy, enthusiasm, or engagement in teaching. The Hunter method of teaching had been the district standard, widely taught in inservice education courses; the presentation of lessons with all the appropriate steps had been the basis for evaluative observations, originally by principals and later by consulting teachers. The district's evaluation form did not consider situational adaptivity or receptivity to new ideas, but all on the governing board agreed that these qualities were what made good teaching.

In effect, the criteria for being a good teacher in Poway changed that afternoon. The review panel recognized the artistic dimension of teaching. Within the next year, consulting teachers coined a new phrase, "in, through, and beyond Madeline Hunter." New teachers are expected to have basic craft skills in lesson presentation, but they are also expected to develop their classrooms as interesting places of learning and inquiry.

In Poway, although not yet in Lompoc, the novice teacher program has been joined by an intervention program for permanent teachers judged to be in "serious professional jeopardy." And during the 1990–91 school year, the district and union instituted an alternative to conventional teacher evaluation that begins with teacher-made goal statements for professional growth. At a conference held early in the fall, teacher and principal meet, discuss, and agree on acceptable goals. They also decide on an alternative means of evaluation, which may include portfolios, peer coaching, classroom action research, participation in structured staff development, or a collaborative group of teachers that self-evaluate.

Organizational Development

Several districts have negotiated organizational development Agreements (see Koppich & Kerchner, 1990, for text of the agreements and details).

The San Juan Unified School District (in Sacramento County) and San Juan Teachers Association have developed an Agreement around site-based management for the district of 40,000 students. The program is designed to provide individual schools with greater flexibility and increased opportunities to solve educational problems the schools identify, following this philosophy:

We believe decisions about educational issues should be made by those closest to the issues and most responsible for their implementation. It is our belief that as school employees become more closely and creatively involved in making decisions, the quality of education improves. Better decisions lead to quality instruction. (Koppich & Kerchner, 1990, p. 53)

The program, now in nine schools, is governed by a districtwide committee of teachers and administrators.

The Morgan Hill Unified School District (5,000 students) and Morgan Hill Federation of Teachers also wrote an organizational development Agreement. The program announcement, issued jointly by the union and superintendent, asked:

If you could explore, with a team of colleagues, alternative ways of organizing teachers and students for increased effectiveness, productivity, and learning, what would you do differently? How would you go about developing a plan for changing the way you deliver instruction? (Koppich & Kerchner, 1990, p. 30)

Interested schools were invited to assemble teams of teachers and administrators and develop action proposals. The union and administration held a joint "bidders conference" where teachers could share ideas and ask questions about the process. A joint committee awarded the grants.

Staff Development

Petaluma City Schools, a jointly managed elementary–high school district with a combined enrollment of approximately 8,500 students, has negotiated two Trust Agreements. The first reorganized the district's staff development efforts. Previously, staff development in Petaluma was run by a central office administrator with little or no teacher involvement. Teachers and administrators chose staff development as an important area because it seemed noncontroversial and relatively straightforward—safe ground on which they could start. The Agreement restructured district staff development days, with a teacher–administrator team planning and executing the event, and placed a new emphasis on nurturing and developing teacher expertise in the district rather than on speeches by outsiders. (I sat with decidedly mixed emotions as the teachers voted not to hire any more professors to run inservice programs.)

On the surface, the Petaluma Agreement is simple, but it has unfrozen teacher expectations of themselves and of their school district (Bascia, 1994). Teachers now expect to be involved in school-level decisions, an expectation that initially was greeted with nervousness by school principals but that has laid the groundwork for a second Agreement on decentralized decision making.

San Francisco Unified School District (60,000 students) and the San Francisco Federation of Teachers have operated a paraprofessional career development project for two years. The project provides flexible work schedules and substantive assistance so that paraprofessionals can complete bachelor's degrees and teacher certification. Eighteen paraprofessionals are in the program this year; seven have completed and are now probationary teachers in San Francisco. The Claire Lilienthal Elementary School has an Agreement for a curriculum project in which decisions about text selection and curriculum organization are made at the school rather than at the district office. More important, the money that would have been spent on textbooks was made available to the faculty to purchase instructional materials of their own choosing.

LESSONS LEARNED

Although it was copied by other districts, such as Cincinnati (King, 1991), the Trust Agreement project failed to grow beyond its pilot project stage in California. From it, one can draw lessons about home-grown reform: If reforms challenge existing hierarchical power relationships, they will be resisted; if they're not glossy enough, they will be ignored. Trust Agreements were too radical for statewide practitioners' organizations, too different for some teachers, and not dramatic enough to gather the acclaim of the educational reformers.

The California Education Association, the dominant teachers union in the state, turned against the project, and its members attempted to decertify the rival union, which was affiliated with the American Federation of Teachers (AFT), in Petaluma. The support of the AFT and its California affiliate also cooled after Miles Myers left the presidency of the CFT. The California School Boards Association and the Association of California School Administrators remained officially supportive, but increasing the scope of relationships between unions and school districts was seen as undermining the authority of school administrators and board members. Trust Agreements made them nervous.

Ultimately, organizational support and foundation support went toward a politically safer mode of labor relations reform represented by the California Foundation for the Improvement of Employee/Employer Relations (CFIER). CFIER has been a highly successful program built around the techniques of reducing conflict in collective bargaining. Unlike the Trust Agreement approach, it makes no alterations in the structure of labor relations or the authority structures within school districts. Its operating assumptions are that the fundamental problem with existing labor relations rests in unnecessary antagonism and that training in conflict reduction will yield more fruitful agreements. What needed to be fixed was how people talked, not necessarily what they talked about.

Trust Agreements started with a different assumption—that the fundamental problem was less a lack of cooperation than a system that failed to focus on important educational problems. Underneath the Trust Agreement idea was a notion of a professional mode of unionism that explicitly departed from many of the beliefs of industrial unionism (Kerchner & Koppich, 1993). It suggested that unions had not only a right to discuss educational policy questions but a duty to engage in the thorny and difficult problems and to make judgments about the distribution of resources for programmatic ideas and the personal gains of its members. It asserted that the command and control hierarchy of school districts was incapable of producing real reform. It confronted the conventional wisdom—and thus was resisted.

Paradoxically, the policy community saw the Trust Agreements as too marginalist. The efforts of teachers to manage their own staff development in a small city such as Petaluma were viewed as quaint by visitors from New York, and the scale of most projects failed to impress those who sought dramatic ways to restructure districts and schools. It was sometimes difficult to see the substance. Much more visible reforms could be found in cities such as Miami, Rochester, Louisville, and Pittsburgh.

From an insider's perspective, the Trust Agreement project had one major failing and one major positive attribute that have not been well recognized or capitalized on.

A Failure to Grab the Purse Strings

The largest structural failure of the Trust Agreement project was our inability to convince school districts and unions to take a noticeable percentage of the school budget and place it in trust for the pursuit of educational projects identified by the district and union. The Trust Agreement projects were not bold enough largely because they were not well funded. The best and most extensive of the projects is arguably the Poway peer review and assessment project, and it was financed by $100,000 set aside annually in the teacher's contract. One can easily observe that the inability to sequester money for educational reform and improvement, particularly in hard times, has undercut most of the reform ventures of the 1980s. In public budgets, reform and experimentation are treated as fiscally expendable. Consequently, a sustained attack on problems that are ambiguous, those which have no certain solution, is nearly impossible to maintain. The history of reform efforts nation-wide during the recession of the late 1980s is a splendid example. When the surplus cash stopped, reform foundered.

The Trust Agreement project made an important strategic error by not making setting aside resources for reform an explicit part of its agenda. As one of the requirements for participation, the project insisted on a written indication of support by union, administration, and school board. It did not ask for a budgetary allocation. Sequestering even 1% of a district's budget for reform would have given Trust Agreements much greater substance, and this process would have tested the will of unions, managers, and school boards to protect teacher-driven reforms during tight fiscal times.

A Stealth Weapon for Change

On the other hand, Trust Agreements appear to be very good vehicles for incremental change. They are quiet and capable of keeping a process of small steps going forward. The Japanese word *kaizen* means the pursuit of continuous, organized self-improvement. The underlying logic is that many small changes add up to a virtual redesign of a product or service. The process is more like intensive gardening than strategic planning. The best of the Trust Agreement projects, five of which continued after the expiration of extramural funding, exemplified this characteristic. These agreements were as much about instituting a process as they were about a discrete product. Participants learned to make tough decisions about educational problems and formed sufficiently strong personal relationships that change efforts continued even during tough times. For example, we found that the process of negotiating a Trust Agreement was substantially different from negotiating a conventional labor contract, and the differences were not captured by the differences between antagonism and friendliness. The dialogue in Trust Agreement negotiations was about solving problems, not dividing up resources. As a result, people brought things rather than taking them away. Because the process was usually fiscally starved, people brought other important resources, particularly time and authority.

Time is probably the most precious commodity in a school district. Buying more of it is usually prohibitively expensive, as school boards and legislatures find when they attempt to extend the school day or the school year. But the Trust Agreement project engendered large gifts of "free time" from teachers and administrators because the workers valued the projects in which they were involved.

Authority, usually the most carefully guarded resource in a bureaucracy, was freely relinquished. One assistant superintendent said proudly of a completed staff development project, "All I did was to pull the curtain in the auditorium; the teachers made all the decisions." People came to value good decisions more than who it was that made them. Relatively effortlessly, participants were able to focus on the problem, not on one another (Fisher & Ury, 1981).

Because Trust Agreements altered authority relationships, they helped produce role changes that redefined leadership for both school administrators and teacher unionists. The gradual adoption of new roles, which was by no means universal, allowed people to engage in programs of school improvement and self-renewal simultaneously.

Linking the capacity for continuous improvement to the organizational structures that allocate resources remains an important but largely unexploited legacy of the Trust Agreement project. It is that capacity that allows teachers a larger measure of control over their work and responsibility for it. In a word: professionalism.

Chapter 11

Text and Context for Professional Development of New Bilingual Teachers

Stephanie Dalton and Ellen Moir

The nation faces a major challenge in reshaping its schools to meet the changing diversity of its population. In California alone, more than 1.2 million students with limited English proficiency, close to 100 different language groups, and dozens of cultural groups are now represented in classrooms (Linguistic Minority Research Institute, 1994). These dramatic changes in student populations in California and elsewhere mean that many teachers work with students whose backgrounds are linguistically and culturally different from their own. Too often, new teachers find themselves unprepared to teach students from diverse backgrounds. Yet preservice programs are typically classroom-based, providing little opportunity for intending teachers to practice applications of what they learn. In preservice education, California's Commission on Teacher Credentialing began to shape new credentialing structures for teachers, which recognize teachers' needs to know more about the students they will be teaching: cross-cultural, language, and academic development (CLAD) and bilingual CLAD certificates embody an effort to provide teachers with the cultural knowledge and language skills necessary for contemporary classrooms.

As the program described in this chapter demonstrates, the promise of new credentialing structures will be realized when preservice and inservice are linked in symbiotic ways to support new teachers' full-time practice in culturally diverse classrooms. In such a relationship, new teacher program support draws on the text of preservice education to assist new teachers in the context of contemporary classrooms. Preservice and inservice programs that come together for mutual benefit relate preservice text to diverse classroom contexts and inform both programs from the perspective of practice. New teacher support programs using this approach provide a means to evaluate the capacity of inservice programs to respond to, and preservice program capacity to prepare, intending teachers.

Evaluation in preservice and inservice teacher education programs offers a largely neglected instrument by which programs and individual teachers can develop responsiveness to rapidly changing student populations and teaching conditions (Dalton & Moir, 1992). A preservice program preparing teachers for bilingual classrooms and responsive to CLAD and bilingual CLAD needs flexibility to stay abreast of current research and adapt to the needs of teachers in changing conditions. In practice, few program evaluations are designed for internal use in program improvement or to increase understanding about developmental processes of either individual teachers or the program itself.

The Santa Cruz County New Teacher Project (SCCNTP) is one of eight programs in California to link preservice education with the first two years of professional teaching. SCCNTP has the dual goal of providing teachers with the skills and experience necessary for them to succeed in today's teaching context and of providing the necessary infrastructure, such as program evaluation, to accomplish teacher support and assistance. SCCNTP is designed to help teachers apply preservice knowledge in the context of culturally diverse classrooms and to increase its own capacity to encourage and facilitate teachers' development in the first two years of teaching culturally diverse students. For SCCNTP, evaluation is different from that in most teacher education programs, where evaluation is usually conducted for accountability reports to accrediting or other external agencies. The relationship between SCCNTP's teacher support and program evaluation components leads to program improvement and affects the preservice program most participating SCCNTP teachers have completed. This symbiotic relationship of teacher support, program evaluation, and preservice program feedback refines SCCNTP's capacity to respond effectively to teacher needs as they emerge in diverse classrooms.

This chapter elaborates SCCNTP's dual approach to providing new teachers with needed support, first of all with feedback about ways to improve, and with preservice education with applications in the context of culturally diverse classrooms. Dropout rates for teachers nationwide are 30% for the first two years, rising to 50% after seven years. After six years, SCCNTP has lost only 5% of the 300 teachers participating in the program. In this chapter, we argue that the key to this accomplishment resides in the effect SCCNTP program evaluation has on the program's capacity to provide sensitive and responsive support for new teachers in classrooms serving linguistically and culturally diverse students. Program evaluation informs SCCNTP's role definitions and structure, which are basic to its capacity to assist new teachers in substantive ways.

PROGRAM CHANGE AGENT: SCCNTP TEACHER ADVISOR

The SCCNTP is a consortium of university faculty, advisors who are bilingual teachers themselves on two-year leaves from their classrooms, new teachers, principals, and superintendents. On the basis of research and ongoing practice, this group determines the program's principles of effective practice and oversees the program's evaluation. Guided by the consortium's principles, the SCCNTP advisors are at the heart of the evaluation process, functioning as change agents. Working shoulder to shoulder with new teachers, and weekly with consortium colleagues, advisors bridge preservice and inservice for the new teachers. Induction as a SCCNTP advisor means joining a community of peers who meet weekly to improve their support and assessment practice. The advisor receives training in coaching strategies, culturally responsive pedagogy, teacher assessment, needs and developmental stages of new teachers, and portfolio development. Advisors play three roles in helping teachers adjust their practice to culturally diverse students: they focus on making the new teachers comfortable in the new setting, they are the educational companion committed to developing the new teacher's professional competence, and they are the agent of change who promotes collaboration, shared inquiry, and networking with colleagues. The advisor also provides feedback to the preservice program. In weekly meetings, the advisors relay to university preservice faculty the strengths and weaknesses the new teachers discovered in the context of practice. In bimonthly consortium meetings, the advisors share with the consortium the midyear and end-of-year new teachers' evaluations in order to assess how the preservice and inservice program might better meet teacher needs.

Each advisor has a caseload of 13 new teachers. Familiarity with students in the class, the overall curriculum plan, and the class structure and organization enables the advisor to provide each new teacher with context-specific praise and suggestions. When in the classroom, advisors teach demonstration lessons, observe, coach, co-teach, videotape lessons, respond to interactive journals, and assist with problems as they arise. Time outside the classroom is spent planning, gathering bilingual materials, and providing emotional support and safe structures for reflection and feedback.

New teachers and their advisors use interactive journals to pose questions, reflect on daily classroom experiences, assess beginning teacher needs, provide assistance for effective practice in diverse classrooms, and support and validate beginning teachers' efforts. In addition to the interactive journal, advisors provide feedback and support by observing other experienced bilingual teachers as well as the beginning teacher and discussing the observations. Finally, they facilitate essential networking opportunities among beginning teachers.

SCCNTP PRINCIPLES OF EFFECTIVE PRACTICE FOR LANGUAGE-MINORITY STUDENTS

Advisors orient their feedback to new teachers according to the content principles established by the consortium. These principles are derived from research literature on culture and education, bilingual research findings, and collegial conversation among consortium members that draws on a practice perspective. The principles comprise the template against which advisors assess new teacher practices and frame their counsel. A sketch of one of the program's content focus areas and an outline of its principles of practice illustrates how research and practice together shape the SCCNTP program.

A central concern that shapes the SCCNTP principles is the question of which language to use in classroom instruction (Garcia, 1990). The SCCNTP promotes bilingualism as an asset and is shaped by the conviction that in view of research findings, a demand for early English competency is seriously misguided. What has been ignored in this policy is the cost to the young learners and their families in primary-language loss—what has been referred to as "subtractive bilingualism" (Wong-Fillmore, 1991). Language-learning research indicates that second-language development is not significantly impeded by native language. In fact, research has shown that human cognition is organized to accommodate new language learning (McLaughlin, 1990). Research supporting bilingualism as an asset to thinking is replacing the notion of bilingualism as a deficit condition (Diaz, 1983; Hakuta, 1986). Cognitive and linguistic research, such as that by Lily Wong-Fillmore and the growing influence of Vygotskian theory, increasingly inform our understanding about the critical role of language and dialogue in the education of language-minority students. Native-language instruction can be a highly effective form of assistance for language-minority students' academic learning. Language instruction in the home language through sixth grade, native-language programs in middle school, and two-way or dual-immersion programs are yielding success. Requiring English competency without commensurate support in students' home languages deprives educators and schools of the means of promoting success for these students. In sum, there is sufficient consensus among educational researchers and practitioners to emphasize language development as a focus for classroom practice and support.

The following principles of SCCNTP focus especially on the issue of the language of instruction relating to culturally diverse student populations:

1. Instruction in students' home language provides valuable assistance for academic learning and second-language learning.
2. Language development in the language of instruction needs continual and strategic emphasis supported by instruction in students' home languages.
3. Effective pedagogy based in activity and conversation is culturally sensitive and responsive to culturally diverse students' funds of knowledge.
4. Teaching, curriculum, and the school itself are contextualized in the experiences, skills, and values of the student and community.

PRINCIPLES OF SCCNTP PROGRAM EVALUATION

SCCNTP's aims are to establish collegial partnerships that support new teachers, provide the program with feedback about ways to improve, and inform preservice education from the perspective of practice in culturally diverse classrooms. Through collegiality and networking teachers have opportunities for problem posing and problem solving, and they are encouraged to reflect on their practice, making revisions to benefit all students, particularly those from linguistically and culturally diverse backgrounds. When evaluation is concerned with program roles and relationships as the means of contextualizing substantive content, it becomes process-focused.

SCCNTP's evaluation design is in keeping with its collegial, nonjudgmental approach to beginning teacher support. Evaluative feedback, whenever possible, is the natural product of support services and the ongoing process of relationship-building between teacher and advisor. An example of such a source is the interactive journal. Other data sources include learning plans, advisor logs, teaching videotapes, student work samples, artifacts/evidences representing teachers' goals, checklists, rating scales, and reviews. For the second-year teachers, sources include professional projects and portfolios. Data are also collected by a questionnaire on teacher demographics, distribution of teacher support-time among advisors, and surveys of advisors' and teachers' beliefs and attitudes. In other words, the evaluation component is participatory and ongoing in order to capture work-in-progress.

SCCNTP's evaluation is designed by consortium members, faculty, and teachers. It reflects the following design principles:

1. Include program participants in program evaluation design in order to promote stakeholding.
2. Use broad-based methods and authentic measures to obtain multiple perspectives from program clients on program experience in order to maximize program responsiveness to feedback.
3. Design professional development program evaluation in order to obtain feedback about program content emphases.
4. Identify, showcase, and share program achievements and ways the program responds to feedback.

Program Evaluation Findings

At SCCNTP, advisors and new teachers use the Continuum of Skills, Knowledge and Attitudes (Moir & Garmston, 1992) to assess the performance of new teachers over time. With the aid of this instrument and the interactive journals, new teachers receive continuous skill-building feedback from the advisors.

The interactive journals are coded along five of the six domains of the continuum: (1) organizing and managing the classroom/creating a positive learning environment, (2) planning and designing instruction, (3) delivering instruction to all students, (4) diagnosing and evaluating student learning, and (5) participating as members of a learning community. In the analysis of journal entries, we found that advisors' thematic emphases for teacher support were similar, indicating a shared perspective and knowledge base. For example, in addition to praising, advisors often used cues from lessons or teacher's previous discussion as ways to offer suggestions, feedback, or validation for teaching activity. Journal entries and interviews indicated that teachers' feedback to advisors is largely extremely positive. The new teachers' positive orientation to the program was also clearly evident in the program's midyear and end-of-the-year evaluations.

The principal message emerging from both evaluation periods was one of harmony between the aims of the project and the goals of the participants. In particular, in both the first (midyear evaluations) and second (end-of-year evaluations) response periods, the supportive presence of the advisor was seen as most beneficial. In addition to the support new teachers receive from their advisors, they also participate in monthly seminar series and five days of professional development. Most of the first-year and all second-year teachers attend a two-day session on cultural diversity. Although the content of these workshops and release days is rated very highly by the new teachers, the opportunities for networking, reflection, and problem solving with other beginning teachers are found to be the most valuable aspect.

In SCCNTP, program evaluation has encouraged review of program-content emphases and process, and has informed the program's change agents, the teacher advisors, as expected. Interactive journals and teachers' evaluations of the program are extremely positive regarding professional relations between the advisors and new teachers. The trust established in this relationship demonstrates that the program is applying its guiding principles in ways that satisfy teachers. Enhanced professional relations producing teacher competence is an effect of assistance that contextualizes new teachers' knowledge and skills in culturally diverse classrooms, where they are needed. Aspects of the program and program relationships can be improved—particularly the linkage with preservice training. Overall, the program's orientation to process has improved relationships within and across programs for the mutual benefit of all.

CONCLUSION

SCCNTP contributes to professional development for teachers of culturally diverse students and illuminates an essential area of professional development practice: support for new teachers to apply what they have learned in preservice training to culturally diverse classrooms in ways that meet teachers' needs to develop through evaluative feedback. From its program evaluation experience, SCCNTP strongly recommends that new teacher support be:

- *Interactive*: The advisor–new teacher relationship engenders responsive dialogue for discussing and reflecting on practice.

- *Contextualized*: Advisors assist applications to practice in the context of diverse classrooms.
- *Co-constructed*: Through regular discourse in person and through journal entries, the new teacher and advisor can construct and review lessons together.
- *Routinized*: The feedback new teachers receive and give is embedded in the routines of daily practice.

Evaluation is a form of program self-reflection and construction. Through evaluation, programs themselves enter a developmental process, responding as a community to make meaning, share learning, and increase program impact.

Chapter 12

Preparing Teachers for Multicultural, Inner-City Classrooms

Grinding New Lenses

Kip Téllez and Myrna D. Cohen

For most teachers, the inner-city school is both familiar and foreign. The essential shell of a U.S. public school is easily recognizable in form and structure. But inside the inner-city school, below the veneer, is a world very different from the "typical" school as it exists in more advantaged communities. Decades of inadequate funding, political neglect, and inept urban school bureaucracies have contributed to the decay of inner-city schools and produced school settings where grime, violence, inadequate materials, and ravaged facilities are the rule. Neither teachers nor students are safe in many inner-city schools, and the environment provided there for public education signals society's disregard for the teachers and young people who work there. Conditions that elsewhere would be considered scandalous are everyday realities in many of America's inner-city schools.

The challenge to teaching and learning in the inner city extends beyond physical facilities, material resources, and visible signs of indifference. The children and youth who come to school in the nation's inner cities bring with them cultures, languages, family circumstances, values, and experiences foreign to many of their teachers. The special demands of children who live in the country's inner-city neighborhoods have long been recognized. In 1909, the progressive thinker Jane Addams (1911/1972) admonished those who could to take responsibility for their welfare and special needs: "It is as though we were deaf to the appeal of these young creatures, claiming their share of the joy of life, flinging out into the dingy city their desires and aspirations after unknown realities, their unutterable longings for companionship and pleasure" (pp. 70–71). Addams maintained that the schools were the only social institution that held any hope for "her" children. More than half a century later, Larry Cuban (1970) echoed Addams's assertion about the special needs of the teachers and students who teach and go to school in inner-city America. Traditional teacher preparation programs, in Cuban's view, could not prepare teachers to work effectively in inner-city schools. Weiner (1993) continued this call for attention to the challenges facing those working in the inner-city school and highlighted the clash between the cultures and experiences of so-called mainstream teachers and those of their urban students. Weiner, with Cuban and Addams, contends that teaching and learning in the inner city requires teachers prepared specifically for the cultures and everyday realities they will meet in their schools and classrooms.

Effective teaching and learning in the context of inner-city classrooms requires that teachers confront and reexamine many of the principles or orthodoxies they were taught in teacher-training programs and move toward practices with which they have little experience. In particular, teachers working in inner-city schools must separate two ideas: (1) what is sound pedagogy for inner-city students and (2) what they believe is good teaching, but which is in fact a suitcase filled with their own cultural heritage.

Few teachers have the experience, training, or personal background to assist them in this difficult task of adapting pedagogy and content to the learners who fill their inner-city classrooms. The cultural background of most teachers has never mirrored the children who attend schools in the inner city, and it now appears that the cultural discontinuity is growing as the number of African Americans and Hispanics who choose a career in teaching declines (Grant & Secada, 1990). Few teachers from traditional middle-class backgrounds have any knowledge of or experience with the often brutal life circumstances of inner-city youth and the multiple pressures they navigate daily. The new urban youth, in fact, arguably are even more stressed, more impoverished, and less well served by schools and society than were the children who so moved Jane Addams. In today's inner-city neighborhoods live children whose lives are often anything but childlike; in this context the common ideals of teaching—care, respect, and the communication of ideas—take on new meaning. Yet teacher education programs rarely prepare teachers for the special needs of inner-city teachers and students. Cursory courses in "Cultural Awareness" or "Urban Youth" often are the only apparent recognition given to the unique environments for teaching and learning found in the inner cities. To be sure, the problem is complex and little experience exists as guide. Teacher educators and policymakers hoping to prepare teachers who can successfully negotiate the urban world face ingrained ideas about "good" practice and few examples of successful multicultural, inner-city classrooms. Traditional practices and perspectives are entrenched. Decades of research on teacher development conclude: We teach the way we were taught (Hollingsworth, 1988; Ryan, 1970). Add to this the fear and uncertainty felt by those unfamiliar with inner cities. Prospective teachers are often frightened of inner-city students of color, especially teenagers, because they have no knowledge of who they are, what they care about, or how to motivate them. The media's portrayal of inner-city youth often encourages such fear. Other anxieties are professional. In the back of their minds, many teachers know that these students are going to require an education different from the one they received, and they feel ill prepared to make the adaptations necessary to succeed in inner-city classrooms and so must continue to rely on traditional routines and assumptions.

"Inner-city youth" is not a generic category. Youth of the inner city have different needs and interests depending on their background, language, and personal circumstances. From one perspective, all these differences in language, ethnicity, family status, and life conditions can be viewed as cultural differences. As educators who work with English as a Second Language teachers and students, we find that the theories and models of second-language acquisition present a particularly useful model for developing the capacity teachers need to teach effectively in the urban school. This chapter elaborates this approach to providing new teachers with a second [or third] "language" and "culture" and illustrates the teacher education program that results from it. Our approach is based on the belief that teacher educators face two fundamental tasks in preparing teachers to work effectively in inner-city schools: grinding new cultural lenses and enabling prospective teachers to learn new cultures.

GRINDING CULTURAL LENSES

Educators take for granted that effective teaching pivots on each teacher's understanding of the particular context in which he or she teaches and that an understanding of one's particular students is probably the most important understanding or knowledge a teacher can have. Without such understanding of students, it would be virtually impossible to implement even the most basic elements of teaching, such as linking prior knowledge and experience to new content, planning for relevant instruction, or even devising successful classroom management systems. Yet since the world views and environments of our inner-city students are typically so disparate from those who teach them, exceptional efforts are needed to provide teachers this understanding.

The cultural disparities between inner-city teachers and their students are not unlike those between peoples of different nationalities. Although other national cultures, notably Latino ones, are certainly represented in student populations of inner-city schools, represented as well are native English-speaking students with their own unique cultural contexts fashioned by family and neighborhood contexts. The social and economic realities of the inner city provide a particular challenge for teachers. We seem to assume that since we all live in the same country and often within close physical proximity of one another, a "foreign culture" comparison between mainstream teachers and these children may be too severe. However, we find it useful to regard inner-city students as we would students of foreign cultures in order to benefit from some of the tools developed to enhance cross-cultural sensitivity and language proficiency.

Second-language acquisition models suggest a number of important parallels between spoken language and cultural understanding. For example, those who successfully speak foreign languages are often more adept at constructing reality in the native speakers' terms than are those limited to their own language. They have the facility to remold their internal systems to accommodate new input, while less successful speakers work the other way around—they force the foreign input to fit their already solidly molded internal systems (Andersen, 1983). Guiora, for example, maintains that it is our culture and language that determine how we organize and construct reality and that to approximate the native speech of a foreign language one must reorganize the reality of the first culture to fit that of the second: "The speaker of every language is obliged, as he talks, to look at the world through a language-specific 'grid' that imposes upon him a particular kind of 'dissection,' a particular conceptualization" (Guiora et al., 1975, p. 57). Speaking another language entails exchanging the grid of the first language for the grid of the second. Switching grids enables one to develop the empathy that leads to authentic speech in the native speaker's terms.

If teachers in inner-city environments were to undergo this process, perhaps they would attain empathy and, consequently, the authentic speech of marginalized students. However, too often teachers, through lack of exposure or expertise, view their students through monocultural lenses that prevent them from viewing the world from the perspectives of those of different cultural orientations.

Viewing multicultural, inner-city youth through traditional lenses often leads to misunderstandings. Latino parents who fail to attend parent–teacher conferences or Parent–Teacher Organization meetings may be labeled as apathetic, while respect for teachers and embarrassment about poor language skills may be a more accurate interpretation of their behavior. Or a child's failure to bring in a few dollars for participation in a school fieldtrip may be considered irresponsible behavior, while in fact pride prevents that child from admitting the hardships the expenditure of those few dollars would cause the family. Monocultural lenses often result in missed opportunities. Abused children unresponsive to disciplinary measures may be erroneously classified as hopeless behavior problems. The conceptions of "appropriate family" attached to mainstream perspectives can mask alternative arrangements that may work for a child while simultaneously lending support to teachers' misconceptions that children from so-called dysfunctional families are less able or willing to learn. (Indeed, we often hear teachers lament that they are unable to educate children whose "parents" are not involved.) If a parent is unavailable or unable to support a child, why not enlist a grandparent or other consistent, reliable adult in a parenting role?

Becoming conscious of the monocultural nature of the lenses through which we see our students is a crucial first step toward this kind of multicultural sensitivity. Switching lenses presupposes the recognition that our own parsing and organization of the world is not the only option and that our particular perception is but one of many possibilities. This switch does not depend merely on intelligence, motivation, or skill (Guiora, Brannon, & Dull, 1972). Rather, it requires altering our language egos. Those who have permeable rather than fixed ego boundaries can move back and forth between languages and in doing so, switch cultural lenses.

The key to softening our ego boundaries is introspection and greater self-knowledge, which, according to Guiora, entails having a well-defined, secure, integrated ego and sense of self. The deeper one's introspective knowledge, the better the chances are for permeability. In fact, increased self-awareness and a strong sense of self are widely recognized as a means for reducing prejudice (Pate, 1988) and are necessary for the empowering "wide-awakeness" described by Greene (1978).

Willingness to explore other cultural perspectives is in itself a way to deepen self-knowledge. We better perceive our own cultural biases once we can compare our parsings with others. Similarly, the grammar and form of our native language become clearer when compared to those of a second language, just as we better understand our ethnocentricity once submerged in a foreign country. Therefore, teachers' attempts to understand the diverse cultures of their students is in itself one way to increase introspection and self-knowledge, which then, in turn, facilitates deeper empathy.

New lenses and languages cannot be acquired simply or even by increasing one's knowledge base about particular cultures, nor can one approach it on a cognitive level. New perspectives cannot be fashioned by adhering to someone else's tips on what to do and what not to do in culturally diverse classrooms, a point we cannot overemphasize. It is a personal undertaking, which entails grinding new lenses that will enable teachers to understand the world through the eyes of their students.

CONSTRUCTING CAPACITY: THE UNIVERSITY
OF HOUSTON PROGRAM

The most important point we must make with respect to building the capacity to work in inner-city settings is that this body of knowledge, whatever it may be, cannot be explicitly taught. An inner-city teacher must learn about culture as an anthropologist does. Indeed, cultural learning is quite different from cognitive learning (Clifford, 1988). Outsiders can only become insiders when they cease "learning" culture and act to "acquire" it. The difference between acquisition and learning is one of conscious involvement, participation, and reflection. Cultural learning cannot be reduced to a fieldtrip, nor can cultural learning come from a book or lecture. "Transmission teaching" works no better in preparing teachers than it does in educating students. As Landes (1965) argued, "separateness from the objects of discussion forfeits the experiences words should mirror" (p. 64). Many teacher educators who have acknowledged the importance of learning culture have placed prospective teachers in inner-city schools in order to gain this understanding. Unfortunately, schools are a poor place to acquire the culture of the children and families associated with them. The often impenetrable boundaries around school typically render them incapable of reflecting the cultural consciousness of the surrounding community. Local, "nontraditional" culture resides not in hegemonic institutions sanctioned and financed by the majority, but on the street corners, in community organizations, and in the living rooms of those whom we wish to understand. Building capacity to teach in the inner city must include a serious investigation into and interaction with the lives of children outside the school. In spite of this fact, teacher educators continue to view inner-city school placements, the earlier the better, as the "perennial panacea" (Weiner, 1993).

Our teacher education program at the University of Houston involves prospective teachers directly in the life of the community where they will be teaching so they can "acquire culture" (Tellez, Hlebowitsh, Cohen, & Norwood, in press). The University of Houston's community service component provides opportunities for students to volunteer in one of many social service agencies across the city, in concert with their observations in urban schools. Some students choose, for example, to work at the Chicano Family Center, while others opt to work in one of the largely African American Baptist churches of inner-city Houston. Intensive, sustained social interaction is key to these experiences and the ability of our students to acquire culture. Meaningful interactions with members of the community force our students to confront their stereotypes and to appreciate the perspective of families struggling with language, culture, poverty, and strains related to "making it" in the inner city.

For example, at an elementary professional development school site, we invited nine teacher education students to offer free English as a Second Language (ESL) instruction to the school's Spanish-speaking parents living in the apartment complex across the street from the school. The apartment unit was typical of many of those found in Houston. Designed and built for the oil boom singles who flooded the city in the 1970s, it was small and flimsy. Before the project began, the students had several fundamental concerns—most importantly, their safety. No teacher at the school had ever visited the apartment complex; some communicated to students that they should think twice about participating in this venture.

It was in these initial stages of developing our community service program that we felt like outsiders, typical "university" educators who fail to understand what teaching is about. A few of the veteran cooperating teachers, we learned, were unimpressed by the adult ESL project. Although the cooperating teachers spoke highly of the professional development program at their school—primarily because it placed the students in classrooms earlier and for longer periods of time than traditional teacher education programs—several saw the adult ESL project as confusing and unnecessary. One even told her student teacher that she was not to leave the classroom during the day to conduct her tutoring sessions.

Our project goal was to bring the parents to a level of oral-language proficiency sufficient for them to speak with teachers regarding their child's progress without the aid of a translator. None of the teachers at the school were proficient enough in Spanish to conduct parent conferences. A dramatic event occurred on the first day that illustrated the importance of the project to prospective teachers. One of the mothers, who was trying to speak to the students in her halting, broken English, began to cry out of frustration. A student journal notes:

> She began to cry as we talked about the limited conversations she has already had with her child's teacher; it is obvious that she loves her little girl very much and wants very badly for them both to assimilate into the school situation.

The isolation and alienation felt when one is not fluent in the dominant language became at once apparent to the students. After that, the students demonstrated a resolute commitment to the project, often working with "their" parents when other pressing matters demanded their attention.

Another student acquired culture as a volunteer at an adult ESL center organized by the local chapter of the Salvation Army. As she tutored her "student," a local Latino high school girl, she learned of Mexican culture from the perspective of a friend, not someone associated with the school system or a university professor. As a result, the myths she had heard about Latino parents were dispelled, she came to realize the wrenching effort that learning a second language required (she began to learn Spanish), and, perhaps most important, she grew close to the girl's family.

These experiences with non-English speakers and those with limited English proficiency benefited our students in several ways. First, our students gained some initial understandings of the challenges facing low-income, limited-English-speaking parents. Second, students became convinced that they must learn to speak Spanish. Third, these direct involvements in the lives of inner-city residents taught our student valuable lessons about the realities of the students they would teach. For example, our students saw that many of the students who live in the complex simply do not have a place for study or homework. A 500-square-foot apartment shared by two families leaves no room for quiet concentration. Nor is there anyone there who can help the children when the work is in English. These volunteer activities enabled our students to better understand the children of the parents they taught.

Other students learned other aspects of inner-city culture. Those who volunteered to work in the homeless shelters serving our region had many of their preconceptions challenged and their understanding of the homeless greatly altered. Some of the Houston shelters serve whole families, while others restrict themselves to women and children. Some allow clients to stay for one month, while others are designed for extended residence. Our students typically are asked to work in the day-care facilities of the shelters, although some have worked with the adult populations as well. Regardless of what tasks they were asked to perform, our students uniformly expressed surprise about ways in which the shelters failed to meet their preconceived notions. Most students were shocked at the clean and convenient living conditions offered. Families, for instance, are given dormitory-type rooms with locks; washing machines are available, as are tutoring services for children, computer rooms, and beauty shops. In addition, our students often reported surprise, and later shame, as their stereotypes of "homeless children" crumbled in the face of increased understanding. For instance, a student at the shelter on a day when the children brought home report cards was amazed that there were many straight-"A" students. All of our students experienced emotional struggles as they wrestled with ideas about the homeless population. For example, one student at first could not relate to one teenage mother who refused to hold her baby or change his diapers. As time progressed, the rage toward the young mother turned to empathy as she revealed what had brought her to this behavior—a lifetime of devastating sexual abuse. Many students could not, at first, reckon how any responsible person could become homeless. Later, they began to question society for allowing this to happen. One student wrote in her journal: "It troubles and saddens me to think that at some point these people were in classrooms, and yet didn't get the skills they needed to succeed."

Our students began to show a true understanding of culture as a complex, ever-evolving construct. After the community-based projects, students were no longer convinced of the easy categories often promoted by so-called experts in multicultural education who peddle lists of characteristics (e.g., "This is the way African American parents deal with their children"). They also learned that the urban world has its share of dangers but that such dangers can be greatly minimized by applying the same precautions used in suburban settings.

Most important, many learned that they could become successful inner-city teachers. Urban teaching may require a greater personal transformation than suburban teaching, but many students find it worthwhile. Approximately 60% of our program's graduates have chosen the urban school setting.

LESSONS FOR TEACHER EDUCATORS

Teacher educators must let the experience do the teaching; they cannot teach about social inequality or cultural differences. Some teacher educators fear that students' initial, and often racist, views will become more entrenched as a result of a community-based experience such as we describe. We argue that a student who continues to "blame the victim" in spite of evidence to the contrary is likely not fit to teach and should perhaps be counseled out of the profession.

Some students object to the additional time and energy demanded by our community volunteer program. Some students maintain that they are "already doing it." For instance, we find that approximately 15% of our students report doing service work with their church or other organization (e.g., sorority); they usually ask if they can simply continue that project as a way to fulfill their community volunteer requirements. We explain that while such projects are worthwhile (e.g., painting homes of the elderly, loading food on trucks for homeless shelters), they lack an engagement with the people who live in the inner city. These projects usually involve "doing for" rather than "doing with." They lack the direct, personal social interaction we want them to experience.

Acquiring new culture and adjusting new lenses is an ongoing, difficult process. While the school and community placements are critical, prospective teachers must have a support group of cohorts who are facing similar challenges. We have observed the critical role of a support network for students who are faced with the challenges of working in inner-city schools. In these network communities, students discuss what they have observed, share lessons, work through their own prejudices, and provide psychological support for one another. For instance, emerging teachers in the University of Houston's Pedagogy for Urban and Multicultural Action (PUMA) program are invited to present portfolios of their teaching to a panel of urban classroom teachers and university faculty. Students are allowed to work together to complete their portfolios. This feature encourages beginning educators to rely on the support of other students in a similar predicament.

In spite of the success of the community-based project, we find ourselves short of the goals we have set. We still certify teachers who opt for suburban districts because they want to teach children whose educational challenges are not so great. These graduates report that they learned much about urban communities and schools and see the need for outstanding urban teachers but that they lack the personal strength to "deal with" urban children day after day. Perhaps they are no less dedicated than our other students, only more honest about their own capabilities. Urban teaching transforms us. It requires us to be at our very best when we think we can no longer give our best. It is often thankless, discouraging, and frustrating. We have come to recognize that not every potential teacher who wishes to work in the inner city can be effective (see also Haberman, 1987). But to meet the needs of those prospective teachers who want to teach in these challenging educational settings, teacher educators must begin to explore how preservice teachers can acquire culture and the understandings necessary for them to succeed. None of us needed a book or template to learn our first culture; we learned it through doing and living it. Prospective teachers and teacher educators are not able to intellectualize the acquisition of culture. The essence of urban teaching cannot be conceived or even perceived without new lenses ground from direct experience.

Chapter 13

Problem-Based Learning

A Promising Approach to Professional Development

Edwin Bridges and Philip Hallinger

You are the new principal of a middle school where one-third of the 950 students are Latino; 100 of those students have limited English proficiency. Ethnic tensions are mounting; the school is considered "a tinder box." You receive a letter from Mrs. Olsen, president of the "Concerned Parents Group":

> Year after year, these same people continue to expect the United States to support their lack of language acquisition. . . . Our concern is with the large numbers of such people who bleed all sorts of funding agencies and, generation after generation, never do learn English. The parents never read English books, never watch English television, and never attempt to speak English. Their children are cut from the same cloth; the only place they try to speak English is at school. . . . Before long these kids from across the border will be classified as "learning-disabled" and receive more attention than kids who are serious about their education. . . . We want you to put these kids in separate classes.

This chapter draws heavily on Chapter 1 in *Implementing Problem-Based Learning in Leadership Development*, Edwin Bridges and Philip Hallinger, Eugene, Oregon: ERIC Clearinghouse in Educational Management, 1995.

A Latino community leader has a different point of view:

> Latino students don't like coming to school. They feel unwelcome.
> They sense that the teachers don't understand them and are not
> making much of an effort to help them adjust to a foreign environ-
> ment or succeed in school. . . . The Anglo students resent the pres-
> ence of Hispanics and harass, tease, and intimidate them daily.
> Overt racial conflict will break out any day if racial relations don't
> improve.

What do you do?

Messy, real-life problems like these provide the starting point for
learning in a radically transformed instructional environment (hereafter
referred to as "problem-based learning"). The "students," prospective
and current principals, jointly decide how to deal with these problems.
In the process of grappling with these real-world challenges, the "students" (hereafter referred to as "participants" or "trainees" to reflect
their adult status) acquire the knowledge and skills needed by principals
who lead by facilitating collaboration and building consensus rather
than by exerting formal authority.

Problem-based learning (PBL), though a newcomer to the field of
educational administration, has been used for more than a decade to
prepare future physicians and other professionals (Boud & Feletti,
1991). As one reads about how PBL has been used in these other fields,
one discovers that it comes in various forms. This variety stems in part
from the differences inherent in the various professional roles for which
the students are being prepared.

Accordingly, the version of PBL discussed in this chapter reflects
the nature of the role that trainees enact when they complete their
professional training in the field of educational administration. This future role, as the reader will discover, influences a host of instructional
decisions—decisions about goals, content, instructional process, and
evaluation.

In discussing this version of PBL for preparing educational administrators, we elaborate the model, illustrate how it has been used to prepare school leaders, foreshadow what researchers are likely to learn as
they study the implementation of this model, and discuss the changes
that must occur for the professional development of administrators to
become rooted in the principles of PBL. Even though we have used PBL
in training veteran, as well as prospective, administrators in both this
country and abroad, we base our discussion mostly on preservice training, where we have had the most experience.

PBL: THE MODEL

Underlying Assumptions

The assumptions underlying traditional preparation in educational administration contrast sharply with those in PBL. Traditional preparatory programs view teaching as transmission of knowledge and learning as acquisition of that knowledge. Program designers make four assumptions about this knowledge: (1) The knowledge is relevant to the trainee's future professional role; (2) learners will be able to recognize when it is appropriate to use their newly acquired knowledge; (3) application of this knowledge is relatively simple and straightforward; and (4) the context in which knowledge is learned has no bearing on subsequent recall or use. Program designers further assume that knowledge is learned most effectively when it is organized around the disciplines and taught through lecture and discussion. Finally, those responsible for the professional development of administrators assume that the central purpose of student evaluation is to ascertain whether trainees can recall the knowledge to which they have been exposed.

PBL rests on an entirely different set of assumptions. PBL proponents assume that learning involves both knowing and doing. Knowledge and the ability to use that knowledge are of equal importance. Program designers also assume that participants bring previously learned knowledge to each learning experience. Moreover, PBL adherents assume that trainees are more likely to learn new knowledge when the following conditions are met:

1. Their prior knowledge is activated and they are encouraged to incorporate new knowledge into their preexisting knowledge.
2. They are given numerous opportunities to use it.
3. They encode the new knowledge in a context that resembles the context in which it subsequently will be used.

PBL teachers further assume that the problems trainees are likely to encounter in their future professional practice provide a meaningful learning context for acquiring and using new knowledge. These problems supply cues that facilitate future retrieval and use of knowledge acquired during their formal education. Finally, PBL instructors assume that evaluation can play a major role in fostering the ability to apply knowledge if evaluation serves learning (formative) and is based on performance of tasks that correspond to the professional tasks participants will face after completing their training.

Major Components

Designing a professional development program based on PBL requires one to consider five interrelated issues: (1) the realities of the workplace, (2) the goals, (3) the content, (4) the process by which the content is taught and learned, and (5) participant evaluation. By attending to these five issues simultaneously, the program designer increases the likelihood that trainees will be able to transfer their newly acquired knowledge and skills to the work context. Let us examine each of these issues more closely.

Realities of the Workplace. Crafting a program rooted in the principles of PBL involves making a number of assumptions about the realities of the workplace. By way of example, we have adopted several key assumptions in designing Stanford University's Prospective Principals' Program. Local school districts are granting each school more latitude in dealing with the problems and challenges it faces. The principal of the school is expected to collaborate with teachers and parents in solving these problems and in creating an educational environment that effectively and humanely responds to the needs of an increasingly diverse student population. Moreover, the problems and the knowledge base relevant to these needs and problems will continually change.

Goals. In light of the workplace realities that we have assumed, the following professional development goals for principals seem appropriate:

1. Familiarize prospective principals with the problems they are likely to face in the future. Such problems should be those with high impact, that is, those that affect a large number of individuals for a relatively long period of time.
2. Acquaint trainees with the knowledge that is relevant to these high-impact problems. Such knowledge likely comes from a variety of disciplines, rather than from a single one.
3. Foster skills in applying this knowledge. Since PBL assumes that knowing and doing are equally important, trainees should be provided with opportunities to use their knowledge and to test its utility in dealing with real-life professional problems. In the process of applying the knowledge, students discover gaps in their understanding and their ability to use the knowledge. This awareness stimulates them to revisit the conceptual material and to solidify their understanding.
4. Develop problem-solving skills. Since the character of future prob-

lems is somewhat unpredictable, attention must be paid to promoting skills in finding, framing, analyzing, and solving problems. Moreover, future principals need to learn how to distinguish between problems and dilemmas and to acquire strategies for dealing with both. While problems generally contain no value conflicts, dilemmas do. Since dilemmas arise from competing values, they resist solution and are likely to surface again and again.

5. Develop skills in implementing solutions. Consistent with the emphasis on doing as well as knowing, trainees should implement their proposed solutions. Simply discussing what one would or should do to solve a problem is insufficient. Implementing a solution to a problem often proves more difficult than anticipated; moreover, the solution may evoke additional problems. Consequently, principals need to acquire skills in anticipating potential problems, assessing their seriousness, and developing preventive or contingency actions for dealing with potentially serious problems.

6. Develop leadership skills that facilitate collaboration. Critical to collaboration are skills in the following: planning and organizing projects, running meetings, achieving consensus, resolving conflict, and listening.

7. Develop an array of affective capacities. Unless principals acquire a strong commitment to collaboration and the patience to use this kind of leadership style, they are unlikely to use their skills in working with others. Moreover, when things go awry, principals need to know how to deal constructively with frustration, anger, and disappointment. Above all, they need to acquire confidence in their ability to handle the many facets of this demanding professional role.

8. Develop self-directed learning skills. With an exploding knowledge base and ever-changing problems, principals need to acquire skills in identifying gaps in their own knowledge, in locating relevant resources, and in evaluating the suitability and appropriateness of the resources for the issues confronting them.

Content. Knowledge (content) in a PBL curriculum is organized around high-impact problems of professional practice. PBL adherents follow this maxim: *first the problem, then the content.* Problems are used as the stimulus for learning new content instead of the context for applying previously learned material. One major criterion guides the selection of content: The content should be *functional* in fostering understanding of the problem, possible causes for the problem, constraints that must be taken into account when considering solutions, and/or possible solutions.

Problem-relevant knowledge comes from a variety of sources: the disciplines, practitioners with relevant expertise and practical wisdom, local district policies and practices, and the trainees themselves. Although the instructor may suggest pertinent reading material, participants exploit an array of sources that may assist them in understanding and dealing with the focal problem—a practice that is consistent with the type of on-the-job learning that PBL seeks to develop.

Instructional Process. In a PBL curriculum, trainees assume major responsibility for their own learning. The process by which they learn the content mirrors the realities of the workplace and the instructional goals. Accordingly, the process affords participants repeated opportunities to practice and refine the skills needed to lead today's schools—skills in promoting collaboration, cooperative problem solving, and implementation of change.

Unlike traditional educational administration programs, the basic unit of classroom instruction is a project. Embedded in each project are a high-impact problem, a set of learning objectives, and a collection of reading materials that illuminate different facets of the problem. The problems are usually messy, ill defined, and representative of the problems the trainees will face as principals.

Trainees are assigned to a project team. The number of teams formed in a class depends on the size of the class and the size of a team (typically five to seven members). Each team is responsible for framing the problem and deciding how to use the knowledge gleaned from the readings to deal with it. Teams have a fixed period of time, usually 9 to 15 hours spread over a period of one to three weeks, to complete the project. One of the trainees is designated as the project team leader; other team members take turns acting as process facilitators and recorders. Class sessions are treated as meetings of the project team, and the leader, in consultation with the facilitator, develops a tentative agenda for each meeting. The agenda for each session reflects what the team intends to accomplish and how it plans to proceed. Following each class session, the recorder prepares minutes of the meeting and distributes them to other team members.

During each meeting (i.e., class session), the instructor moves among the teams and acts as an unobtrusive guide on the side, rather than as a sage on the stage. At times the instructor may raise questions, answer questions, engage the participants in reflecting on their process, or provide feedback to them about their use or understanding of the problem-relevant knowledge. If instructors sense that the team is headed in the wrong direction or developing an unsound solution to the problem, they do not intervene. Missteps or mistakes represent occasions for learning and often provide valuable insights into the problem, the problem-solving process, the solution, the implementation, the group's functioning, or the participants' own sense of self.

Evaluation. Participant evaluation, like the goals, content, and instructional process, reflects the realities of the workplace. As part of each PBL project, participants are expected to perform tasks and to create products that approximate what they would do while solving the problem on the job. The students' performance during a project, as well as their products, provides the basis for formative evaluation. Accordingly, trainees receive feedback from peers, the instructor, and practitioners about their performance. When providing feedback to the trainees, everyone underscores what they have done especially well and raises questions for them to ponder in relation to their performance. Given the nature of the PBL projects, trainees may receive feedback on their performance relative to any of the eight goals described earlier.

As a way of encouraging trainees to consolidate what they have learned and to think about transferring their newly acquired knowledge to their future role, each participant prepares a reflective essay at the end of each project. This essay details what they learned and how they intend to use the insights, knowledge, and skills in the future.

PBL: EXAMPLES

To illustrate how some of the major components of PBL operate in the classroom, we have chosen two projects, one related to the opening vignette and the other related to teacher selection. The instructional materials for these two PBL projects appear in Bridges and Hallinger (1992, pp. 144–159). A case study detailing what happened during the teacher selection project also appears in Bridges and Hallinger (1992, pp. 29–57).

Example 1: In English, Please

This PBL project centers on a middle school undergoing transition from a monolingual to a multilingual student population. The vignette at the beginning of this chapter highlights several of the numerous sub-problems embedded in the problematic situation featured in the project. In addition to the description of this messy, real-world problem, participants receive information about the school district, a fact sheet distributed by school leaders to parents and pupils, and a description of the district's proposed newcomer center for Hispanic students. Participants also receive a set of readings that cover such topics as theory and research on bilingual education, translating language-acquisition theory into educational practice, historical accounts of how language minorities have been treated in this country, the legal requirements for students with limited English proficiency, and the needs of recent immigrants.

Members of the project team are responsible for developing a packet of materials to be circulated to the school's Bilingual Advisory Committee prior to its first meeting. The team is expected to include the following materials in this packet:

1. A statement that describes the committee's charge
2. A tentative plan for how the committee should proceed to accomplish its charge
3. An agenda for the meeting that clarifies what the content and the process will be for the meeting
4. A two-page statement that attempts to provide committee members with pertinent background information about bilingual education

At the end of this 15-hour project, each team presents its packet of materials to a group of bilingual program coordinators and principals of linguistically diverse schools. This group of practitioners reads the same problem and background material that the team did, reviews the materials prepared by the project team, and meets with team members to raise questions and to provide feedback on the contents of their packet. Team members also have an opportunity to ask questions about issues that arose during the project.

Example 2: Teacher Selection

In this PBL project, participants serve on a teacher selection committee. The committee has been appointed to fill a vacancy for a fourth-grade teaching position. Committee members are furnished with information about the school, the teaching position, and the district, including its teacher evaluation system. Besides this background information, committee members receive reading materials on a range of related topics—recruitment, theory and research on employee selection, legal aspects of selection, treatment of new teachers, and misassignment.

Committee members design and implement a selection process for choosing the fourth-grade teacher. Since the district requires its teacher selection committees to interview and to observe demonstration lessons before making a recommendation, the committee must incorporate these two procedures into its selection process. During the last phase of the project, the committee interviews three "finalists" for the position and observes each of them teaching a group of 20 pupils. These students closely resemble those who will be in the teacher's fourth-grade class.

Following the interviews and the demonstration lessons, the committee meets to evaluate each candidate against the criteria it established. When the committee completes its deliberations, it prepares a report to the personnel director that contains the following: (1) the recommendation of the committee, (2) an overview of its selection process, (3) a justification for its recommendation, and (4) a description of the steps to be taken to ensure that the candidate succeeds once hired.

At the conclusion of the project, committee members receive feedback from two sources: the three candidates and the faculty. Unbeknownst to the committee, a faculty member has interviewed each of the three applicants immediately following the selection activity. The interview includes questions like these: If you were offered this position, would you accept it? Why? What did the committee do that you especially liked? How might the selection committee improve its process? The faculty member later shares the answers to these questions with the members of the selection committee. During this feedback session, committee members learn whether their preferred candidate will accept the job offer. This information stimulates the committee to reflect on its process and how it might be improved in the future.

PBL: FORESHADOWED OUTCOMES

Since PBL represents a radical departure from the traditional way in which school administrators have been prepared, one question often arises: How does this innovative instructional strategy impact the learner, the content of instruction, the teacher, and the classroom climate? To provide a partial answer to this important question, we draw primarily, though not exclusively, on our own experiences with this approach. Thus far, most of the research on PBL has been conducted in the field of medical education, not educational administration. The most comprehensive review of research on using PBL to train future physicians appears in Albanese and Mitchell (1993).

Classroom Environment

Our rendering of PBL creates a more intense learning environment than in traditional educational administration programs. This intensity stems in large part from the project nature of the PBL curriculum. Project teams work without the active facilitation of an instructor; the facilitator, as we mentioned earlier, is one of the team members. Moreover, teams must reach consensus on how to deal with the problem and are required to implement their problem in a context similar to the one they will encounter later as administrators. Although the context is contrived, the vast majority of participants do not experience it as such. Rather, the context has the "feel" of the real thing, and that "feel" produces a rather high level of performance anxiety.

Learner

Despite the more intense and stressful PBL classroom environment, participants report high levels of satisfaction. They also view their leadership preparation as much more realistic, practical, and meaningful than that of their counterparts in traditional programs. However, when asked "Would you like the portion of the curriculum that is taught using PBL [roughly 40% at Stanford] to increase, decrease, or remain the same?", participants consistently answer "Remain the same." According to them, PBL is too intense to be increased and too valuable to be decreased. (See Bridges & Hallinger, 1992, pp. 117–133, for a description of the entire Prospective Principals Program curriculum at Stanford.)

In a PBL environment, participants often learn more than formal knowledge, the kind of knowledge emphasized in traditional leadership programs. Some adopt new perspectives on leadership. For example, following a project, one individual wrote:

> At the beginning of the project I had little confidence in participative leadership. I doubted that a group could efficiently produce a product in a timely manner using consensus. . . . I gained a new perspective on the role of the leader. Midway through the project I realized I was feeling very stressed about the project. I felt I must determine the "right" answer and then sell it to the group. Reflecting on this, I concluded that wasn't my responsibility as the leader. Problem-solving was the group's responsibility. . . . I can improve (as a leader) by continuing the participative style I tried in this experience—an agenda open to revision by the group, decision-making through a mixture of consensus and majority-rule, equal par-

ticipation of group members, meeting closure with a review of accomplishments, and followup actions. (Bridges & Hallinger, 1992, p. 70)

Still other participants learn how to deal with disappointment and the importance of balancing the demands in one's life. By way of illustration, one project leader wrote:

> As to pressure and priorities, I give too much authority to external authorities—bosses, assignments, etc.—and so lose sight of people priorities outside of the job. To be specific, during this experience I sacrificed my family relationships at a crucial time (for them). This was irresponsible. . . . I have to learn how to put the job in better perspective with the rest of my life and with the world context. Furthermore, by making the assignment and my responsibility for it too big a deal in my own mind, I also limited my creativity in trying to help the group to be more creative and less stressed. . . . I find it difficult to fail, but no one died, and if I can learn about making mistakes and carrying on creatively despite them, particularly in not letting difficulties get me down, that will be progress. (Bridges & Hallinger, 1992, pp. 78–79)

As participants' exposure to a PBL environment broadens and deepens, most become comfortable in working with adults and internalize the value of collaboration. An alumnus of the Stanford program captured these affective outcomes when she was asked to comment on the essays that students prepare following each project. These essays give a sense of what students say and feel about their performance on specific projects. They are intentionally deeply reflective and thoughtful, and so do not convey the enthusiasm people have about this program and the PBL method.

> The affective outcomes are not emphasized—the amazing camaraderie, the sensitivity to others, the change of intolerance to tolerance to acceptance to appreciation of different viewpoints—all these are important in the operational goal of the program, and in developing a new breed of administrator who won't settle for the isolation so characteristic of the principalship. (Bridges & Hallinger, 1992, p. 68)

Content

Given that each project confronts trainees with multiple goals (i.e., acquire problem-relevant knowledge, reach consensus on how to deal with the focal problem, and implement their solution), less content is covered in PBL than in conventional programs. Moreover, there is the ever-present danger that participants will lose sight of the learning objectives and concentrate on solving the problem. Unless instructors take steps to ensure that trainees grapple with the content and how it applies to the focal problem, participants may overlook the learning resources that are provided.

Teacher

Faculty generally find PBL a satisfying way to teach. When describing their experiences with PBL, most highlight the participants' level of motivation, the quality of their work, and their engagement with the classroom tasks. However, some instructors miss lecturing and become frustrated while watching their trainees grope and struggle with the messy realities of the problem. A few instructors express concerns about the interpersonal problems that sometimes arise in project teams and the "free-rider" problem (letting other members do the work) that occurs when individuals are not held accountable.

In a PBL classroom environment that emphasizes doing as well as knowing, instructors may make discomforting discoveries. By way of example, one professor wrote:

> The major discovery is how much I have learned as a professor about the quality of my instruction. The last group of students who solved a problem in my class were critiqued severely by a panel of superintendents. The students got defensive, but I realized that I did not prepare them well enough. . . . Students could write beautiful descriptions of how they would deal with problems . . . *but they couldn't do anything!!!* Problem-based learning, especially with problems that require a reaction from a panel of experts, has caused me to look very carefully at my own teaching.

For other professors, the discoveries are similarly enlightening but less painful. Two professors who experimented with our approach described their experiences as follows:

> Here was where we discovered one of the fundamental requirements of an effective PBL approach—the concept of "front-loading." We realized quite early that preparation for this course would mean a significant investment of time prior to the beginning of the class. . . . We discovered as soon as the class began how valuable front loading was. . . . We found that we were able to play different roles as instructors. Instead of believing we were obligated to "perform" each day in front of the class (and thereby

convince ourselves that we were giving students their money's worth), we became more relaxed and under less pressure. Our role quickly evolved into one of a "coach," although we also had to be careful not to "over-coach" or "hover" as we called it. . . .

In one of our post-class sessions one day, while discussing how the class had affected each of us, one of us termed the experience as transformative. By that he meant that he had come to see that with adult learners especially, a much different approach was necessary. For years he had taught the same way that one would use to teach novitiates—that is, a heavy emphasis on content taught in a very didactic style. It became clear however in teaching this class that such an approach was inappropriate. (Chenoweth & Everhart, 1994, p. 428)

GETTING THERE FROM HERE

Since PBL represents a radical departure from current practice, most instructors and trainees in educational administration are unfamiliar with this instructional approach. As a result, moving to a program of professional development that is rooted in the principles of PBL poses challenges to institutions, instructors, and trainees alike. In the balance of this chapter, we will foreshadow what some of these challenges are and how they might be met.

Institutions

If a program elects to adopt or to experiment with PBL, certain institutional conditions will facilitate this transition. PBL classes require longer blocks of time, rather than the more typical one- or two-hour training sessions. Depending on the size of the training group, the institution may need to allot more classrooms to PBL classes because team meetings may interfere with the deliberations of other teams if they are in the same room. In addition, institutions will need to provide funds for instructors to purchase supplies and equipment (see Bridges & Hallinger, 1992, for what is needed). Since developing PBL instructional materials requires considerable preparation up front, the institution needs to provide planning time for instructors to create these materials or to review and adapt ones developed elsewhere (see Bridges & Hallinger, 1995, for an extended discussion of these issues).

Ideally, the norms within the host institution should support risk-taking and efforts by faculty to improve the preparation of practitioners. Unless colleagues favor, or at least tolerate, innovative instructional approaches, instructors are unlikely to invest the time and effort required to implement a PBL program successfully. Active support and encouragement from the administration also play an important role in creating a climate conducive to trying, even on a limited basis, an innovation like PBL.

Instructors

The central figure in implementing PBL in the classroom is the instructor. To implement PBL, instructors require functional knowledge, motivation, and skills. Unless they possess these prerequisites, PBL is unlikely to flourish even if the institution creates the enabling conditions that we discussed in the preceding section.

Through experience, we have discovered that an effective way for instructors to begin the process of acquiring these prerequisites is for them to learn about problem-based learning by actually doing it. By way of illustration, two years ago the Danforth Foundation invited us to make a presentation on PBL to 150 professors and staff developers. Instead of lecturing about this approach, we asked the Foundation to provide us with a three-hour block of time, the facilities, and the equipment needed to implement PBL in the classroom.

The project that we developed to teach PBL ("Wisdom Can't Be Told," in Bridges & Hallinger, 1995) centered on an issue being confronted by many of the participants—declining revenues and budget cuts. To make this issue concrete, we constructed the following problem:

> The President of Midwestern University has announced a 10 percent budget cut for each academic unit. In response to this announcement, the Dean has reviewed each department. Her review reveals that the enrollments in your department show a downward trend over the past four years and that the graduates are extremely critical of their preparation. The alumni maintain that the content lacks any relevance to professional practice and that the professors rely much too heavily on two methods of instruction— lecture and teacher-led discussion. The Dean shares her review with the department chair and asks him to develop a plan that responds to the declining enrollments and student criticisms. Unless the department develops a reasonable plan, it may suffer a much larger cut than 10 percent and be phased out or merged with another program.
>
> As a first step, the department chair creates three sub-committees to look into problem-centered strategies: case method, case incident, and problem-based learning. The sub-committee investigating PBL has the following charge:
>
> 1. Review the literature on PBL
> 2. Make an oral report to the other sub-committees (in this case another project team) that contains (a) what the team has learned about PBL;

(b) what the department should do next (e.g., drop the idea of using PBL, study the idea in more depth, noting what they want to know more about, or use PBL on a limited, trial basis); (c) why that course of action seems justified. (pp. 162–168)

The 150 participants were assigned to teams consisting of six or seven members. We designated three of the team members to serve in one of the following capacities: leader, facilitator, and recorder. The materials that we provided each team contained the learning objectives, the problem, the subcommittee charge, and the pertinent readings about PBL (related theory, research, and an example of PBL in the classroom). After reading the materials, team members discussed and reached consensus about the items contained in their charge. The project culminated with one member of the team presenting its views to another team while the remaining members listened to and discussed another subcommittee's report.

By using problem-based learning to teach it, we discovered that most participants obtained a clear understanding of the approach and experienced firsthand how much students can learn in a PBL curriculum. Many became motivated to try the approach and cognizant of the skills required to implement PBL in the classroom. Merely reading about PBL or listening to someone who is using it is insufficient. Unless potential users participate in a PBL project, they are unlikely to be persuaded that this approach is worth trying in their own classroom.

Trainees

Since PBL involves a radical change in the role of trainees, they, like instructors, need some special knowledge and skills to function in this environment. One of the most important prerequisites is skill in running meetings. In addition to skills in managing meetings, trainees can benefit from prior preparation in problem framing and problem solving. If time permits, these foundation skills can be learned within the context of a PBL format to further heighten trainees' understanding of this approach. If participants possess these skills, their transition to a new kind of role proceeds more smoothly.

CONCLUSION

As we have argued, PBL represents a bold, radical departure from the traditional way of preparing educational administrators. In our judgment, this approach can play an important, instrumental role in ensuring the success of educational reforms now under way. Administrators, like teachers, are being asked to move away from command and control models of leadership to "transformational" styles. Moreover, the kinds of teaching and learning advocated by reformers (teaching and learning for understanding) require administrators who act in ways consistent with these expectations and understand what active learning comprises. Problem-based learning holds promise for preparing the kind of leaders who can facilitate, rather than obstruct, these reforms.

Chapter 14

School–University Partnership

Getting Broader, Getting Deeper

Lynne Miller and Cynthia O'Shea

Partnership can be a powerful mechanism for thinking about and transforming educational institutions, or it can be just another buzzword of school reform that promises much but delivers little. To be successful, a partnership has to accommodate all its members. It needs to be responsive to developing concerns and interests yet hold steadfast to its guiding principles and values. This becomes more difficult as a partnership endures over time and as it increases in size. At any given time, some members in a partnership may be on a "fast track," others may be slow to start and liable to take a circuitous route, still others may be just beginning to raise the questions and identify the problems that some are in the process of answering for themselves. The challenge is to continually develop ways to include all members as active participants; to provide appropriate and multiple opportunities for professional learning, growth, and support; and to move the school reform agenda forward. This tension between breadth and depth has been a driving force in our own experience as members of a school–university partnership. Our intention here is to describe the ways in which the tension has appeared and reappeared in our own work and to identify some of the issues it

Reprinted with permission of The NETWORK, Inc., from "Partnership: Getting Broader, Getting Deeper" by Lynne Miller and Cynthia O'Shea. © 1994. This work is part of the Studies of Education Reform program, supported by the U.S. Department of Education, Office of Education Research and Improvement, under contract number RR 91172009. The program supports studies and disseminates practical information about implementing and sustaining innovation in American education. The opinions in this chapter do not necessarily reflect the position of policy of the U.S. Department of Education, and no official endorsement should be inferred.

uncovers about the very nature of partnership as an organization and as a vehicle for collaboration and change.

THE SOUTHERN MAINE PARTNERSHIP
AND ITS BEGINNINGS

The Southern Maine Partnership is now in its ninth year of continuous operation. It began when a university professor of education and his dean approached six local school superintendents and invited them to create a new kind of organization. Influenced by John Goodlad's (1988) conception of a school–university partnership as "a device for bringing together institutions that need each other for the solution of tough problems" (p. 26), the eight people who met together established the Southern Maine Partnership. Each district agreed to pay annual dues of $1,000. The university contributed support by making the directorship of the new program part of the faculty member's workload.

The Partnership began by inviting educators from the participating districts to join one of four educator groups. The groups had a specific focus (early childhood, mathematics, middle level, secondary education), and each met monthly over dinner to discuss ideas together. These groups had no agenda for action. They were designed as a way for people to talk about and play with big ideas. The groups became the central focus, indeed the heart, of the Partnership and remained so for many years.

In addition to the group meetings, there was a monthly meeting of the superintendents, who had committed themselves to active involvement in the Partnership. Principals also had their own group, ensuring that at all levels educators had a opportunity to experience Partnership principles and practice simultaneously. This structure of monthly meetings involving teachers, principals, and superintendents became the accepted mode of operation for the Partnership.

The authors of this article share a history in the Partnership. Cynthia O'Shea was an original member of groups on early childhood education and leadership. As principal of Narragansett School in Gorham, Maine, she was an active Partnership participant. Lynne Miller joined the Partnership as its executive director two years after its inception. She holds faculty rank at the University of Southern Maine and is released from one-third of her teaching load for her Partnership work. We have chosen to write this piece together because we think that the dual perspective we bring offers a balanced and complex view of the Southern Maine Partnership, its struggles, and its successes. Throughout this chapter, we alternate voice and perspective as we tell our story.

The School Perspective

Located less than a mile from the University of Southern Maine, the Narragansett School serves 450 first-, second-, and third-grade children. The staff is a typical mix of age groups, educational backgrounds, and experiences. Situated just outside of Portland, the town of Gorham is a rural farming community transforming into a suburb. The longstanding relationship between the university and the town's schools has had its ups and downs over time. For the most part, the university was seen by practitioners as the "ivory tower" where professors were researchers far removed from the reality of classroom practice. There was an amiable tolerance for one another's roles and contributions, but not much collaboration and exchange. The Southern Maine Partnership served to dramatically change this dynamic.

Narragansett School's renewal efforts began simultaneously with the creation of the Southern Maine Partnership. The major impetus of school renewal was a new superintendent's fundamental respect for the tacit knowledge and wisdom of the teaching staff. She encouraged teachers to come together to identify major issues within the school and to initiate reform. The Gorham system was awarded a small state grant for the purpose of "raising the teacher's voice" (Gorham, 1985). Teachers began participating in monthly Partnership meetings almost concurrently with the awarding of the grant. The grant allowed a small group of teachers to tape-record discussion sessions that revolved around their classroom practice and then to receive the transcripts for review and reflection. The process was designed to allow teachers to participate in cross-grade-level and cross-district discussion. At the same time, the Partnership was also encouraging teachers to raise their voices and was showing respect for the professionalism of practitioners. In a departure from past practices, the university did not invite teachers to learn from its professors. Rather, the invitation was to learn to question practice, identify common areas of concern, and support each other through the change process. This approach led to a stronger sense of professionalism, one that encouraged teachers to question, to accept or reject ideas and research based on how they related to child development and learning. Most powerful of all, it laid the groundwork for teachers to become innovators.

As members of the Partnership, teachers were invited to monthly dinner meetings to discuss current research and educational practice with educators from several other school districts. Up until that point, talking about and reflecting on one's practice was *not* a routine part of teaching. Some new skills needed to be acquired. The monthly Partnership meetings provided teachers the opportunity to learn where to access current literature on child development, learning theory, and pedagogy. Even more basic, it gave teachers a safe and nonjudgmental forum for discussing their practice.

The group meetings became the vehicles through which teachers gained confidence in their own knowledge and abilities. Rarely in schools is there an effort to help teachers acquire the skill of articulating what they do and why they do it. With the emphasis on reflection and discussion, it became the norm that teachers would talk about what they were doing and why they were doing it. It should be noted that along with reflection and discussion came discomfort. It became apparent (and somewhat embarrassing) that much of existing practice was done from routine and tradition rather than from an understanding of child development and learning theory. It also became apparent that everything teachers do in the classroom must be based on what they know about children and how they learn. It was slow to come, and painful to acknowledge, that what teachers often did in the classroom was not consistent with what they thought they were doing or what they wanted to do. With that major breakthrough and acceptance, it became increasingly uncomfortable to continue with the status quo.

The relationship within the Partnership was one of equality. The Southern Maine Partnership was never formed to tell educators what they were doing wrong and what they should be doing. Instead it was formed to facilitate bringing knowledgeable people together to question, to discuss, to solve problems, and to access pertinent information. It was accepted and welcomed that answers to questions would not be handed down by professors. Instead, the answers would come from group problem solving and individual initiatives.

The process of inquiry and open reflection was encouraged, valued, and seen as a means of understanding and identifying what needed to change in the school. It was imperative that the staff see themselves as learners and as teachers. The connection with the university became a natural part of being a learner and a teacher. Joint and compatible efforts within the district and within the Southern Maine Partnership laid the groundwork for reflection and identification of issues, and proceeded to make school renewal seem possible.

The Partnership Perspective

The early Partnership enthusiasts were a small but powerful lot. They were articulate, intellectually engaged, and willing to challenge one another and themselves. They were often people who felt isolated in their own schools and found in one another the colleagues they had long sought. One of the effects of this kind of success was the creation of an in-group of educators. And whenever there's an in-group, there's an out-group. For many teachers and principals whose districts were members, the Partnership was not a welcoming and safe place. Some were uncomfortable with the ambiguity of the groups; others valued action over talk; still others wanted concrete examples and suggestions about what to do the next day. This issue of inclusiveness versus exclusivity emerged early in the Partnership's history.

Among the superintendents, issues were emerging as well. It was difficult, from the beginning, to find a *modus operandi* for the superintendents' meetings. While the school groups usually began conversation from an article read in common, the superintendents were not so comfortable with this approach. Transcripts of early meetings (1985–87) show a group not at ease with itself and unable to sustain a focused discussion. Digressions, speeches, and silences punctuated the instances of engagement and reciprocal sharing. While in the teacher groups there was much openness and revelation, here there was protectiveness and a public relations stance.

It should be clear from the discussion above that the Partnership's early success in bringing people together and in breaking down the hierarchical relation between the university and schools was significant; it was also problematic. At the end of its initial years, the Partnership was struggling with how to broaden its sphere to include more university faculty and diverse public school educators and how to deepen its work by engaging all levels of school districts in dialogue and action leading to school change as well as individual development.

FORGING AN AGENDA: 1987–1990

The Partnership's next three years were marked by growth and expansion. Membership increased to include a total of fifteen districts and two private schools. The State Department of Education began to promote school reform, and many schools were actively engaged in or seeking to understand what came to be called "restructuring." Of ten state grants awarded for restructuring in 1988, six went to Partnership schools. The Partnership continued to operate through educator groups that fostered collegial interaction and reflection.

The School Perspective

With reflection the norm, teachers got very good at discussing practice and identifying issues. But change remained an individual, rather than schoolwide, concern. It was one thing to be current in the research, to reflect on practice, and to identify issues that needed changing and yet another to actually make significant changes as a whole-school faculty.

The initiation of school change would have been impossible if the partnership were formed for teachers alone. For a school system to become a member of the Southern Maine Partnership, the superintendent had to agree to commit himself or herself and principals to their respective monthly partnership meetings as well as to encourage teachers to attend. This made the chain complete. It was equally important for superintendents and principals to discuss issues and practice, see the need for change, sense the possibilities for the future, and support teachers as they became ready to make significant changes in schooling. In this particular situation, the equal participation of superintendent, principal, and teachers was essential. The superintendent attended many of the Partnership groups and was an active participant in teacher discussions. She provided an environment in which questions were valued above answers, where risk was encouraged and the status quo discouraged.

The first formal opportunity for schoolwide action came when, in 1988, the State Department of Education offered restructuring grants. By that time, teachers at the Narragansett School were ready to put their beliefs into writing—for example, about developing the school as a center of inquiry (Schaefer, 1967)—and commit to a plan to make changes that would benefit student learning. Instead of writing a definitive reform plan, the Narragansett staff, with support from the superintendent, saw greater possibilities and were more comfortable asking the state to support their efforts to become a center of inquiry (Cox & DeFrees, 1991).

Our work in the Partnership helped clarify what type of school structure we wanted to create for children and for teachers. We came to believe that in order to make lasting and fundamental change, we needed to create a flexible structure that supported ongoing inquiry into what is important for children to learn, how children learn, and how children can best demonstrate their skills and abilities. We were firm in our stand that we should be doing what is best for children and that our knowledge would continue to grow from year to year. While the whole-language philosophy and the Math Their Way approach made sense, we knew that they were not the answers to school reform. Schools should be able to accept new information, materials, and approaches. They must also be able to discard outdated practices whenever they see a better way. These were all lessons we had learned through our involvement in Partnership groups. The state's grant application provided the opportunity for us to come together as a staff, to commit to a body of shared ideas, and to announce our vision of school and schooling to our public. We were successful in our grant-writing effort and were awarded $150,000 over three years to create the type of school we envisioned.

The most significant change we made was, quite simply, a change in mind-set. As a staff, we had come to see ourselves as continuous learners, reflective practitioners, and stewards of student learning. We spent a significant amount of time studying the concept of multiple intelligences and other theories of how children learn. We also came to value the knowledge children bring to school and what they know about themselves. We designed a program that focused on self-awareness, self-esteem, and metacognition. It was not good enough for teachers to know how children learn. It also was important for *children* to know how they learn and to be able to articulate this knowledge so they could advocate for their own needs.

As the mind-set of teachers changed, it became necessary to redesign and sometimes to invent structures that support professional learning. Teacher duties were reduced to one per week; class sizes were kept at manageable levels; and paraprofessionals assumed new support roles for classroom teachers. Perhaps our most unique invention was the role of teacher scholar. This is a teacher who comes out of the classroom for a year to support other teachers as they change their practice. The teacher scholar seeks out and conducts research, volunteers to teach demonstration lessons in class, observes children, and generally is available for on-site, as-needed, personalized staff development.

Our staff developed a new kind of relationship with the Partnership. Many of our teachers became resources to other member schools by giving workshops, providing consultation, and making presentations. They felt empowered and confident. They made connections with like-minded teachers in similar schools and made efforts to learn and share from one another. In addition, the school staff developed ongoing relationships with university faculty who served as "critical friends," advocates, and documenters of progress.

At the same time, participation in Partnership groups decreased. Teachers no longer felt the need to read and reflect for its own sake. The action taking place at the school had became more engaging than the conversations taking place within the Partnership. Many teachers found the Partnership groups lacking in challenge. While supportive of other teachers' growth, the groups no longer spoke to the needs of teachers so intensely involved in school reform.

The Partnership Perspective

During the third, fourth, and fifth years of its existence, the Southern Maine Partnership grew in size and reputation. This may have been due to the fact that of ten state grants awarded for restructuring, six went to Partnership schools. Another contributing factor was the Partnership's identification with John Goodlad. Still another was the opportunity it provided for ongoing professional interaction and intellectual exchange. The reality was that while motivations were varied, the Partnership was viewed as "where the action is" and districts joined in large numbers.

As new districts sought admission to the Partnership, it became necessary to establish a procedure for joining. The superintendents' group, the designated decision-making body, assumed responsibility for this task. The procedure was, in a word, perfunctory. Any superintendent who wrote a formal letter of application, and who was willing to pay the annual dues, was admitted. The result was that in just three years, the Partnership almost doubled in size. The educator groups grew as well. Instead of three groups, all convened by the director, there were now five university faculty involved in seven groups. A new director had been appointed who wanted to extend the Partnership and its work.

The Partnership thrived with its new members and momentum. The monthly group meetings were well attended and bustling with activity and engagement. Along with reflective practice, restructuring became an explicit part of the agenda. In effect, the Partnership was developing a dual focus: individual educator development and whole-school restructuring. This agenda emerged from the work of member educators and schools over time.

There were negative consequences of expansion as well. The superintendents' group, which had not functioned particularly well in its initial stages, was now not only more diverse, but also more confused. The norm of full participation of superintendents failed to take hold in this new iteration. In fact, some superintendents were not clear about the Partnership's mission and saw the organization as a vehicle for teacher development, not their own. As time went on, it became obvious that some had joined the Partnership under pressure from staff or school board, with no real commitment on their own part.

Among teachers, there was a sense of gain in the participation of more educators from a wider range of schools. But there was also a sense of loss of the "we-ness" that the original group members had so strongly felt. For some of the original members, there was a retreat from the Partnership and into the work of their schools. With a more heterogeneous mix of educators, many teachers became impatient with repeating old learnings for new members. They wanted to push the school reform agenda forward, not re-create it for others. On the other hand, some new members felt they were entering closed conversations where the vocabulary was unfamiliar and the atmosphere unwelcoming to strangers.

Though the Partnership had been in existence for several years, it had not been successful in including the university as a full partner. The discussion groups required that university professors find new ways of interacting with school people. The groups bore no resemblance to university courses. The agenda was emergent; participation varied from meeting to meeting; and the role of the faculty convener was clearly different from that of lecturer, seminar leader, or transmitter of information and knowledge. The university people who were involved in the Partnership thrived, but they continued to represent their own interests, not those of their home institution.

It was becoming obvious at the end of the Partnership's fifth year that even as it was growing and thriving, it was also beginning to unravel. Its assumptions and structures no longer were able to accommodate its ambitious mission or its growing membership. In order to survive, the Partnership needed to find answers to questions about accommodating diversity, promoting school reform as well as individual development, and maintaining the old norms of reflection and exchange while establishing new norms for application and action. In addition, the Partnership needed to look at its expectations for membership and to pay attention to the university as an equal partner in restructuring. The Partnership had learned to get broader; it now had to go deeper.

GETTING DEEPER, GETTING BROADER: 1990–93

In 1990, the Partnership was awarded a grant of $1.1 million over five years from the UNUM foundation. The grant was intended to assist in the restructuring of schools and of the university's teacher education program. For the first time, the Partnership could support a staff and offer resources to schools. The Partnership had clearly entered a new phase. The Partnership continued to grow in size until it included twenty-three districts, three private schools, and an additional institution of higher education.

The School Perspective

Just as the Narragansett School's involvement with the Partnership and school renewal began simultaneously, Narragansett continued to establish connections and relationships with other organizations as its reform efforts evolved. Naturally the relationship between teachers and the Partnership changed. With a sense of professionalism and purpose, the Narragansett teachers felt comfortable seeking out other relationships that would extend their learning and their practice.

The Gorham superintendent who initiated the relationship with the Partnership had received her doctoral degree from the Harvard School of Education. Just as she had introduced the Narragansett teachers to Schaefer's notion of the school as a center of inquiry, she also introduced us to the work of Harvard faculty Eleanor Duckworth and Howard Gardner. It was not long before teachers in the school were working on a regular basis with Project Zero and its staff. Individual classroom teachers were supported as they took what they were learning about the theory of multiple intelligences, curriculum and assessment, and portfolio development and wove it into their practice. Individual efforts led to broad-based school reform and eventually had an impact on the district's ability to establish a K–12 framework for improvement. This framework led to the district's identification as one of three ATLAS communities in the New American Schools Development Program.

Some teachers who began their professional growth with the Partnership's inception were now leading Partnership groups. Others joined newly formed discussion groups within the Partnerships. A large number of Narragansett teachers became involved in the Partnership's new assessment group and took an active role in a minigrant program that awarded funds for teachers to develop nontraditional classroom assessments. The new Foxfire program engaged a few individual teachers in reconstructing their own teaching. Others stopped attending the Partnership altogether, finding other venues for professional dialogue and support. This was a time of expansion, experimentation, and consolidation. The one group seemingly left out was the newly hired teachers; they had no way to capture the excitement of the start-up period in the Partnership's history. This left those teachers beginning their career at the Narragansett School without a structured environment in which to nurture their abilities to reflect on learning theory and practice. Many teachers began to feel a need for a new cycle of Partnership activities to introduce people to the concepts of collegial reflection, problem solving, and support.

As their roles in the Partnership changed and as their connections with other professional groups developed, it was evident that teachers had gradually assumed another role—that of teacher leaders. It became apparent in the district that the most significant hope for increasing our school's and our district's capacity for change was through teacher initiation and leadership. Teacher-led initiative had been well received and teacher leadership acknowledged, yet nothing had been provided by the district for training or support as teachers assumed this new role. It was through the Partnership that the Gorham system was introduced to trustees of the Noyce Foundation. Eventually the Noyce Foundation and Intel Corporation sponsored a four-day leadership development seminar for 50 teacher leaders in the Gorham district.

Teachers at Narragansett also began to assume leadership in teacher education. The Partnership's director had spearheaded a drive to reform the university's teacher education program. The new model of teacher education that was adopted and implemented was based on authentic partnership with schools so that groups of preservice teachers were placed in Partnership schools where restructuring efforts were in full force. Narragansett became an intern site, and many of our teachers served as mentor teachers, course instructors, or members of the teacher education steering committee. Some teachers were granted adjunct faculty status at the university. A truly different kind of school–university relationship was being developed.

Teacher leadership has its roots in the respect for teachers' abilities and knowledge that the Partnership promoted from its onset. The Narragansett School staff and students have benefited from that basic premise of respect. Teachers have become reflective practitioners, innovators of change in classroom practice and school reform, and leaders in their profession. They are comfortable in both the local and national reform movements and accept the responsibility that significant change comes from within. They clearly see themselves as part of the solution to a very complex problem—making schools significantly better for students. They are particularly fond of a quote attributed to John Sculley: "The best way to be ready for the future is to create it."

The Partnership Perspective

With the support of outside funds and the notoriety that they generated, the Partnership was in even greater demand than previously. Districts were requesting admission to membership in large numbers, and it became incumbent upon the superintendents to revisit their procedures for admission. Although not wanting to appear exclusive, the superintendents were also eager to maintain the integrity of the organization. They decided that in order to join the Partnership, a superintendent had to write a letter describing how the district's work to date fit into the Partnership's agenda of school restructuring and educator development. In addition, they asked that the school board in each district vote approval for membership. These new requirements were not particularly stringent, but they accomplished their goal. Only half of those districts making new inquiries about membership actually pursued that interest.

Over the next three years, the Partnership grew to include twenty-three districts, three private schools, and the Maine College of Art. As we write this chapter, two other districts are preparing their application letters, and the superintendents are meeting to consider a mission statement to help guide this and other decisions. This mission statement is important because it represents a clear articulation of purpose, establishes a focus, and delineates expectations of member districts. It is worth noting that the need for a mission statement did not emerge until the *ninth* year of the Partnership's existence. It was developed in response to a question that the organization had to face: We say we are committed to linking school reform and teacher development, but to what end? The mission statement describes the end this way: "to create and maintain learner-centered schools" (Southern Maine Partnership, 1993). Learner-centered schools are defined as moving toward new definitions of schoolwork, teacher development, community, governance, and accountability. The superintendents intend to use the mission statement to make Partnership decisions and to guide the work of their districts. Principals and teachers will review the statement, recommend ways to improve it, and decide how to use it to help frame their individual work in classrooms and collective work in schools and districts.

Throughout the Partnership, people were continuing to struggle with how to develop structures and opportunities to meet the diverse needs of the organization. The problems of accommodating teachers at different stages of awareness and development, of combining reflection and action, of focusing on both individual and schoolwide concerns, and of involving the university as an equal partner were all begging for response. The UNUM money provided a window of opportunity to tackle these issues, but we recognized that money was not the answer. We had to depend on the ideas, insights, and commitment of our members. Below, we highlight some of the ways in which we came to address concerns about both breadth and depth.

Educator Groups. At its height, the Partnership had over 15 educator groups meeting monthly. The topics were very broadly cast from the original early childhood, mathematics, middle level, and secondary foci to issues of social responsibility, multiculturalism, fine arts, the nature of built environments, and special education.The Partnership's office became a clearinghouse for meetings, dissemination of materials, and resource gathering. Just when the groups seemed to be firmly established as the chief mechanism for Partnership involvement, they stopped working. Attendance dropped, meetings were canceled, interest waned. This all happened during the Partnership's eighth year. What had been the essential, galvanizing structure of the Partnership had suddenly become irrelevant.

We held focus-group meetings to find out what had gone wrong. We found that the reasons for the groups' demise were diverse. For some people, the drive to the university where the groups met was too long. For others, the work that was going on at the school level was so time-consuming and engaging that there was simply not enough time or energy to do anything else. For still others, new opportunities inside and outside the Partnership replaced the function the groups had served. As we enter our ninth year, we have only a handful of educator groups in operation in addition to the superintendents' and principals' meetings. We are experimenting with new ways to bring people together for reflective conversation and exchange across schools and districts. The groups have lost their magic, and we have to seek new forums for conversation.

Consultations. Consultants serve both individuals and schools in negotiated relationships that promote and support the diffusion of knowledge, learning, and expertise across the Partnership. Individuals and schools that are in the middle of solving an important problem are identified through self-examination and peer recommendation. By way of seminars, site visits, presentations, demonstrations, and structured conversations, the consultants provide technical assistance, information, and inspiration to others.

Foxfire. An approach to education based on Dewey's principles of experience and education, Foxfire became an important vehicle for engaging teachers in individual classroom change. With UNUM grant support, we were able to hire a veteran school practitioner and gifted group facilitator to introduce Foxfire to the Partnership. The response was immediate. Beginning with a summer institute for 24 people, the Foxfire Partnership Teachers Network now involves more than 110 teachers in more than 40 schools. Key to the success of Foxfire is the intellectual integrity of the initial institute, the provision of classroom support, the accessibility of a skilled coordinator, and the participation of teachers as leaders in the work. Additional grant funding has allowed us to hire three Partnership Foxfire teachers, on leave from their schools, to assist in program development, on-site assistance, and assessment and documentation.

Assessment Minigrants. Small grants allowed us to award money to individuals and groups of teachers to develop nontraditional assessments in their classes. The money is usually used to buy teacher time to develop and test these assessments. This past year, we awarded two different kinds of minigrants: level one grants for people who are getting started in designing new assessments and level two grants for those who are ready to refine their work and disseminate it to others in publishable form. When the peer review group met to award the grants, it decided to support a third category that was targeted to prepare teachers to think about assessment in new ways so that a larger pool of educators would be in a position to compete for the grants in years to come.

Demonstration Schools. Three Partnership schools have committed themselves to "planning backwards" from outcomes and assessments. These demonstration schools (one elementary, one middle, and one high school) are developing outcomes and assessments in one content area and in the area of "global and personal stewardship." With the on-site assistance of three Partnership staff (two university faculty and an assessment associate) and the resources of a small grant, the schools have developed strategies and products that they are now ready to share with other Partnership schools. In fact, seven districts have committed themselves to this approach to school development and are working closely with the demonstration schools as models of the process.

Teacher Education. Long the domain of the university, teacher education has become a major component of the Partnership's work. In 1989 the university eliminated its undergraduate teacher preparation program and replaced it with an extended program that grants certification after a postgraduate year and awards a master's degree after two years of teaching and study. The director of the Partnership was asked to lead the new program from planning to implementation. Beginning with a pilot class in 1990, the Extended Teacher Education Program (ETEP) evolved. ETEP is based on the notion of partnership. There are five ETEP intern sites, each a Partnership district. The program is decentralized, so that each site's steering committee (composed mostly of public school teachers and at least one university faculty member) makes decisions about program delivery and student placement. Each site is co-directed by a university faculty member and a public school faculty member on half-time assignment to the program.

ETEP represents a marked departure from business as usual in teacher education. It involves the university as a full member in the Partnership, not as a collection of individuals but as an institution. Most important, it acknowledges that teaching is a shared profession involving both school and university faculty, with each having a stake in teacher education and knowledge about how to do it.

School Quality Review. Our newest initiative involves whole schools in examining their practices and outcomes and fosters a model of accountability that is especially appropriate for members of a partnership. Still in its formative stages, School Quality Review will generate a template of learner-centered practice and desired student outcomes. Schools will then volunteer to undergo a formal review of their practices and agree to develop an improvement plan based on its findings. We believe that the quality review has the promise to influence state policy on learner outcomes and school accountability. It is a risky undertaking, but one well worth pursuing.

WHAT WE'VE LEARNED ABOUT PARTNERSHIP

From our experience, we've come to see that a partnership is not so much an institutional arrangement as it is a set of reciprocal relationships among members. In a partnership, one member cannot *fix* or *heal* another. Through conversation, interaction, and common work, members find ways to influence one another, to provide collegiality and support, and to encourage self-empowerment and progress.

In a partnership, relationships are egalitarian. No one person, group, or institution has privileged access to knowledge or power. If, as Goodlad (1988) suggests, partnerships are forged from tough problems that need resolution, then all members are equal in that they have problems to pose and solutions to seek. In our case, partnership establishes a "third culture," neither school nor university, where institutional roles are left at the door. Partnership is a place where certitude is less valued than doubt and where ideas are considered practical. It is an alternative to business as usual.

When one conceives of partnership as relational rather than institutional, the solution to the problem of simultaneously getting broader and deeper rests on the quality of interaction among members. In our nine-year history, we have learned some powerful lessons about struggle, change, and endurance in partnership and about how to simultaneously get broader and deeper in our work. Among our learnings are the following.

Partnership Is Emergent. It is not fixed. The structure, norms, mission, and activity of a partnership are in the process of continuous development. They respond to the needs of members. And the needs of members change for many reasons. We have found that it is important that we don't fall so in love with the structures we create that we are not able to see their shortcomings. For instance, in our partnership, the educator groups were at the center of our work. They seemed to be an intrinsic part of our identity. Yet, over time, the groups stopped serving the needs of our members. We had to look critically at the groups and invent new ways to keep conversation alive in the partnership, to draw in new voices, and to challenge old ones.

It is no accident that we did not develop a mission statement until our ninth year of operation. Until then, we didn't need one. In fact, such a statement would have been more restrictive than enabling. Our focus, like our structures, became refined and clarified over time. This way of working is not linear, but it is rational. It assumes that people engaged in authentic conversation and shared work can create and re-create organizational form and focus for themselves.

Partnership Is Forgiving and Accommodating. Unlike so many other organizations, partnership depends on personal commitment and voluntary engagement. There are no extrinsic rewards, such as course or inservice credit, attached to participation. Because of this, a partnership cannot impose sanctions on people who miss meetings or drop out of projects. Rather, partnership creates an ambiance of forgiveness and accommodation that keeps it alive.

In our partnership, one of the most difficult adjustments that university faculty had to make in convening the educator groups was coming to terms with their shifting memberships. Every meeting had an array of new, veteran, and lapsed members. As one teacher said, "I've been away for three months, but I knew I'd be welcomed back without issue. The Partnership is just a forgiving organization."

Forgiveness means that it is all right for individuals or whole schools to "drop out" of the Partnership for a period of time and to reenter when they think it is appropriate to do so. Many teachers at Narragansett School, for instance, stopped attending Partnership activities and redirected their energies toward school-based reform or national projects. In a few years' time, these same people returned to Partnership involvement as group leaders, teacher consultants, and minigrant designers. Multiple entry and exit points not only ensure forgiveness, they encourage renewal.

Along with forgiveness comes accommodation. Because structures are emergent, they are by nature responsive and flexible. When there is a wide array of activities involving different degrees of commitment, it is more likely that there is an appropriate starting place for just about everyone. Our own development from depending exclusively on the educator groups to offering a range of programs, projects, and activities bears witness to the importance of multiple opportunities for engagement. We now talk of offering three kinds of forums for member involvement: conversations, consultations, and networks. Each requires different degrees of participation and commitment; each offers a different point of entry for members.

Partnership Focuses on Individual and Organizational Development. Because partnership provides multiple opportunities for entry, it recognizes that "one size does not fit all" when it comes to professional development. It also must recognize that there is no one right way to change schools and schooling. In our case, the goal has been defined as "creating and maintaining learner-centered schools." While debate looms large among researchers and school reformers about whether individual development precedes organizational development (Loucks-Horsley & Steigelbauer, 1991) or whether belief precedes practice (Guskey, 1986), partnership needs to acknowledge and support both individual and school development and influence both practice and belief. There is, quite simply, no one best way to engage people and keep them engaged.

In our work, the educator groups, the emerging conversations, and the Foxfire Network focus on individual growth, while the assessment minigrants, demonstration schools project, and school quality review are geared toward whole-school development. Teachers, principals, and superintendents are engaged as both individuals and as representatives of schools and districts. They can use the Partnership to fulfill personal, professional, or institutional needs—depending on where they are at any given moment.

Partnership Draws on Its Own Members for Leadership and Expertise. One of the unique aspects of partnership is that it develops an internal cadre of leaders and experts. While it is important to maintain connections with national movements and the people who lead them, it is even more important to recognize and use the experience, talent, and knowledge that is home-grown and local. As an example, our consultant program draws on our own members as experts in learning, curriculum, and assessment. Not only is the approach more affordable in economic hard times, it also has proven to be more effective than relying on outside experts who don't understand our context or share our commitments.

Teacher leadership is another key element in our partnership. Most of our initiatives are teacher-designed and -motivated. We also make every effort to involve teachers as leaders in Partnership work. Whether as group conveners, consultants, or conference presenters, teachers assume leadership that is both visible and formally acknowledged. More important, whenever we secure funding for specific projects, we draw on practicing teachers to lead these efforts. At present, there are five teachers on leave to the Partnership as assessment and Foxfire associates. In addition, there are five Partnership teachers who co-lead the new teacher education program. It is now Partnership policy that all new positions are advertised internally and assumed by one of our members. We have found that the active engagement of teachers as experts and leaders keeps the Partnership fresh. When teachers sit around the table, it ensures that the teacher's voice is heard. And that voice guards against the organization becoming too distant or too self-satisfied.

Partnership Involves All Partners in Finding and Solving Problems. In order to be a partnership, the organization needs to attend to both the self-interests of each member and the collective interest of the whole. It is too easy in a school–university partnership for the university to assume a didactic or helping stance toward schools. In the early days of our Partnership the educator groups, convened by university faculty, conveyed the tacit message that problems lie in the schools and that university people can help solve them. This began to change when school faculty assumed group facilitator roles and found other paths to leadership. It changed even more dramatically when the university identified the problem of teacher education as one that required public school input in finding a solution. The Extended Teacher Education

Program that was developed as a university–school collaboration established a parity in relationships that had long been missing.

We have come to believe that it is not until all members acknowledge their individual problems and seek help in solving them that a partnership has fulfilled its potential. This is a long and hard road for partnership members, but it is one well worth traveling.

Partnership Seeks Connections Beyond Its Boundaries. Any organization can become ingrown. This is especially true of partnership. Based on notions of reciprocity and local knowledge development, a partnership can turn in on itself and shut out good ideas and practices that are generated outside its own boundaries. We believe that our partnership began to find solutions to the tension between getting broader and getting deeper when it looked outside of itself for ideas and opportunities for engagement. The Foxfire network and the school quality review are the direct result of conversations and collaborations with organizations outside of Maine. They brought new initiatives to our work and new structures to support them. Our partnership efforts in nontraditional assessment have benefited from involvement and dialogue with people on a national level. Narragansett's connections to Project Zero and the ATLAS communities not only deepened its own work, but influenced the work of other members and of the Partnership as a whole. It has become obvious that as networking is beneficial within a partnership, it is also useful across and among partnerships and other existing affiliations.

Partnership Is Self-critical and Reflective. A partnership needs to engage itself in the same degree of problem finding and problem solving it promotes in its members. Such engagement helps maintain the critical edge and freshness that are so vital to partnership work. It is easy for a long-enduring partnership, like any organization that has gained recognition and positive attention, to become complacent. Even the most innovative organization can embrace business as usual. Like schools that blame their students for not meeting unrealistic expectations, partnerships can easily blame their members for not using their services well.

Our partnership "hit the wall" in its eighth year of operation. Having prided itself on being responsive, flexible, and inventive, the Partnership was in danger of becoming redundant and irrelevant. The decisions to hold focus-group meetings, to raise the issue of focus and inclusion with the superintendents, and to involve teachers as leaders and experts all helped the organization find its way. The new structures that were developed, alongside the traditional vehicles for dialogue and action, have infused new energy into the Partnership's work.

Perhaps the most important lesson we have learned as active participants in a partnership is that we need to become "critical friends" to
each other, to hold ourselves to the norms and values that the partnership espouses, and to be always ready to incorporate new ideas and new
forms into our work.

SCHOOL AND UNIVERSITY WORK:
THE INFLUENCE OF PARTNERSHIP

The Partnership has had considerable influence on how the University of Southern Maine and Narragansett School both think about and
construct their work. The university's teacher education program has
been completely transformed as a result of the Partnership. Preservice
teachers no longer take coursework that is isolated from the realities
of practice, nor do they enter a student teaching experience that is
disconnected from and contradicts academic study. Rather, our interns
live out the tension between theory and practice in daily interaction
with children, public school educators, parents and community residents, and university faculty. The university and the schools have joined
together to develop a new breed of teacher—one who is suited to the
demands of teaching and learning in renewing schools. Our program
graduates are hired in record numbers and are beginning to have an
impact on the lives of children in schools throughout the southern
Maine region and the entire state.

Narragansett School has also changed. Some of this change can be
attributed to the Partnership, some to other influences—among them
the superintendent and her vision of schooling, a positive state environment for restructuring, the development of internal talent and support
for invention, and connections to organizations outside the Partnership
and outside of Maine. How has Narragansett changed? Over the course
of ten years, the school has become a true "center of inquiry" for
teachers and students. Students are encouraged to engage in active learning, to demonstrate what they know and are able to do to a public
audience, and to reflect on what they've learned and how they've
learned it. Multiage and multi-grade-level classes operate alongside each
other. Students and their parents make choices about placement, selecting from a variety of options in regard to learning and teaching style and
patterns of classroom organization. Special education students are fully
included in the life of the school; the most severely handicapped children interact and learn in regular classrooms with nonhandicapped students as their peers.

Perhaps the most palpable change in Narragansett School is in the way that student learning is displayed and assessed. Explicit performance standards are in place for all content areas. There are clear and public criteria for student work. Portfolios are used to track student progress, and rehearsals and performances are built into every aspect of the academic program. Student juries, as well as community panels, take an active role in evaluating student work. More important, students are expected to talk about, critique, and evaluate their own work. There are no surprises for students or parents when conferences are held or when progress reports are issued. In fact, the entire district has adopted a policy, K–12, which provides for 30 minute parent/student/teacher conferences using portfolios as the basis for assessment.

What Narragansett has accomplished in the areas of learning, teaching, and assessment is significant; it is setting the standard for other schools in the Partnership. The school models intellectual engagement, learner-centered practice, and norms of inquiry and reflection. Narragansett represents what can happen when a school looks at itself critically and embarks on a path of continuous improvement in the company of colleagues and friends.

PART V

AN EMERGENT
PARADIGM FOR
PRACTICE AND POLICY

Images of new practices and new policies are evolving from practitioners' and policymakers' struggle with the implications of the reform agenda. Part V sketches dimensions of this emergent paradigm for
practice and policy. Ann Lieberman, in Chapter 15, and Linda Darling-
Hammond and Milbrey W. McLaughlin, in Chapter 16, summarize key
lessons and principles from practices such as those detailed in the body
of this book.

"Break-the-mold" classroom practices, Ann Lieberman argues, require break-the-mold professional development practices that cast
change as key to learning. Lieberman extracts core principles for professional development activities consistent with teaching and learning for
understanding.

Darling-Hammond and McLaughlin focus on the policy implications of these new institutional arrangements and the infrastructure indispensable to teachers' development and efforts to change. The challenge to policy in this reform era extends beyond invention of new
opportunities and support. Equally important is the fit between reformers' image of practice and the policy system in which it is embedded.
The authors offer guidelines for aligning the signals and incentives existing in the system, as well as design principles that can be used to assess
the promise of policies and practices proposed in support of teachers'
professional development.

Chapter 15

Practices That Support Teacher Development

Transforming Conceptions of Professional Learning

Ann Lieberman

BREAKING THE MOLD: FROM INSERVICE TO PROFESSIONAL LEARNING

This chapter is concerned with the limitations of traditional approaches to teacher development and the new learnings that are informing the field. These might be summarized in this way:

- Teacher development has been limited by lack of knowledge of how teachers learn.
- Teachers' definitions of the problems of practice have often been ignored.
- The agenda for reform involves teachers in practices that have not been a part of the accepted view of teachers' professional learning.
- Teaching has been described as a technical set of skills, leaving little room for invention and the building of craft knowledge.
- Professional development opportunities have often ignored the critical importance of the context within which teachers work.
- Strategies for change have often not considered the importance of support mechanisms and the necessity of learning over time.
- Time and the necessary mechanisms for inventing as well as consuming new knowledge have often been absent from schools.

- The move from "direct teaching" to facilitating "in-school learning" is connected to longer-term strategies aimed not only at changing teaching practice but also at changing the school culture.
- Networks, collaborations, and partnerships provide teachers with professional learning communities that support changed teaching practices in their own schools and classrooms.

As opportunities increase for professional learning that moves away from the traditional inservice mode toward long-term, continuous learning in the context of school and classroom with the support of colleagues, the idea of professional development is taking on new importance (Lieberman & Miller, 1992a; Little, 1993b). For if teacher learning takes place within the context of a professional community that is nurtured and developed from both inside and outside of school, the effects may be not only an expanded conception of teacher development but also the accomplishment of significant and lasting school change.

Learning by Changing: Teacher Development and School Development

This expanded view of professional learning, of necessity, is both personal and professional, individual and collective, inquiry-based and technical (Darling-Hammond, 1993; Hargreaves, 1994). While we have no definitive roadmaps that lead us directly to how these dualities are negotiated, we do have a growing body of evidence from some schools that have discovered the power and critical importance of professional development when viewed as an integral part of the life of the school. By studying these schools, we can deepen our understanding of how teachers acquire the experience that encourages them to grow and change in the context of school reform (Darling-Hammond, Ancess, & Falk, 1995; Lieberman, 1995; Murphy & Hallinger, 1993).

For example, some organizational and pedagogical changes in these schools put new and experienced teachers together to learn from each other; create common periods for planning so that connections can be made across subject areas; use staff expertise to provide leadership for in-house workshops or meetings (Lieberman, Falk, & Alexander, 1994); have self-contained teams where the organizational structure (a team) encourages constant staff learning (Darling-Hammond et al., 1995); or develop curricular changes that encourage interdisciplinary studies for short periods of time, involving staff in discussion of curriculum and pedagogy (Ancess, in press).

Numerous curricular, pedagogical, and assessment approaches to student learning also provide powerful professional learning for teachers, involving them in rethinking their role with students while at the same time expanding the way students interact with content and the problems of learning. Many instances of professional learning come about as a result of starting with meetings about subject-matter content, pedagogical approaches, new means of assessment, or simply learning (Lieberman, 1995). What makes the difference for teachers is that the content of the curriculum, the context of each classroom within the school, and the context of the school itself are all considered, with teacher participation central to any changes in the functioning of the school.

From Direct Teaching to Learning in School

Most of the inservice or staff development that teachers are now exposed to is of a more formal nature; unattached to classroom life, it is often a melange of abstract ideas with little attention paid to ongoing support for continuous learning and changed practices. By contrast, the conception of teacher development that ties together student-centered pedagogy with opportunities for teacher learning, supported by favorable and durable organizational conditions, is now being tried in many places (Fine, 1994; Grimmett & Neufeld, 1994; Lieberman, 1995). By constructing a continuum of the actual practices that encourage teacher growth, we see that such a continuum involves moving from direct teaching—the dominant mode of inservice—to practices that involve learning in school as well as learning out of school. The change from "teaching" to "learning" is significant, since it implies that teacher development opportunities must become integral to the restructuring of schools. This will, of necessity, involve strategies and mechanisms that are more long-range, more concerned with groups' and individual teachers' interactions, and often original and unique to the particular contexts in which they are invented (see Table 15.1).

This broader approach moves teachers beyond simply hearing about new ideas or frameworks for understanding teaching practice, to being involved in the decisions about the substance, process, and organizational supports for learning in school, to finding broader support mechanisms—such as networks or partnerships—that provide opportunities and innovative norms from groups outside the school.

Because direct teaching is currently much of what the public and many districts consider staff development, it is important that teachers, administrators, and policymakers become aware of new and broader

TABLE 15.1. **Teacher Development and Professional Learning**

A Continuum		
Direct Teaching	**Learning in School**	**Learning out of School**
• Inspirationals	•Teacher Scholars	•Reform Networks
•Awareness Sessions	•Teacher Leaders	•School/University
•Basic Knowledge	•Critical Friends	Partnerships
•Initial Conversation	•School Quality Review	•Subject-Matter Networks
•Charismatic Speakers	•Peer Coaching	•Informal Groups
•Conferences	•Action Research	•Collaborations
•Courses and Workshops	•Story Telling	•Teacher Centers
•Consultations	•Sharing Experience	•Impact II
	•Teaching Each Other	•NEA and AFT
	•Problem Solving Groups	Collaborations
	•Descriptive Reviews	
	•Portfolio Assessment	
	•Experiencing Self as	
	Learner	
	•Proposal Writing	
	•Case Studies of Practice	
	•Standard Setting	
	•Journal Writing	
	•Working on Tasks	
	Together	
	•Writing for Journals	
	•On-line Conversations	
	•School Site Management	
	Team	
	•Curriculum Writing	

conceptions of professional development. At present many districts have from one to seven days of inservice education in the school year when teachers are introduced to new ideas (e.g., new math standards, new forms of assessment). Some districts run workshops on themes or particular subjects, often hiring consultants to handle the "implementation" of these ideas. While learning about new ideas that affect both the content and the processes of teaching is important, ideas, when unrelated to the organization and context of one's own classroom, have a hard time competing with the dailiness of work—even when teachers are excited about and committed to them.

There are times when direct teaching can play an important role in building a constituency for change. The more members of the educational community who are knowledgeable about the educational changes taking place, the more support there will be for these changes. When, for example, schools move toward performance assessments, cooperative learning strategies, or project work, parents should know why these are important teaching and learning strategies so that they will come to support rather than resist them.

But if reform plans are to be made operational, enabling teachers to really change the way they work, then teachers must have opportunities to talk, think, try out, and hone new practices, which means they must be involved in learning about, developing, and using new ideas with their students. This can happen in a number of ways:

- *Building new roles*: Teacher leaders, critical friends, teacher scholars (Miller & O'Shea, Chapter 14, this volume)
- *Inventing new relationships*: Peer coaching, doing action research
- *Creating new structures*: Problem-solving groups, school site decision-making teams, descriptive reviews
- *Working on new tasks*: Journal and proposal writing, learning about assessment, creating standards, analyzing or writing case studies of practice, communicating "on-line" about particular topics (Jervis, in press; Wood & Einbender, in press)
- *Creating a culture of inquiry*: Professional learning eventually comes to be expected, sought after, and an ongoing part of teaching and school life (Lieberman, 1995; McClure, 1991; McLaughlin, 1991; Smith & Wigginton, 1991)

What characterizes these examples of professional learning is that their life span is not one or two days; rather, they become a part of the expectation for the teacher's role and an integral part of the culture of the school. Learning and development become as varied and engaging for teachers as they are supposed to be for students. Experiencing and helping to produce new knowledge becomes as compelling as consuming already existing knowledge—in fact, one feeds the other. Being involved as a learner and participant provides openings to new knowledge, broadening the agenda for thought and action (e.g., teachers involved in action research, looking at their own practice, often seek affiliation with their colleagues, who subsequently may themselves participate in some form of problem-solving activity). In important ways, such activities link professional learning that is solo and personal to learning that is also collegial and communal.

Teachers who engage in these new professional opportunities often find themselves in an exciting and powerful cycle: The more they learn,

the more they open up to new possibilities and the more they seek to
learn more. Unfortunately, other teachers, despite the failures of their
students to learn in school, are often satisfied with what they know, do
not seek opportunities to learn, and, in the worst of situations, block
those who are trying to make changes. The problem then becomes one
of how to engage these teachers in activities that bring an awareness
of the possibilities for student learning inherent in new pedagogical
approaches.

TEACHER DEVELOPMENT PRACTICES:
EXPANDING OUR CONCEPTIONS

Several examples illustrate the connection between teacher learning
and the mechanisms to support these in-school efforts.

Learning by Observing Children

The Primary Language Record (PLR), a guide for collecting evidence to aid teachers' understanding of how students become literate in
the primary grades, encourages teachers to observe student habits and
choices as they are involved in learning tasks. Using this guide involves
teachers in interviewing parents and students concerning students'
study habits and interests both at home and in school. It provides teachers with greater breadth of information about their students, helping
them to become aware of and plan for student differences in learning
styles. Most important, by observing children closely (with the help of a
guide), teachers see that students learn differently, think differently,
and engage with their fellow students in a variety of ways. It does not
tell teachers what to do but rather expands their understandings of what
is possible. The record, focusing attention on student strengths, enables
teachers to better use their own professional judgment to build more
effective teaching programs. Networks of teachers from New York to
California support one another in using this tool to integrate child development knowledge with their observations of their students (Falk &
Darling-Hammond, 1993).

In another example of teachers learning by observing children,
teachers who keep daily journals of classroom activity find themselves
better able to understand their students: their work habits, ways of
approaching tasks, developing interests, as well as satisfactions and frustrations with their classroom work. Participating in action research or
writing case studies of their own practice—whereby teachers write,

think about, and share their experiences with other teachers concerning their students' patterns of learning in their classroom—are other ways in which teachers gain knowledge and insights into the effects they are having on their students (Cochran-Smith & Lytle, Chapter 9, this volume; Wood, 1992). The information and evidence that teachers gather provide a powerful form of self-generated feedback.

New Pedagogical Approaches to Subject Matter

There have been new and innovative approaches to subject-matter teaching that are involving teachers in pedagogical as well as curricular changes. These include:

- The writing process approach, which engages teachers in writing, revising, and polishing their own work and thus experiencing what it means to learn to write
- Whole-language approaches to integrating language arts, which involve teachers in planning for blocks of time for students to read, write, listen, and speak; when teachers and their students integrate ways of thinking about content and how it is learned, teachers often revise their class schedules to allow for larger blocks of work time and more opportunities for students to work together and independently
- The Foxfire approach, which encourages teachers to use students' interests and choices to involve them in planning and carrying out their own learning—gaining skills and subject knowledge as they seek information, write, edit, and produce work in a variety of subject areas using projects of their own making

These new pedagogical approaches encourage teachers to be learners as well as teachers, experiencing for themselves the struggle for personal and intellectual growth that is an essential part of the learning process and sensitizing them to the nuances of learning and the needs of individuals and groups. These approaches to student learning do not downgrade the learning of basic knowledge; they use the interests and abilities of students and teachers to invigorate this learning. Instead of simply memorizing lectures or texts, these approaches involve teachers and their students in using learned skills and abilities to identify and pose problems, and to seek perspectives and methodologies that help to find answers to these problems. Inevitably this means increasing student content knowledge, since solutions to problems depend on such knowledge and the skills and analytical tools developed in the process.

Strategies for Learning Together

The "descriptive review," a process that focuses on looking carefully at one student at a time, brings teachers together in a group to talk about particular students that individual teachers are finding difficult to reach or teach. In the process of understanding these difficulties, a teacher tells what she or he knows about the child, while the other teachers then speak to strategies that they have found successful in similar situations. Teachers share their knowledge with one another, learn from one another, and, by extension, take responsibility for the growth and development of all children in the school (Carini, 1986).

There are many less structured informal strategies that bring teachers together, encouraging individual and group development. Peer coaching, one teacher helping another learn new strategies or refine old ones, legitimates and makes possible the use of valuable expertise within a school faculty that is not usually exploited. Writing curriculum together, forming problem-solving groups, telling stories of difficulties as well as successes in practice, organizing parent presentations, participating in discussions with the board of education about proposed new practices, working together on proposals for state or federal funding—all are means of providing avenues for teachers to interact as professionals. They have opportunities to work through problems of practice, explore pedagogical and organizational strategies, develop understanding of the change process, and give and receive help in public ways that reach out from and penetrate into the privacy of their own classrooms. Taken together these strategies provide the basis for creating norms of collaboration and colleagueship, as well as providing processes and content that contribute to professional learning.

Learning by Integrating Assessment and Curriculum

Through their involvement in new patterns of student assessment, teachers learn by organizing the curriculum in ways that reflect their rethinking of what students should know and be able to do to demonstrate the breadth and depth of their learning. Portfolios, which are exhibitions of a student's knowledge and skills, embrace diverse forms of expression, including science and social science research reports, constructions, multimedia presentations, original works of art, and writing or dramatic presentations (Darling-Hammond, Einbender, Frelow, & Key-King, 1993). An important example of this process is the work done in the Central Park East Secondary School (CPESS) linking "habits of mind" with portfolio assessment (see Darling-Hammond et al., 1995, for details). "Habits of mind" is defined as a set of five principles that involve examining evidence critically, looking at multiple viewpoints, making connections, seeking alternatives, and looking for meaning. These principles serve as a foundation on which to build a pedagogy that teaches students to use their minds well in order to enable them to live socially useful and personally satisfying lives. They form the basis for ongoing discussions about breadth versus depth, core versus individualized knowledge, and for developing the kinds of courses and educational experiences to achieve these ideals. The assessment process, which is integral to this work, uses portfolios as a means to involve teachers as "coaches" of their students: serving as critics and supporters of their work, connecting them to subject areas, guiding them toward completion of graduation requirements, and always helping them to build "habits" of mind and work that will last beyond graduation.

The organic relationship between portfolios and the principles of "habits of mind" forms the basis for learning for teachers as well as students. The school involves the faculty in continuous work on the definitions and parameters of core subjects; portfolio content and measurements of competent work; what it means to be a coach, advisor, and supporter of student work; students' responsibilities for creating, revising, and completing academic work; and the kind and quality of social responsibility and interaction with students and their families as well as with one another. Although this is a particularly ambitious example, it shows how significant changing the method of assessment can be to teacher learning and development when this becomes an integral part of the daily work of school transformation that is not seen in isolation from the problems and questions that are a part of teachers' daily lives.

Efforts to reform assessment practices may be among the most ambitious of all reform efforts, since methods of assessment have great significance in determining how teachers teach as well as powerfully affecting their own learning and development. Reforming assessment not only involves teachers in looking at *what* and *how* they are teaching; it also confronts them with what students are really learning. Whether considering the uses of portfolios or working together to set standards of practice, teachers come to question in fundamental ways the quality of students' learning experiences and, considering the different interests and abilities of individual students, what work is "good enough." Contentious issues such as depth versus breadth, quality versus quantity, direct versus indirect methods of teaching, or measurements of success based on the amount of growth of a particular student versus a universal standard of excellence—all become part of the daily work of school transformation (Darling-Hammond & Snyder, 1992). Pursuing solutions to these issues provide endless possibilities for growth, development, and change (Jervis, in press; Wood & Einbender; in press).

The Role of Partnerships, Coalitions, and Networks in Teacher Development

Although up to this point we have been dealing with professional learning for teachers that takes place inside the school, there is growing evidence that important and potentially powerful organizational arrangements exist outside the school as well. These networks, collaboratives, coalitions, and partnerships offer teachers professional opportunities that are different in quality and kind than those that have been available inside the school or in traditional professional development programs (Lieberman, 1986a, 1986b; Lieberman & McLaughlin, Chapter 7, this volume; Little & McLaughlin, 1991; McLaughlin & Talbert, 1993; Miller & O'Shea, Chapter 14, this volume; *Teacher Leadership*, 1989, 1990). Unlike most professional development strategies, with a "one size fits all" orientation, networks and/or coalitions and partnerships provide opportunities for teachers to commit in small and large ways to topics that are of intrinsic value to them or that develop out of their work (Little & McLaughlin, 1991). In addition to formal learning they may, by joining informal groups, develop stronger voices to represent their perspectives, learn to exercise leadership among their peers, use their firsthand experience to create new possibilities for students through collaborative work (Jervis, in press; *Teacher Leadership*, 1989, 1990), and, perhaps most importantly, develop a community of shared understanding that enriches their teaching while providing the intellectual and emotional stimulation necessary for personal and enduring growth and development (Lieberman & McLaughlin, Chapter 7, this volume; Wood & Einbender, in press). These important opportunities for teacher development more readily exist in environments free from the constraints of the cultures of university and school-based educators, providing a level of flexibility and collaborative work not usually possible in existing organizations.

The following examples help us to understand the variety of contexts, content, and collaborative arrangements possible when teachers are learning out of school.

The Center for Collaborative Education (CCE). This urban network of schools—the New York City affiliate of the Coalition of Essential Schools (a national school reform network established in 1985 by Ted Sizer)—was formed under the leadership of Deborah Meier to link together a small number of public elementary and secondary schools committed to democratically run, learner-centered schools. From its beginnings in one district (District 4) in one elementary school (Central Park East I), the network has grown to 20 schools in New York City, plus 10 more schools in the surrounding area.

The values that these schools hold in common are evident in their small size, diverse populations, thematic organization of the curricula, and active approach to student learning and adult participation (see Table 15.2). Each of these schools has from 200 to 400 students, yet their populations reflect the socioeconomic, racial, and ethnic diversity of New York City. Organized into heterogeneous, multiage classes, they are structured to encourage and enhance collaboration between and among faculty, students, and their families. Classroom environments promote active involvement with materials and experiences, while the pedagogy encourages individualized project work, peer interaction, and an interdisciplinary approach to learning.

One of the CCE schools—Central Park East Secondary School—is also a "partnership school," having joined a group of other schools that have been given permission by the State Board of Education to develop local innovative assessment and accountability systems for state approval. Whereas the schools in the network were initially seen as "alternative" and marginal, they are now part of New York State efforts to create systemwide reform in its New Compact for Learning. The CCE network thus serves not only as a support system for its member schools but also as a resource for other schools in the state that are attempting to change.

As a part of the ongoing work of developing and deepening the practices that support their stated principles, the schools in the network continually examine their own practices, as well as how they can help others who want to join them. Since the network's inception it has published a newsletter, *Connections*, which communicates to member schools, students, parents, and staffs about work issues and other areas of concern, such as assessment, standard setting, the changing nature of responsibility, and accountability). The network sponsors local conferences, organizes professional development opportunities, and is involved in New York City's creation of small new secondary schools—such as the recently created Campus Coalition Schools Project, a group of six new high schools on the CCE model that have opened in New York City.

Attempting to expand their connections with other schools, the network has recently created several categories of membership:

TABLE 15.2. Essential Principles: The Center for Collaborative Education, NYC Affiliate of the Coalition of Essential Schools

1. **Purposes:** The school should focus on helping young people learn to use their minds well. Schools should not attempt to be "comprehensive" if such a claim is made at the expense of the school's central intellectual purpose. To this end each school needs to clarify the essential skills, areas of knowledge, and habits of mind that it believes are central to the students becoming well-educated members of our society.

2. **Academic Standards:** Teaching and learning is personalized, but the general course of study should be unified and universal. While the school's goals should apply to all students, the means to these goals will vary as the students themselves vary. High expectations must be held for all. All students, not just some, should be expected to be in a position to grapple with important issues, to be able to participate fully in the larger community as citizens and workers, to have the skills and competencies to hold useful and decently paid employment, and to live satisfying personal lives.

3. **Curriculum:** Three principles guide our curriculum: (1) that the curriculum should respect the intradisciplinary nature of human activity; (2) that the curriculum should respect the diverse heritages that encompass the society in which our students live and must respond to; and (3) that the curriculum be mindful of the concept that "less is more"—that it is better to know well a few important and powerful ideas/topics rather than cover many superficially.

4. **Size/Personalization:** In order to educate well, teachers must know the work of their students and their colleagues. Furthermore, the level of staff governance necessary to develop a CCE/CES plan requires a community small enough to easily meet and talk together. No high school teacher should therefore be expected to deal with more than 80 students a year. Each student should be known well by one faculty member who is responsible for no more than 30 students. No school (or independently organized subschool) should have more than 500 students; and learning units should be organized so that students and adults remain together in considerably smaller communities over several years so they can get to know each other well. Furthermore, the principal and teachers should perceive themselves as generalists first and specialists second, and should expect multiple obligations as teacher-counselor-manager and a sense of commitment to the entire school.

5. **Student-As-Worker/Student-As-Citizen:** Learning is not an observer sport! The student must be an active participant in his/her own learning. Student-as-worker and teacher as coach and mentor is our metaphor. Students must—in collaboration with their teachers and families—also be active citizens in creating the tone, standards, and quality of life of the school. A school should be a living example of communal responsibility. Students, staff, and families should have ways to actively contribute to the well-being of their school and the larger community.

6. **Assessment:** Students should be evaluated on the basis of their performance, not hours spent or credits earned. Performance assessment should be as direct and authentic as possible. Thus indirect and normative testing should be replaced, as soon and as far as possible, by alternative performance-based assessment methods. Graduation from elementary school and high school should be based on demonstrated mastery over clearly stated competencies related to the school's general plan of education.

TABLE 15.2. continued

7. **Tone/Values:** The tone of the school should explicitly and self-consciously stress values of unanxious expectation ("I won't threaten you, but I expect much of you"), of trust (until abused), and of decency (the values of fairness, generosity, and tolerance).
8. **Families:** Families need to have ways to have input into school policies and decisions, as they affect both their own children and the school as a total community. The development of mutual respect and trust between the staff and families is a key to the education of students.
9. **Decision Making:** The people who implement policies should have maximum feasible decision-making power over their design. Therefore the internal life of such schools and learning communities must provide the teacher staff with power and responsibility to govern its own practices, to select its own teacher leaders, and to participate in all those decisions that affect their working/teaching success. This must include, however, collaboration between all those affected—particularly students and their families.
10. **Diversity:** Each school, learning community, and classroom should represent as fully as possible the range of racial, ethnic, and economic backgrounds, as well as academic competencies, of NYC school children. Efforts should also be made to build a racially and ethnically mixed staff.
11. **Choice:** A school community is best served by participants who are voluntarily committed to it. Every effort should be made toward the end that no one need be a member of a CCE school community against his/her wishes. Such choice should not, however, operate as a vehicle for creating inequities or elitism.
12. **Budget:** Ultimate administrative and budget targets should include, in addition to providing student loads per teacher as described in #4 above, substantial time for collective planning by teachers, competitive planning by teachers, competitive salaries for staff, and an ultimate per pupil cost not to exceed that at traditional schools by more than 10 %. In the case of high schools this may require phased reduction or elimination over time of some activities now provided in many traditional comprehensive secondary schools.

1. *Exploring schools*, that is, those in the beginning stages that are rethinking their priorities and practices by engaging in conversations among staff and parents about the CCE principles
2. *Networking schools*, which must have drafted a plan of action that could include performance assessment, changing curriculum and pedagogy, or developing criteria for grouping students
3. *Member schools*, which are fully committed to implementing CCE's 12 principles and are ready to provide information, professional development, and additional forms of support to other CCE schools

CCE's progression—from a loosely affiliated group of public schools trying to change while working within the school system, to a small network made up of schools subscribing to common principles of pedagogical and organizational development, to a larger network that is not only expanding its membership and influence within its own school system but has become a national resource in the movement for school reform—is an important example of the latent power that networks of educators can mobilize and develop.

The Foxfire Network. The Foxfire network grew out of a teacher's discovery that, in order to interest students in learning in his English class, he had to involve them in areas of their own interest and choice. The dramatic story of how this happened has been recorded elsewhere (Wigginton, 1985). But what concerns us here is how one teacher's struggle was transformed into a strategy for the creation of teacher networks to provide professional learning beyond the boundaries of one classroom, one school, and one locale. Beginning as a teacher outreach program, the Foxfire network invited teachers to participate in classes during the summer. Because they themselves were teachers, the original Foxfire group modeled the techniques that teachers might try with their students during the school year: from encouraging students to choose their own topics to research and write about, to involving them in identifying their own learning needs—with teachers serving as guide, coach, and counselor. Understanding that meaningful learning needed to be supported over time, they started networks in a few places where the Foxfire course had been given and where there were growing relationships with groups of teachers. These groups, meeting throughout the year, have become a formal part of the Foxfire teacher outreach program, growing from five initial networks to twenty. These networks now exist across the country, and while in some cases they are connected to colleges and universities, they continue to be centers for professional learning created by teachers for teachers (Smith & Wigginton, 1991).

The Four Seasons Network: Authentic Assessment. This network was organized by the National Center for Restructuring Education, Schools and Teaching (NCREST) to bring together teachers from three reform networks: the Coalition of Essential Schools, Foxfire, and Project Zero. The purpose of the network was to bring teachers together to learn about authentic assessment by learning from experts, by learning from each other, and by creating new modes of assessment in their own classrooms and schools. It was created to be a collaboration to support and encourage teacher participation and leadership in the area of assessment. Teachers from ten different states were brought together initially during two summer workshops, while continuity and support was provided year-round through the use of an electronic network. This electronic network enabled teachers to share current stories of practice, discuss their struggles around the creation of portfolios and exhibitions of student work, and give each other support and encouragement for taking risks (Wood & Einbender, in press). Since problems of assessment are crucial to all teaching and learning, this network, by involving teachers from previously existing networks, has helped them all to expand the breadth of their reform work.

These are a few examples of networks and partnerships created to deal with complex educational problems that defy simplistic solutions and pat answers. By bringing groups of teachers together—whether in regard to particular subject areas, articulated principles for reforming schools, new pedagogical techniques, or changed teacher education programs in schools and universities—these networks provided them with access to new ideas and a supportive community for the very difficult struggle of translating these ideas into meaningful changes in teaching and learning in each school and each classroom. In the process, teachers have helped to build an agenda that is sensitive to their contexts and concerns, have had opportunities to be leaders as well as learners, and have often committed themselves to goals that are broader and more inclusive than their initial concerns.

NEW PRACTICES TO HELP WITH OLD DILEMMAS

This chapter has suggested that the need for a more comprehensive view of professional learning has led to a wider range of teaching practices and broader conceptions of teacher development. Strategies for learning in school and learning out of school are beginning to connect teachers' personal needs for growth and development with professional needs to restructure schools, individual teacher learning with the collective learning of peers, and the dynamics of inquiring into one's own practice with acquiring appropriate technical skills and abilities.

The apparent dualities in these new strategies, opening up new possibilities for teacher learning, reveal the organic relationship between the way change takes place and how teaching practices unfold over time. Consider, for example, the Four Seasons teachers described above, who came together from a variety of different locations to learn about new forms of student assessment. Many of the participants in this network used this opportunity not only to learn about assessment but also to return to their schools and organize other teachers to work with them on assessment issues. These teachers realized that they needed to understand how to create supportive conditions in their schools and districts to accommodate the needs of new assessment systems; assessment and the building of support structures therefore became part of the agenda of the network. In the process, as they became more knowledgeable and articulate about assessment practices, some teachers began to assume new roles and responsibilities in their schools and districts. An electronic network slowly grew to include a sizable group of teachers who felt comfortable enough to share their strategies, their struggles, and their newfound knowledge (see Wood & Einbender, in press).

Inquiring into their own practices, in this case, made the teachers aware of skills and abilities they needed to learn, such as how to organize their classrooms when students were working on individual projects, how to deal with standards (rather than standardization) when students were at different places in their understanding, and how to think differently about coverage versus depth in the curriculum. Unfortunately, replacing old routines with new ones never comes easy, but identifying with like-minded peers helps teachers to take the necessary risks. Networks, even if initially focusing solely on inquiry, provide the impetus for teachers to try working differently with their students. The network agenda grows as a consequence of teachers' sharing their new experiences honestly and openly within a supportive community that values learning from one another. Joining intellectual inquiry about learning to teachers' firsthand experiences with their students creates a powerful synthesis of knowledge and commitment to change both school and classroom practice.

Strategies that emphasize learning within the school context are important; they serve to break the isolation that a teacher feels when she or he learns something outside and tries to bring it inside, and they help to legitimate collective learning, which is a critical step in helping to make professional learning an accepted norm in the life of a school. However, networks, collaboratives, and other informal groups are often the catalysts that provide knowledge and inspiration for in-school learning strategies (Lieberman, 1992). When the climate of a school is difficult, they provide teachers with knowledge, support, and identity with a broader community that enables them to persevere. They have partners in the struggle in which they are engaged, and this struggle is recognized and expected, not frowned upon or denied; status differences and taboos are fewer and norms of friendship and support come easier; leadership functions are more broadly shared and practiced; asking questions, admitting problems and failures, and describing the dilemmas of practice are acceptable, encouraging the acquisition of more knowledge and technical skills; and both information and support is available when needed, rather than being given at arbitrary times in rationed amounts. It is for these reasons that serious school reform has a greater chance of succeeding over time when there are teachers (and principals) inside school who belong to reform networks from outside school.

Chapter 16

Policies That Support Professional Development in an Era of Reform

Linda Darling-Hammond
and Milbrey W. McLaughlin

The vision of practice underlying the nation's reform agenda requires most teachers to reconceptualize their practice, to construct new classroom roles and expectations about student outcomes, and to teach in ways they have never taught before and probably have never experienced (Nelson & Hammerman, Chapter 1, this volume). The success of this agenda turns ultimately on teachers' success in accomplishing the serious and difficult tasks of *learning* the skills and perspectives assumed by new visions of practice and, often, *unlearning* practices and beliefs about students or instruction that have dominated their entire professional lives. Yet few occasions and supports for such professional development exist in teachers' environments.

Because teaching for understanding relies on teachers' abilities to see complex subject matter from the perspectives of diverse students, the know-how necessary to accomplish this vision of practice cannot be prepackaged or conveyed by means of traditional, top-down, teacher-training strategies. The policy problem for professional development in this reform era extends beyond mere support for teachers' acquisition of new skills or knowledge to providing occasions for teachers to reflect critically on their practice and fashion new knowledge and beliefs about content, pedagogy, and learners (Nelson & Hammerman, Chapter 1, this volume; Prawat, 1992).

Teacher development focused on deepening teachers' understandings about the teaching/learning process and the students they teach must begin with preservice education and continue throughout a teacher's career. Effective professional development involves teachers both as learners and as teachers, and allows them to struggle with the uncertainties that accompany each role. It must be:

- Experiential, engaging teachers in concrete tasks of teaching, assessment, observation, and reflection that illuminate the processes of learning and development
- Grounded in inquiry, reflection, and experimentation that are participant-driven (that is, learners take responsibility for posing questions and exploring answers)
- Collaborative and interactional, involving a sharing of knowledge among educators and a focus on teachers' communities of practice rather than individual teachers
- Connected to and derived from teachers' work with their students
- Sustained, ongoing, and intensive, supported by modeling, coaching, and collective problem solving around specific problems of practice
- Connected to other aspects of school change

Professional development of this kind signals departure from old norms and models of teacher training or inservicing to new images of what, when, and how teachers learn. These new images bring a corresponding shift from policies that seek to control or direct the work of teachers to strategies intended to *develop the capacity* of schools and teachers to be responsible for student learning. Capacity-building policies view knowledge as constructed by and with practitioners for use in their own contexts, rather than as something conveyed by policymakers as a single solution for top-down implementation.

Though the outlines of a new policy paradigm for professional development are emerging (Cohen, McLaughlin, & Talbert, 1993; Darling-Hammond, 1993), the hard work of developing concrete exemplars of policies and intersecting practices that model "top-down support for bottom up reform" has just begun. The changed curriculum and pedagogy of professional development requires *new* policies that foster new structures and institutional arrangements for teachers' learning, as well as *strategic assessment of existing policies* in terms of their compatibility with a vision of learning as constructed by teachers and students and of professional development as a lifelong, inquiry-based, collegial activity (Lieberman, Chapter 15, this volume). Both broad policy responses are essential. New approaches to teachers' professional education are needed; they require new structures and supports. New initiatives cannot by themselves promote meaningful or long-term change in teachers' practices if they are embedded in a policy structure at odds with the visions of student and teacher learning that reforms seek to bring alive. In other words, both new wine and old wine require new bottles or else incentives and supports for teachers' development and change will be working against one another.

This chapter looks first at new institutional forms that support teachers' professional growth in ways consistent with conceptions of teaching and learning for understanding. We then look at ways in which existing arrangements can be rethought or redesigned to support reformers' visions of practice and teachers' professional growth. Finally, we consider aspects of the larger education policy context that foster or impede teachers' incentives and ability to acquire new knowledge, skills, and conceptions of practice.

NEW STRUCTURES AND INSTITUTIONAL ARRANGEMENTS

Efforts to redesign education ultimately require rethinking teachers' preparation and professional development. New course mandates, curriculum guidelines, tests, or texts cannot produce greater student learning and understanding without investments in opportunities that provide teachers access to knowledge about the nature of learning, development, and performance in different domains as well as firsthand opportunities to integrate theory with classroom practice. Like students, teachers learn by doing, reading, and reflecting; collaborating with other teachers; looking closely at students and their work; and sharing what they see. This kind of learning enables teachers to make the leap from theory to accomplished practice. Such learning requires settings that support teacher inquiry and collaboration as well as strategies grounded in teachers' questions and concerns and a theoretically powerful base of knowledge. To understand deeply, teachers must learn about, see, and experience successful learning-centered and learner-centered teaching practices. Sustained change in teachers' learning opportunities and practices will require investments in the infrastructure of reform—development of the institutions and environmental supports that will promote the spread of ideas and shared learning about how change can be attempted and sustained.

New Forms for Teacher Preparation

A growing number of teacher education programs are inventing new structures for preservice teacher education that bring together all of the learning strands described above in new institutional arrangements called professional development schools (Darling-Hammond, 1994; Lieberman & Miller, 1990; Sykes, 1985). Since the late 1980s, more than 200 professional development schools (PDSs) have been created as collaborative efforts that simultaneously restructure schools and colleges of education through teacher development programs co-constructed by university-based and school-based educators. The most forward-looking of these professional development schools are engaged in preparing prospective and beginning teachers in settings connected to major school reform networks like the Coalition of Essential Schools and the Comer School Development Program. These networks engage the schools and teachers in inquiry that supports their mutual work and learning.

PDSs create settings in which novices enter professional practice by working with expert practitioners, while veteran teachers renew their own professional development as they assume roles as mentors, university adjuncts, and teacher leaders. Professional development schools also provide serious venues for developing teaching knowledge by enabling practice-based and practice-sensitive research to be carried out collaboratively by teachers, teacher educators, and researchers (Cochran-Smith & Lytle, Chapter 9, this volume). PDSs enable teachers to interact in a collegial manner—to become sources of knowledge for one another—and learn the important roles of colleague and learner.

Some reform models, such as those offered by the Holmes Group (1986), the Carnegie Forum on Education and the Economy (1986), and the National Board for Professional Teaching Standards (1991), call for all prospective teachers to do their student teaching and a more intensive internship in professional development schools. Ideally, many of these would be located in central cities, where teacher demand is high and the need for reinvented schools is great. Here they serve two purposes: providing excellent education for central-city students and opportunities for prospective teachers to learn to teach diverse learners effectively. Despite this visible, prestigious support for PDSs, significant policy supports and changes will be required if PDSs are to take root. The viability of PDSs as new forms for teacher preparation depends centrally on state acknowledgment that they are part of the infrastructure for a strong education system and funding through basic aid allocations, just as teaching hospitals receive formula adjustments to acknowledge the special mission they perform. Some states, including Minnesota and Michigan, are considering how to incorporate PDS-based internships as part of initial preparation and licensing, and they are funding pilot programs. However, states undertaking such reexamination of credentialing and preparation structures are still in the minority.

PDSs also will need to become part of the licensing structure for entry into teaching and to be taken into account in procedures for approving and accrediting teacher education institutions. These policy changes are under discussion as states increasingly envision internships as part of the teacher preparation process, and as the National Council on Accreditation of Teacher Education (NCATE) develops standards for the clinical preparation of teachers. But PDSs remain outside the mainstream teacher education policy structure.

Teachers prepared in these kinds of settings will have a learner-centered frame for the ongoing development of their practice, as well as appreciation for the fact that learning about teaching is a lifelong process. However, encouraging and sustaining these attitudes, roles, and practices in the classroom require other structures and supports, both outside and inside school.

New Institutional Arrangements
for Professional Development

New structures for individual and organizational learning must replace the usual notions of training, inservicing, or dissemination with possibilities for knowledge sharing anchored in problems of practice. To serve teachers' needs, professional development must embrace a range of opportunities that allow teachers to share with one another what they know and what they want to learn, as well as to connect their learning to the contexts of their teaching. Professional development activities must allow teachers to actively engage in experiences with others that are sustained over time, to reflect on the process as well as the content of what is actually being learned.

Key to this kind of professional growth are structures that break down isolation, empower teachers with professional tasks, and provide arenas for thinking through standards of practice. Opportunities for teachers' learning exist inside and outside school; they range from professional organizations and standards boards that have more formal roles in the educational policy structure, to "critical friends" relationships and more collaborative professional roles outside and within schools, which can take many different forms.

New Structures and Opportunities Outside School. A powerful form of teacher learning comes from belonging to professional communities that extend beyond classrooms and school buildings (Lieberman, 1995; Talbert & McLaughlin, 1994). These communities can be
organized across subject-matter lines, around significant pedagogical issues, or in support of particular school reforms. They legitimate dialogue and support the risk-taking that is part of any process of significant
change. Examples include:

- *School–university collaborations* engaged in curriculum development, change efforts, or research. When such relationships emerge
  as true partnerships, they can create new, more powerful kinds of
  knowledge about teaching and schooling, as the "rub between theory
  and practice" produces more practical, contextualized theory and
  more theoretically grounded, broadly informed practice (Dalton &
  Moir, Chapter 11, this volume; Miller & O'Shea, Chapter 14, this
  volume).
- *Teacher-to-teacher and school-to-school networks* that provide "critical friends" to examine and reflect on teaching and opportunities to
  share experiences associated with efforts to develop new practices or
  structures (Jamentz, Chapter 6, this volume; Szabo, Chapter 8, this
  volume). Such networks demonstrate that help helps. They are powerful learning tools because they engage people in collective work on
  authentic problems that emerge in their own efforts, allowing them
  to get beyond the dynamics of their own schools and classrooms to
  encounter other possibilities as well as people experiencing and solving similar problems (Lieberman & McLaughlin, Chapter 7, this
  volume).
- *Partnerships with neighborhood-based youth organizations*, such as
  club programs, theater groups, literacy projects, museums, or sports
  groups, that provide teachers with important—and sometimes other-
  wise unavailable—information about their students' homes and neighborhood settings, insight into students' nonschool interests and accomplishments, as well as opportunities for coordination between
  school and youth organization activities to promote students' learning (Heath & McLaughlin, 1994; Téllez & Cohen, Chapter 12, this
  volume).
- *Teacher involvement in district, regional, or national activities*,
  such as task forces, study groups, and standard-setting bodies engaged
  in developing standards, revising curriculum frameworks, or assessing teaching or school practices. Examples include work on curricu-

lum and teaching standards such as those developed by the National Council of Teachers of Mathematics and state or local committees involved with developing new curriculum frameworks, as well as participation in reviews of school practices through peer review processes such as the School Quality Review being piloted in New York and California. Such activities create new lenses for examining practice, while building the norms of the profession. Similarly, teachers who have engaged in powerful forms of teacher assessment, such as the year-long reflection and documentation they undertake in building a portfolio for the National Board for Professional Teaching Standards (1991), claim they have learned more through this process than in any other staff development activity during their entire careers.

These strategies create new communities of practice within and across levels of the policy system, while they involve new actors and new agencies in teachers' learning and growth. They also depart from traditional notions of institutionalization and institutional relationships, which assume teaching is shaped and structured primarily by school systems. These extra-school structures and supports more broadly represent the profession and partnerships on behalf of children; their concerns extend beyond institutional maintenance and implementation to concerns for deepening the capacity of teachers to make change and for enabling the profession as a whole to advance knowledge.

Policies That Support Extra-School Learning Communities. While some of these structures take on institutional forms—such as the Center for the Development of Teaching (Nelson & Hammerman, Chapter 1, this volume) or collaborations developed by schools and universities (Miller & O'Shea, Chapter 14, this volume)—others are more fluid and informal. *All* must be flexible and dynamic, responsive to the specific, changing needs of teachers or the profession. They must start where teachers are, building from their knowledge, skills, and classroom contexts. A network or resource effective in one community or for one school site likely will operate differently in another. Or the collaborative relationship that was successful last year in supporting teachers' learning may fall short this year. A highly successful mathematics collaborative in one urban district, for example, disintegrated after five years of operation. Organizers worried that this signified failure, but a closer look at participants' responses suggested that it came to an inevitable end because it had accomplished its objectives and was no longer useful as it existed. Other networks have evolved, changed focus, and reconsidered relationships as the needs of their participants have shifted over time. Such networks are best managed through "systematic ad hocism"—a process of moving toward shared goals with enormous flexibility in strategy (Miller & O'Shea, Chapter 14, this volume).

Policies in support of teachers' learning communities allow such structures and extra-school arrangements to come and go, to change and evolve, as necessary and useful, rather than insisting on plans or promises of permanence. What does need to be a permanent addition to the policy landscape is an infrastructure or "web" of professional development opportunities that provides multiple and ongoing occasions for critical reflection and that engages teachers in challenging content.

The policy implications associated with sustaining healthy extra-school opportunities for professional collaboration and growth are threefold: First, policy must create a significant professional role for teachers in many areas of practice—curriculum and assessment development, standard setting, and evaluation of practice—that have previously been managed by others in the bureaucracy. These roles carry powerful, authentic opportunities for teachers to learn from others, reexamine their practices, and acquire new knowledge.

Second, funding must be directed to these components of a professional infrastructure to support teacher participation and learning. A climate rich with sustained and relevant opportunities for teachers' learning resembles a "web," where networks, seminars, meetings, and focus groups crisscross one another to provide an array of in-school and extra-school opportunities for teachers to pursue their interests. Occasions and opportunities for teachers' continuous intellectual renewal must be multiple and diverse rather than generic and discrete if they are to be responsive to specific content-based or learner-based concerns.

Third, policy supports must focus on stimulating an *environment* that nurtures high-quality teachers' learning communities, rather than on particular institutional forms or promises of permanence. Effective professional development activities are fluid and have various "life cycles." The focus of policy concern should be the quality of teachers' general environment in terms of opportunities to learn; the richness and relevance of the overall "menu" is what matters. Sometimes demands for rigid institutionalization can lead to meaningless activities and out-of-date structures down the road.

Opportunities for Professional Development Within Schools.
Inside schools, teachers' workplace, habits, and cultures must foster critical inquiry into practices and student outcomes—communities of practice that enable teachers to meet together to solve problems, con-

sider new ideas, evaluate alternatives, and frame schoolwide goals. Key to such learning opportunities are occasions in which teachers look at practice collectively and through new lenses (Szabo, Chapter 8, this volume).

Opportunities for such learning and reflection already exist in many aspects of school-day routines. Everything that goes on in school, arguably, presents an opportunity for teachers' professional development. The extent to which gatherings of colleagues play an educative role depends on their intent and the perspective with which they are viewed. Department meetings, for example, can be an administrative bore, or they can operate as "miniseminars," engaging faculty in examination of materials, student work, and curriculum plans (Grossman, Chapter 4, this volume). Student teachers can be viewed as professional responsibility or opportunity (Tatel, Chapter 5, this volume). Committees to develop instructional plans or review assessments can be viewed as "hardship duty," or as research agencies and occasion for critical review (Jamentz, Chapter 6, this volume). Even usually mundane or tedious tasks such as student assignments or creation of a master schedule contain opportunities to reflect on norms, assumptions about practice, and organizational goals. Where teachers' professional growth is a top priority for teachers and administrators, all manners of opportunities become apparent in the daily lives of schools. Mind-set matters (Szabo, Chapter 8, this volume).

In addition to such "on-the-ground" opportunities for teachers to reflect on practice and new ideas, activities new to teachers' roles stimulate learning and growth and merit acknowledgment in the school workplace. *Teacher-as-researcher*, for example, puts teachers in charge of inquiry and analysis of their workplace. School-based research and inquiry occurs not only in professional development schools but also as part of many restructuring efforts. Some states (Iowa and Maine, for example) support such research as part of restructuring efforts.

Peer reviews of practice afford often intense occasions for deliberation about practice and can occur in many forms. Teachers learn as they collectively examine aspects of their curriculum or other practices; look at particular problems or concerns within the school, develop and participate in peer evaluation and peer coaching activities, and participate in assessments of students. Similarly, teacher engagement in teacher-driven assessments of teaching and learning are proving to be powerful tools for learning: Looking closely at authentic work—one's own or someone else's—stimulates tremendous growth (Darling-Hammond & Ancess, 1994; Jamentz, Chapter 6, this volume). Questions at the heart of such inquiries about school effectiveness and student learning constitute the basis for transformative learning—learning that enables teachers to change their models for what schools and teaching might look like and accomplish.

Policy Supports for Professional Development Within Schools.

School organizational structures must be redesigned so that they actively support staff learning and collaboration around serious problems of practice. This requires rethinking schedules, staffing patterns, and grouping arrangements to create blocks of time for teachers to work and learn together. In addition, schools must be organized around small, cohesive units that structure ongoing collaborative work among groups of adults and students (e.g., teaching teams or clusters, houses, advisories) so that teachers have shared access to students and shared responsibilities for designing their work. Many restructured schools have accomplished this smaller workplace scale in a variety of ways, ranging from block scheduling of students and teachers to reallocations of staff so that nearly all have direct responsibilities for students, creating more time for shared teacher work (Darling-Hammond, Ancess, & Falk, 1995).

Teachers cannot reconceive their practice and workplace culture in isolation, yet almost everything about school is oriented toward going it alone professionally. While it may be possible for teachers to learn some things alone, rethinking old norms requires a supportive community of practice. The traditional school organization separates its personnel from one another and from the external environment. Inside school, teachers are inclined to think in terms of "my classroom," "my subject," or "my kids." Few schools are structured to allow teachers to think in terms of shared problems or broader organizational goals. A collaborative culture of problem solving and learning must exist to challenge these norms and habits of mind; collegiality itself must be valued as a professional asset (Szabo, Chapter 8, this volume).

New structures for teaching may not include supervision as usually defined in bureaucratic organizations: a one-to-one relationship between a worker and his or her presumably more expert superordinate charged with overseeing and correcting the work. Instead, organizational strategies for team planning, sharing, evaluating, and learning may create methods for peer review of practice that—like those used in other professional organizations and restructured businesses—may better fill the needs for feedback, oversight, and evaluation.

These same needs for collaborative inquiry and learning exist for other educators, including school leaders (principals, teacher directors, and other emerging leaders) and other support staff, from school psychologists and counselors to teachers' aides. They should be included, as appropriate, in these in-school and outside-school efforts and activities to examine teaching practice and learner outcomes. Cross-role participation in professional development activities stimulates shared understandings of school goals and new approaches more effectively than do activities that treat teachers, principals, counselors, and others as separate groups for whom different conversations and topics are thought to be relevant (Fullan, 1991). For example, extended institutes for school-based teams of teachers, administrators, and parents have proved to be critical for launching school reforms in cities like Hammond, Indiana, and Louisville, Kentucky (Lieberman, 1995). Participation of counselors, school psychologists, and parents, as well as teachers and principals, in shared development activities is central to the work of successful initiatives like James Comer's School Development Program, Henry Levin's Accelerated Schools, and the Coalition of Essential Schools founded by Theodore Sizer, which embrace all roles in the education environment. This contributes to a common sense of purpose and practice among all of the members of the school community, rather than reifying the professional Balkanization that already exists.

District policies matter to what goes on behind the schoolhouse door in terms of learning and development opportunities for teachers (Talbert & McLaughlin, 1994). Here, too, perspective and priorities are crucial. Policies consistent with the notions of teachers' learning outlined here assume teachers' professional development as integral, rather than adjunct, to the school workplace. A major task for district leadership involves encouraging and sustaining reflective communities of practice both within and among schools, as well as making resources available for teachers to use according to their needs and preferences.

ALIGNING THE POLICY CONTEXT TO SUPPORT PROFESSIONAL DEVELOPMENT

The policy environment in which teachers work sends a myriad of often conflicting signals about how schools are expected to do business and what behaviors and skills are valued and rewarded. Messages about more or less preferred teaching practices and learner outcomes issue explicitly or implicitly from all the major education policy domains, including those that shape curriculum, assessment, teacher and administrator licensing and evaluation, and accountability requirements. Existing policies and practices must be assessed in terms of their compatibility with two cornerstones of the reform agenda: *a learner-centered view of teaching and a career-long conception of teachers' learning.*

Does a new curriculum framework stress "implementation of texts," thereby describing a passive teacher and student role, or are teachers assumed to participate in the construction of practices that start with students' experiences and needs and aim at student outcome standards? Does an assessment system evaluate student understanding, or does it test for rote recall of disconnected facts? Do teacher evaluation systems look for teaching behaviors aimed at keeping students quiet or for practices that engage students actively in their learning? Do administrator licensing standards require that principals know how students learn and how teachers teach for understanding, or do they stress noninstructional matters? Do school accountability requirements enforce current, highly fragmented bureaucratic structures and uses of time, or do they allow for more integrated and student-centered forms of staffing and fund allocations?

Schools and teachers aiming to adopt new practices must contend with the "geological dig" (Darling-Hammond, 1990) of previous policies that produce contradictory signals in their environment and prevent a complete transformation of practice. Some of these are familiar, such as state standardized testing policies that continue to deflect time and attention from more challenging forms of learning, forcing a march through content coverage that prevents more in-depth projects and creating a focus on multiple-choice thinking that undermines extended writing, discourse, and problem solving (Madaus, 1993). These tests, along with mandated textbooks and basal readers, prescriptive curriculum guides, and "old paradigm" teacher evaluation measures, create incentives to continue traditional forms of teaching that emphasize superficial understanding and rote learning rather than higher-order thinking and performance skills.

Both the content and form of curriculum policy must change, so that what is required is compatible with teaching for understanding and provides reasons for teachers to rethink their practices and assumptions about teaching and learning. Likewise, in those few key, strategic areas where state regulation of curriculum and testing is deemed necessary—for example, in curriculum frameworks and occasional student assessments for state monitoring purposes—policies should encourage in-depth learning around major, powerful concepts and ideas. States and districts should explicitly evaluate their current curriculum and testing policies to remove prescriptions that conflict with one another and that are grounded in misunderstandings about how students learn well and how good teaching occurs.

Teacher education institutions figure prominently in the policy context that surrounds professional development both as purveyors of teacher education and as determinants of what counts as "knowledge," "expertise," and successful performance—and, by extension, what is important for professional standards and development. Providing clear guidance for schools of education about the demands of teaching for understanding, along with supports and incentives that enable them to meet new standards, will be important. For the most part, current policies governing teacher education, especially the content of teacher licensing and testing requirements, fail to fully incorporate the kinds of teacher knowledge and understanding described throughout this volume.

Likewise, licensing, testing, and evaluation for teachers require grounding in new understandings about student learning and effective teaching, and they must be connected to other professional standards for teaching. The demands of teaching for understanding—as represented through such work as the National Council of Teachers of Mathematics curriculum standards and those of other professional associations—are incorporated into the standards and assessments for accomplished practice recently developed by the new National Board for Professional Teaching Standards and by related model standards for licensing beginning teachers developed by the Interstate New Teacher Assessment and Support Consortium. The National Council for the Accreditation of Teacher Education has also incorporated these standards into its accreditation requirements. Policies that provide incentives for teachers to become National Board-certified, for states to enact compatible licensing standards and assessments as well as standards for approving teacher education programs, and for schools of education to become NCATE-accredited could help create a coherent approach to preparing teachers to teach for understanding, reducing some of the disjunctures between existing teacher development policies and current reforms of curriculum.

Similarly, the policies that structure the ongoing evaluation of teachers and teaching practice must also support teaching for understanding and teacher learning. In most teachers' workplaces, teacher evaluation activities act as powerful disincentives to honest examination of practice, problem solving, or learning. "Needs improvement," after all, is about the lowest grade a teacher could be given on an evaluation of practice. Yet ongoing improvement and critical inquiry are fundamental to learning and change. In addition, many evaluation forms and processes continue to be based on a conception of teaching as the implementation of routines that can be observed and checked off in a brief inspection system. The type of teaching anticipated by evaluation forms is teaching for transmission rather than teaching for understanding, and the assumption undergirding the desired teaching behaviors is that students are passive, standardized participants in the classroom (Darling-Hammond with Sclan, 1992).

To support teaching for understanding and the professional development necessary to it, new forms of teacher evaluation will need to emphasize the *appropriateness* of teaching decisions to the goals and contexts of instruction and the needs of students, rather than focusing on teacher's adherence to prescribed routines. Evaluation must be conceived not as a discrete annual event conducted by supervisors making brief visits bearing checklists but as a constant feature of organizational and classroom life for practitioners.

Relatedly, the leadership roles of administrators in schools structured to support teacher learning and student understanding would change. Administrators' evaluations by central office staff typically have little if anything to do with teachers' effectiveness in establishing and supporting a culture of learning and inquiry at their school. Guidelines for administrator evaluation in most districts give no attention to an administrator's responsibility for the quality and vitality of workplace culture and community of practice (McLaughlin, 1993). A critical role for administrative leadership involves creating and sustaining settings in which teachers feel safe to disclose aspects of their teaching, admit mistakes, try and possibly fail, and continue to seek out advice and counsel.

To fulfill these new roles and expectations for leadership, however, administrators require opportunities to understand what the conceptions of teaching and learning that motivate the nation's reform agenda look like in classrooms, as well as how these visions of practice relate to teachers' opportunities to learn. Administrators, no less than teachers, urgently require opportunities to rethink practice and learn new perspectives and skills consistent with reformers' visions of teaching and learning for understanding (Bridges & Hallinger, Chapter 13, this volume).

All of these things require time for teachers' professional work as part of their normal responsibilities. Time for teachers can only be bought by rethinking the ways in which schools are staffed, funded, and managed. Compared to other countries, the United States has invested in a relatively smaller number of lower-paid teachers who are directed, supervised, and supplemented by large numbers of administrative staff and nonteaching specialists, populating several layers of bureaucratic structures. In 1986, U.S. school systems employed approximately one administrative staff person for every two-and-one-half teachers and spent only 38% of their funds on teachers' salaries, with less than an additional 1% going to professional development (Feistritzer, 1983; U.S. Department of Labor, 1986–1987). After several decades in which the number of administrative staff increased at twice the rate of teachers, by 1991 only half of U.S. education employees were classroom teachers (National Center for Education Statistics, 1993). This staffing pattern stands in contrast to many European and Asian countries, where teachers constitute 80% or more of the education work force (Organisation for Economic Co-operation and Development, 1990). Additional investment in teachers seems a critical element of an agenda to enact reformers' visions of teaching and learning.

Finally, through waivers, incentives, grants, and changed formula allocations for personnel and dollars, policymakers can reallocate existing resources to enable and encourage school restructuring that provides time for teachers' collegial work and learning, expects and enables teacher participation in curriculum- and assessment-building and school reform, and anticipates teachers' needs for strong communities of practice or collegial learning. Policies that anticipated these needs would move away from traditional credit-for-seat-time staff development accounting to develop incentives for professional development that involves and credits teachers for participation in networks, professional assessments, and peer review activities.

Policies consistent with this view of professional development would encourage site-level integration of the various bundles and baskets of categorical resources flowing from state or national programs. Current categorical boundaries and accounting lines discourage teachers from addressing whole-school goals or the needs of the whole child. Instead, special projects accounting requirements foster a problem-focused strategy of allocation that fragments a faculty as well as the needs of an individual student—an approach inconsistent with teachers' learning to work successfully with all the learners who fill contemporary American classrooms.

POLICY GUIDELINES FOR PROFESSIONAL DEVELOPMENT

Reformers of all stripes press an agenda of fundamental change in how teachers teach and students learn. Envisioned are schools where students learn to think creatively and deeply, where teachers' ongoing learning forms the core of professional activities, and where students and teachers alike value knowing why and knowing how to learn (Nelson & Hammerman, Chapter 1, this volume; Falk, Chapter 2, this volume; Brooks & Brooks, Chapter 3, this volume). These visions and expectations for practice assume fundamental change in the educational policy setting if teachers are to make and sustain the challenging and sometimes painful changes required of them. Yet the policy paradigm necessary to foster and sustain teachers' learning and ongoing professional growth has only begun to be filled out.

Contributors to this volume elaborate the diverse and important ways in which existing activities—student teaching, assessment, planning, preservice education—and new institutional forms—professional development schools, networks, collaborations, restructured schools—can function as powerful venues for teachers' learning and change. These experiences suggest several important building blocks and design principles to assist in constructing a policy paradigm that supports learner-centered schools and teachers' lifelong learning.

Recognition of the embeddedness of education policy domains is critical to the development of a new model for professional development. The significant interdependencies between expectations for teachers' change and the various domains of education policy—curriculum, assessment, evaluation, credentialing, and so on—have obvious implications for teachers' ability and willingness to change. Expectations and supports for teachers' professional development cannot be understood separate from this broader context.

The successful and diverse activities described here demonstrate the strength and necessity of locally constructed responses to specific teacher and learner needs. Detailed solutions imported from afar or mandated from above predictably will disappoint; effective practices evolve from and respond to specific instructional settings. The situation-specific nature of teaching and learning envisioned by reformers comprises the key challenge for teachers' professional development and, by extension, the key obstacle to policymakers' efforts to engender systemic reform. But the situational character of effective practice does not mean that change must proceed uninformed by experience elsewhere. The effective professional development efforts featured in this volume suggest design principles to guide national and state officials struggling to devise "top-down support for bottom-up change," as well as local actors rethinking existing policies and devising new ones.

Proposed and existing policies can be "interviewed" to assess their correspondence with factors central to teachers' learning and change. For example, does the policy:

- Reduce teachers' isolation, or perpetuate teachers' experience of working alone?
- Encourage teachers to assume the role of learner, or reward tradi-

tional "teacher as expert" approaches to teacher-student and supervisor-teacher relations?

- Provide a rich, diverse menu of opportunities for teachers to learn, or invest primarily in episodic, narrow "training" activities?
- Attach professional development opportunities to meaningful content and change efforts, or construct generic inservice occasions?
- Establish an environment of professional safety, trust, and problem solving, or exacerbate the risk of serious reflection and change and thereby encourage problem hiding?
- Provide opportunities for everyone involved with school to understand new visions of teaching and learning, or focus only on teachers?
- Enable restructuring of time, space, and scale within schools, or expect new forms of teaching and learning to come about within conventional structures?
- Focus on learner-centered outcomes that place priority on learning how and why, or emphasize memorization of facts and rote skills?

Other "interview questions" doubtless will emerge as experience accumulates with policies and practices aimed at developing the capacity of schools and teachers to create effective learning environments. The challenge for policymakers and educators is to align the signals and incentives existing in the system that shape school organizations, teachers' practices, role expectations, and assumptions about student and teacher learning.

Appendix

Participants at the July 1993 Pew Forum on Education Reform

Anthony J. Alvarado, Superintendent, Community School District #2, New York City

Gordon M. Ambach, Executive Director, Council of Chief State School Officers

Alain Bouvier, Director, University Institute for Teacher Education, Lyon, France

David K. Cohen, Professor of Education and Social Policy, Michigan State University

Ernesto J. Cortes, Jr., Southwest Regional Director, Industrial Areas Foundation, Austin, Texas

Linda Darling-Hammond, Professor of Education, Teachers College, Columbia University

Michelle Fine, Professor of Psychology, City University of New York Graduate Center

Chester E. Finn, Jr., The Edison Project, Whittle Schools

Edward B. Fiske, author and education writer, Westport, Connecticut

Booth Gardner, former Governor, state of Washington

David Green, Her Majesty's Inspector of Schools, England, and Consultant for New York State Department of Education

Peter Grimmett, Associate Professor, Faculty of Education, Simon Fraser University, British Columbia

Ellen Guiney, Chief Education Advisor, Senate Committee on Labor and Human Resources

Terry Hartle, Vice President for Governmental Relations, American Council on Labor and Human Resources

Kati Haycock, American Association for Higher Education

Sonia Hernandez, Director, Education Office of the Governor, Austin, Texas

Dorte Heurlin, General Inspector of Education, Upper Secondary Department Ministry of Education and Research, Denmark

Eugenia Kemble, Assistant to the President for Educational Issues, American Federation of Teachers

Thomas W. Langfitt, President, The Pew Charitable Trusts

Milbrey W. McLaughlin, Professor of Education and Public Policy, Stanford University

Lallie O'Brien, Program Officer, The Pew Charitable Trusts

Hugh B. Price, Vice President, Rockefeller Foundation

Bella Rosenberg, Assistant to the President, American Federation of Teachers

Alan Ruby, First Assistant Secretary, Schools and Curriculum Division, Department of Employment, Education, and Training, Canberra, Australia

Robert B. Schwartz, Program Director for Education, The Pew Charitable Trusts

Albert Shanker, President, The American Federation of Teachers

Marshall S. Smith, Undersecretary, U.S. Department of Education

Diane Snowball, Staff Developer, Community School District #2, New York City

Vivien Stewart, Program Officer, Carnegie Corporation of New York

Fran A. Streets, Vice President, Wells Fargo Bank, San Francisco

David S. Tatel, Partner, Hogan & Hartson, Washington, D.C.

Edith S. Tatel, Education Consultant, Washington, D.C.

P. Michael Timpane, President, Teachers College, Columbia University

Thomas Wilson, Research Associate, Education Department, Brown University

Ron Wolk, Editor, *Education Week*

Pew Forum staff located at Stanford University School of Education included: Cathy Casserley, Ralph Levine, Jennifer O'Day, Dorothy Shipps, and Lori White.

References

Addams, J. (1972). *The spirit of youth and the city streets*. Urbana: University of Illinois Press. (Original work published 1911)

Albanese, M., & Mitchell, S. (1993). Problem-based learning: A review of literature on its outcomes and implementation issues. *Academic Medicine, 68*(1), 52–81.

Ancess, J. (in press). *Learner-centered accountability in an urban high school: A case study of the Urban Academy*. New York: National Center for Restructuring Education, Schools and Teaching.

Andersen, R. (1983). Introduction: A language acquisition interpretation of pidginization and creolization. In R. Andersen (Ed.), *Pidginization and creolization as language acquisition* (pp. 1–56). Rowley, MA: Newbury House.

Apple, M. (1986). *Teachers and texts: A political economy of class and gender relations in education*. New York: Routledge & Kegan Paul.

Argyris, C. (1993). *Knowledge for action*. San Francisco: Jossey-Bass.

Ball, D. L. (1988). *Knowledge and reasoning in mathematical pedagogy: Examining what prospective teachers bring to teacher education*. East Lansing: Michigan State University.

Ball, D. L. (1991). Research on teaching mathematics: Making subject matter knowledge part of the equation. In J. Brophy (Ed.), *Advances in research on teaching: A research annual* (pp. 1–48). Greenwich, CT: JAI Press.

Ball, S. J. (1981). *Beachside Comprehensive*. Cambridge, England: Cambridge University Press.

Ball, S. J., & Bowe, R. (1992). Subject departments and the "implementation" of national curriculum policy: An overview of the issues. *Journal of Curriculum Studies, 24*(2), 97–115.

Barnett, C. (1991). Building a case-based curriculum to enhance the pedagogical content knowledge of mathematics teachers. *Journal of Teacher Education, 42*(4), 263–272.

Barth, R. (1990). *Improving schools from within*. San Francisco: Jossey-Bass.

Bascia, N. (1991, April). *The trust agreement projects: Establishing local professional cultures for teachers*. Paper presented at the annual meeting of the American Educational Research Association, Chicago.

Bascia, N. (1994). *Unions in teachers' professional lives*. New York: Teachers College Press.

Belenky, M. F., Clinchy, B., Goldberger, N., & Tarule, J. M. (1986). *Women's ways of knowing*. New York: Basic Books.

Berthoff, A. (1987). The teacher as researcher. In D. Goswami & P. R. Stillman (Eds.), *Reclaiming the classroom: Teacher research as an agency for change*. Upper Montclair, NJ: Boynton/Cook.

Beyer, L. (1986). Critical theory and the art of teaching. *Journal of Curriculum and Supervision, 1*, 221–232.

Borko, H. M., Eisenhart, M., Brown, C. A., Underhill, R. G., Jones, D., & Agard, P. C. (1992). Learning to teach hard mathematics: Do novice teachers and their instructors give up too easily? *Journal for Research in Mathematics Education, 23*(3), 194–222.

Boud, D., & Feletti, G. (1991). *The challenge of problem-based learning*. New York: St. Martin's Press.

Boyer, E. L. (1983). *High school: A report on secondary education in America*. New York: Harper Colophon Books.

Branscombe, A., Goswami, D., & Schwartz, J. (1992). *Students teaching, teachers learning*. Portsmouth, NH: Boynton/Cook Heinemann.

Bridges, E., & Hallinger, P. (1992). *Problem-based learning for administrators*. Eugene, OR: ERIC Clearinghouse on Educational Management.

Bridges, E., & Hallinger, P. (1995). *Implementing problem-based learning in leadership development*. Eugene, OR: ERIC Clearinghouse on Educational Management.

Britton, J. (1987). A quiet form of research. In D. Goswami & P. Stillman (Eds.), *Reclaiming the classroom: Teacher research as an agency for change*. Upper Montclair, NJ: Boynton/Cook.

Brophy, J., & Evertson, C. (1976). *Learning from teaching: A developmental perspective*. Boston: Allyn & Bacon.

Bruer, J. T. (1993). *Schools for thought*. Cambridge, MA: MIT Press.

Bruner, J. S. (1966). *Studies in cognitive growth*. New York: Wiley.

California Center for School Restructuring (CCSR). (1992). *Creating powerful learning for all students: Habits that help*. San Mateo: San Mateo County Office of Education.

California Center for School Restructuring (CCSR). (1993). *Guidelines for the protocol: Examining student work for what matters most*. San Mateo: San Mateo County Office of Education.

Carini, P. (1986). Building from children's strengths. *Journal of Education, 168*(3), 13–24.

Carini, P. (1987). *On the value of education*. New York: The City College Workshop Center.

Carnegie Forum on Education and the Economy. (1986). *A nation prepared: Teachers for the 21st century*. New York: Author.

Carpenter, T. P., Fennema, E., Peterson, P., & Carey, D. (1988). Teachers' pedagogical content knowledge of students' problem-solving in elementary arithmetic. *Journal for Research in Mathematics Education, 19*(3), 385–401.

Carr, W., & Kemmis, S. (1986). *Becoming critical*. London: Falmer.

Carter, B. (1991, April). *The Stanford/Schools Collaborative: Building an inquiring community of practitioners and researchers.* Paper presented at the annual meeting of the American Educational Research Association, Chicago.

Case, R., & Bereiter, C. (1984). From behaviorism to cognitive behaviorism to cognitive development: Steps in the evolution of instructional design. *Instructional Science, 13,* 141–158.

Cazden, C., Diamondstone, J., & Naso, P. (1989). Teachers and researchers: Roles and relationships. *Quarterly of the National Writing Project, 2,* 1–3, 25–27.

Chenoweth, T., & Everhart, R. (1994). Preparing leaders to understand and facilitate change: A problem-based learning approach. *Journal of School Leadership, 4*(4), 414–431.

Clark, C. (1988). Asking the right questions about teacher preparation: Contributions of research on teacher thinking. *Educational Researcher, 17,* 5–12.

Clifford, J. (1988). *The predicament of culture.* Cambridge, MA: Harvard University Press.

Cochran-Smith, M. (1991). Learning to teach against the grain. *Harvard Educational Review, 61,* 279–310.

Cochran-Smith, M., Larkin, J. M., & Lytle, S. L. (1990). *Network of new and experienced urban teachers* (first annual report to the Fund for the Improvement of Post-secondary Education). Washington, DC: U. S. Office of Education.

Cochran-Smith, M., & Lytle, S. L. (1990). Research on teaching and teacher research: The issues that divide. *Educational Researcher, 19*(2), 2–11.

Cochran-Smith, M., & Lytle, S. L. (1993). *Inside/outside: Teacher research and knowledge.* New York: Teachers College Press.

Cohen, D. K. (1990). A revolution in one classroom: The case of Mrs. Oublier. *Educational Evaluation and Policy Analysis, 12,* 327–345.

Cohen, D. K., & Ball, D. L. (1990). Policy and practice: An overview. *Educational Evaluation and Policy Analysis, 12*(3), 233–240.

Cohen, D. K., McLaughlin, M. W., & Talbert, J. E. (1993). *Teaching for understanding: Challenges for policy and practice.* San Francisco: Jossey-Bass.

Confrey, J. (1985, April). *A constructivist view of mathematics instruction: Part 1. A theoretical perspective.* Paper presented at the annual meeting of the American Educational Research Association, Chicago.

Cox, P., & DeFrees, J. (1991). *Work in progress: Restructuring in ten Maine schools.* Andover, MA: The Regional Laboratory for Educational Improvement of the Northeast and Islands.

Cuban, L. (1970). *To make a difference: Teaching in the inner-city.* New York: Free Press.

Cuban, L. (1990). Reforming again, again, and again. *Educational Researcher, 19,* 3–13.

Dalton, S., & Moir, E. (1992). Evaluating limited English proficient (LEP) teacher training and in-service programs (Proceedings of the Second National Research Symposium on Limited English Proficient Student Issues: Focus on evaluation and measurement). Washington, DC: U.S. Department of Education, Office of Bilingual Education and Minority Languages Affairs.

Damasio, A. (1994). *Descartes' error: Emotion, reason and the human brain.* New York: Putnam's.

Darling-Hammond, L. (1990). Instructional policy into practice: The power of the bottom over the top. *Educational Evaluation and Policy Analysis, 12*(3), 233–241.

Darling-Hammond, L. (1993). Reframing the school reform agenda: Developing capacity for school transformation. *Phi Delta Kappan, 74*(10), 752–761.

Darling-Hammond, L. (1994). National standards and assessments: Will they improve education? *American Journal of Education, 104*(2), 478–510.

Darling-Hammond, L., & Ancess, J. (1994). *Authentic assessment and school development.* New York: National Center for Restructuring Education, Schools, and Teaching.

Darling-Hammond, L., Ancess, J., & Falk, B. (1995). *Authentic assessment in action: Studies of schools and students at work.* New York: Teachers College Press.

Darling-Hammond, L., Einbender, L., Frelow, F., & Key-King, J. (1993). *Authentic assessment in practice: A collection of portfolios, performance tasks, exhibitions, and documentation.* New York: National Center for Restructuring Education, Schools and Teaching.

Darling-Hammond, L. with Sclan, E. (1992). Policy and supervision. In C. D. Glickman (Ed), *Supervision in transition.* Alexandria, VA: Association for Supervision and Curriculum Development.

Darling-Hammond, L., & Snyder, J. (1992). Framing accountability: Creating learner-centered schools. In A. Lieberman (Ed.), *The changing contexts of teaching* (pp. 11–36). Chicago: University of Chicago Press.

Dewey, J. (1916). *Democracy and education.* New York: Macmillan.

Dewey, J. (1956). *The child and the curriculum.* Chicago: University of Chicago Press. (Original work published 1902)

Diaz, R. M. (1983). The impact of bilingualism on cognitive development. In E. W. Gordon (Ed.), *Review of research in education* (pp. 23–54). Washington, DC: American Educational Research Association.

Duckworth, E. R. (1991, April). *Teaching and research in one: Extended clinical interviewing.* Invited address presented at the annual meeting of the American Educational Research Association, Chicago.

Edelsky, C. (1988). Living in the author's world: Analyzing the author's craft. *California Reader, 21*, 14–17.

Edmundson, P. J. (1989, August). *The curriculum in teacher education* (Technical Report No. 6). Seattle: Center for Educational Renewal, University of Washington.

Eisner, E. W. (1991). What really counts in schools. *Educational Leadership, 48*(5), 10–17.

Elbow, P. (1973). *Writing without teachers.* New York: Oxford University Press.

Elmore, R. F., & McLaughlin, M. W. (1988). *Steady work: Policy, practice and the reform of American education*. Santa Monica, CA: Rand Corporation.

Emig, J. (1983). *The web of meaning*. Upper Montclair, NJ: Boynton/Cook.

Erickson, F. (1986). *Qualitative methods in research on teaching*. Lansing: Institute for Research on Teaching, Michigan State University.

Falk, B., & Darling-Hammond, L. (1993). *The primary language records at P.S. 261: How assessment transforms teaching and learning*. New York:. National Center for Restructuring Education, Schools and Teaching.

Fecho, R. (1993). Reading as a teacher. In M. Cochran-Smith & S. L. Lytle (Eds.), *Inside/outside: Teachers, research and knowledge* (pp. 265–272). New York: Teachers College Press.

Feistritzer, C. E. (1983). *The condition of teaching: A state by state analysis*. New York: Carnegie Foundation for the Advancement of Teaching.

Fennema, E., Carpenter, T., Franke, M., & Carey, D. (1993). Learning to use children's mathematical thinking: A case study. In R. B. Davis & C. A. Maher (Eds.), *Schools, mathematics, and the world of reality* (pp. 93–117). Boston: Allyn & Bacon.

Fine, M. (1991). *On charters: Creating uncommon communities for urban adolescents in their public high schools*. Unpublished manuscript.

Fine, M. (Ed.). (1994). *Chartering urban school reform: Reflections on public high schools in the midst of change*. New York: Teachers College Press.

Fish, S. (1980). *Is there a text in this class?* Cambridge, MA: Harvard University Press.

Fisher, R., & Ury, W. (1981). *Getting to yes: Negotiating agreement without giving in*. Boston: Houghton Mifflin.

Fosnot, C. T. (1989). *Enquiring teachers, enquiring learners: A constructivist approach for teaching*. New York: Teachers College Press.

Franke, M. L. (1991, April). *Understanding teachers' knowledge of addition and subtraction: Application of a personal construct approach*. Paper presented at the annual meeting of the American Educational Research Association, Chicago.

Fullan, M. (1991). *The new meaning of educational change*. New York: Teachers College Press.

Fullan, M. (1993). *Change forces: Probing the depths of educational reform*. London: Falmer.

Fullan, M., & Miles, M. (1992). Getting reform right: What works and what doesn't. *Phi Delta Kappan, 73*(10), 745–752.

Gagne, R. M. (1968). Learning hierarchies. *Educational Psychologist, 6*(4), 2–9.

Garcia, E. E. (1990). Educating teachers for language minority students. In W. R. Houston (Ed.), *Handbook of research on teacher education* (pp. 717–729). New York: Macmillan.

Gardner, H. (1983). *Frames of mind: A theory of multiple intelligences*. New York: Basic Books.

Gardner, H. (1985). *The mind's new science*. New York: Basic Books.

Geertz, C. (1973). *The interpretation of cultures*. New York: Basic Books.

Giroux, H. (1984). Rethinking the language of schooling. *Language Arts, 61,* 33–40.

Goddard, J. (1994, April 20). College admissions and the high school psyche. *Education Week, 13,* 34.

Goodlad, J. (1984). *A place called school.* New York: McGraw-Hill.

Goodlad, J. (1988). *School–university partnerships in action.* New York: Teachers College Press.

Gorham. (1985). Grant to Maine State Department of Education.

Goswami, D., & Stillman, P. (1987). *Reclaiming the classroom: Teacher research as an agency for change.* Upper Montclair, NJ: Boynton/Cook.

Grant, C. A., & Secada, W. G. (1990). Preparing teachers for diversity. In W. R. Houston (Ed.), *Handbook of research in teacher education* (pp. 403–422). New York: Macmillan.

Greenberg, J. B. (1989, April). *Funds of knowledge: Historical constitution, social distribution, and transmission.* Paper presented at the annual meeting of the Society for Applied Anthropology, Santa Fe, NM.

Greene, M. (1978). *Landscapes of learning.* New York: Teachers College Press.

Greene, M. (1986). Reflection and passion in teaching. *Journal of Curriculum and Supervision, 2*(1), 68–81.

Griffin, G. (1986). Clinical teacher education. In J. V. Hoffman & S. A. Edwards (Eds.), *Reality and reform of teacher education* (pp. 1–24). New York: Random House.

Grimmett, P., & Neufeld, J. (Eds.) (1994). *Teacher development and the struggle for authenticity: Professional growth and restructuring in the context of change.* New York: Teachers College Press.

Grossman, P. L. (1992). Teaching to learn. In A. Lieberman (Ed.), *The changing contexts of teaching: Ninety-first yearbook of the National Society for the Study of Education* (pp. 179–196). Chicago: University of Chicago Press.

Grossman, P. L., & Stodolsky, S. S. (1993, April). *Adapting to diverse learners: Teacher beliefs in context.* Paper presented at the annual meeting of the American Educational Research Association, Atlanta, GA.

Grossman, P. L., & Stodolsky, S. S. (1994). Considerations of content and the circumstances of secondary school teaching. In L. Darling-Hammond (Ed.), *Review of research in education* (Vol. 20; pp. 179–221). Washington, DC: American Educational Research Association.

Guiora, A. Z., Brannon, R. C. L., & Dull, C. Y. (1972). Empathy and second language learning. *Language Learning, 22*(1), 111–130.

Guiroa, A. Z., Paluszy, M., Beit-Hallahmi, B., Catford, J. C., Colley, R. E., & Dull, C. Y. (1975). Language and person studies in language behavior. *Language Learning, 25*(1), 43–61.

Gumperz, J. (1982). *Discourse strategies.* Cambridge, England: Cambridge University Press.

Guskey, T. R. (1986). Staff development and the process of teacher change. *Educational Researcher, 15*(5), 5–12.

Haberman, M. (1987). *Recruiting and selecting teachers for urban schools.* ERIC Documentation Reproduction Service No. ED 242 942.

Hakuta, K. (1986). *Mirror of language: The debate on bilingualism.* New York: Basic Books.

Hargreaves, A. (1989). *Contrived collegiality and the culture of teaching.* Paper presented at the Canadian Society for Studies in Education conference, University of Laval, Quebec.

Hargreaves, A. (1994). *Changing teachers, changing times: Teachers' work and culture in the postmodern age.* New York: Teachers College Press.

Harris, J. (1989). The idea of community in the study of writing. *College Composition and Communication, 40,* 11–22.

Heath, S. B., & McLaughlin, M. W. (1994). The best of both worlds: Connecting schools and community youth organizations for all-day, all-year learning. *Educational Administration Quarterly, 20*(3), 278–300.

Hollingsworth, S. (1988, April). *Toward a developmental model of learning to teach reading.* Paper presented at the annual meeting of the American Educational Research Association, New Orleans.

Holmes Group. (1986). *Tomorrow's teachers: A report of the Holmes Group.* East Lansing, MI: Author.

Howe, K., & Eisenhart, M. (1990). Standards for qualitative (and quantitative) research: A prolegomenon. *Educational Research, 19,* 2–9.

Hymes, D. H. (1974). *Foundations in sociolinguistics.* Philadelphia: University of Pennsylvania Press.

Inverness Associates. (1994). *Draft outline: Year one preliminary report for the study of SB 1274 restructuring.* Unpublished draft paper prepared for the Legislative Analysts Office, Sacramento, CA.

Jackson, P. (1990). The functions of educational research. *Educational Researcher, 19,* 3–9.

Jervis, K. (in press). *Eyes on the child: Three portfolio stories.* New York: National Center for Restructuring Education, Schools and Teaching.

Johnson, S. M. (1990). *Teachers at work.* New York: Basic Books.

Johnston, P. (1990, March). *A shift in paradigm: As teachers become researchers so goes the curriculum.* Paper presented at the Ethnography and Education forum, Philadelphia.

Joyce, B., & Showers, B. (1988). *Student achievement through staff development.* New York: Longman.

Joyce, B., Showers, B., & Rolheiser-Bennett, C. (1987). Staff development and student learning: A synthesis of research on models of teaching. *Educational Leadership, 45,* 77–87.

Kerchner, C. T., & Koppich, J. E. (1993). *A union of professionals: Unions and management in turbulent times.* New York: Teachers College Press.

Kerchner, C. T., & Mitchell, D. E. (1988). *The changing idea of a teachers' union.* London: Falmer.

King, B. (1991). *Cincinnati: Betting on an unfinished season.* Claremont, CA: The Claremont Graduate School, Claremont Project VISION.

Knoblauch, C., & Brannon, L. (1988). Knowing our knowledge: A phenomeno-logical basis for teacher research. In L. Z. Smith (Ed.), *Audits of meaning: A* Festschrift *in honor of Ann E. Berthoff* (pp. 17–28). Portsmouth, NH: Boynton/Cook.

Kofman, F., & Senge, P. (1993). Communities of commitment: The heart of learning organizations. *Organizational Dynamics, 22*(2), 5–23.

Koppich, J., & Kerchner, C. (1990). *Educational policy trust agreements: Connecting labor relations and school reform.* Annual Report. Berkeley: Policy Analysis for California Education.

Ladwig, J. G., & King, M. B. (1992). Restructuring secondary social studies: The association of organizational features and classroom thoughtfulness. *American Educational Research Journal, 29,* 695–714.

Lambert, L. (1989). The end of an era of staff development. *Educational Leadership, 18,* 78–83.

Lampert, M. (1985). How do teachers manage to teach? Perspectives on problems in practice. *Harvard Educational Review, 55,* 178–194.

Lampert, M. (1987). *Teachers' thinking about students' thinking about geometry: The effects of new teaching goals* (Educational Technology Center, Issue Paper TR-88-1). Cambridge, MA: Harvard Graduate School of Education.

Lampert, M. (1990). Connecting inventions with conventions. In L. P. Steff & T. Wood (Eds.), *Transforming children's mathematical education: International perspectives* (pp. 253–265). Hillsdale, NJ: Erlbaum.

Landes, R. (1965). *Culture in American education.* New York: Wiley.

LaPointe, A. N., & Mead, A. (1989). *A world of differences: An international assessment of mathematics and science.* Princeton, NJ: Educational Testing Service.

Lather, P. (1986). Research as praxis. *Harvard Educational Review, 56,* 257–277.

Lave, J., & Wenger, E. (1991). *Situated learning: Legitimate peripheral participation.* New York: Cambridge University Press.

Lichtenstein, G., McLaughlin, M. W., & Knudsen, J. (1992). Teacher empowerment and professional knowledge. In A. Lieberman (Ed.), *The changing contexts of teaching: National Society for the Study of Education Yearbook* (pp. 37–58). Chicago: University of Chicago Press.

Lieberman, A. (1986a). Collaborative research: Working with, not working on . . . *Educational Leadership, 43*(5), 28–32.

Lieberman, A. (1986b). Collaborative work. *Educational Leadership, 43*(5), 4–8.

Lieberman, A. (Ed.). (1986c). *Rethinking school improvement.* New York: Teachers College Press.

Lieberman, A. (1992). School/university collaboration: A view from the inside. *Phi Delta Kappan, 74*(2), 147–156.

Lieberman, A. (Ed.). (1995). *The work of restructuring schools: Building from the ground up.* New York: Teachers College Press.

Lieberman, A., Falk, B., & Alexander, L. (1994). *A culture in the making: Leadership in learner-centered schools.* New York: National Center for Restructuring Education, Schools and Teaching.

Lieberman, A., & Miller, L. (1990). Teacher development in professional practice schools. *Teachers College Record, 92*(1), 105–122.

Lieberman, A., & Miller, L. (1992a). The professional development of teachers. In M. Alkin (Ed.), *The encyclopedia of educational research* (6th ed.; Vol. 3; pp. 1045–1053). New York: Macmillan.

Lieberman, A., & Miller, L. (1992b). *Teachers, their world and their work: Implications for school improvement.* New York: Teachers College Press. (Original work published 1984)

Linguistic Minority Research Institute (LMRI). (1994). LMRI Newsletter (Vol. 4, No. 2). University of California, Santa Barbara.

Little, J. W. (1982). Norms of collegiality and experimentation: Workplace conditions of school success. *American Educational Research Journal, 19,* 325–340.

Little, J. W. (1987a). *Staff development in California: Public and personal investments, programs, patterns and policy choices.* San Francisco: Far West Laboratory and Policy Analysis for California Education.

Little, J. W. (1987b). Teachers as colleagues. In V. Richardson-Koehler (Ed.), *Educators' handbook* (pp. 491–518). New York: Longman.

Little, J. W. (1989, April). *The persistence of privacy: Autonomy and initiative in teachers' professional relations.* Paper presented at the annual meeting of the American Educational Research Association, San Francisco.

Little, J. W. (1992). Norms of collegiality and experimentation: Workplace conditions of school success. *American Educational Research Journal, 19,* 325–340.

Little, J. W. (1993a). Professional community in comprehensive high schools: The two worlds of academic and vocational teachers. In J. W. Little & M. W. McLaughlin (Eds.), *Teachers' work: Individuals, colleagues, and contexts* (pp. 137–163). New York: Teacher College Press.

Little, J. W. (1993b). Teachers' professional development in a climate of educational reform. *Educational Evaluation and Policy Analysis, 15*(3), 129–151.

Little, J. W., & Bird, T. D. (1987). Instructional leadership close to the classroom in secondary schools. In W. Greenfield (Ed.), *Instructional leadership: Issues, concepts, and controversies* (pp. 118–138). Boston: Allyn & Bacon.

Little, J. W., & McLaughlin, M. W. (1991). *Urban math collaboratives: As the teachers tell it.* Stanford, CA: Center for Research on the Context of Teaching.

Lord, B. (1991, April). *Subject area collaboratives, teacher professionalism and staff development.* Paper presented at the annual meeting of the American Educational Research Association, Chicago.

Lortie, D. (1975). *Schoolteacher.* Chicago: University of Chicago Press.

Loucks-Horsley, S., & Steigelbauer, S. (1991). In A. Lieberman & L. Miller (Eds.), *Staff development for education in the 90s* (pp. 15–36). New York: Teachers College Press.

Lytle, S., & Cochran-Smith, M. (1990). Learning from teacher research: A working typology. *Teachers College Record, 92*, 83–104.

Lytle, S., & Cochran-Smith, M. (1991, April). *Teacher research as a way of knowing.* Paper presented at the annual meeting of the American Educational Research Association, Chicago.

Lytle, S., & Fecho, R. (1991). Meeting strangers in familiar places: Teacher collaboration by cross-visitation. *English Education, 23*(199), 5–28.

Madaus, G. (1993). *The influence of testing on teaching math and science in grades 4–12. Executive summary.* Boston: Center for the Study of Testing, Evaluation, and Educational Policy, Boston College.

Madzimoyo, V. (1992). Urban mathematics collaborative promotes teacher professionalism. *EDC* (Educational Development Center) *News, 2*(1), 5.

McClure, R. (1991). Individual growth and institutional renewal. In A. Lieberman & L. Miller (Eds.), *Staff development for education in the 90s* (pp. 221–241). New York: Teachers College Press.

McDiarmid, G. W., & Wilson, S. M. (1991). An exploration of the subject matter knowledge of alternate route teachers: Can we assume they know their subject? *Journal of Teacher Education, 42*(2), 93–103.

McLaughlin, B. (1990). Development of bilingualism: Myth and reality. In A. Barona & E. Garcia (Eds.), *Children at risk: Poverty, minority status and other issues in educational equality* (pp. 65–76). Washington, DC: National Association of School Psychologists.

McLaughlin, M. (1991). Enabling professional development: What have we learned? In A. Lieberman & L. Miller (Eds.), *Staff development for education in the 90s* (pp. 61–82). New York: Teachers College Press.

McLaughlin, M. (1993). What matters most in teachers' workplace context? In J. Little & M. McLaughlin (Eds.), *Teachers' work* (pp. 79–103). New York: Teachers College Press.

McLaughlin, M. W., & Talbert, J. E. (1993). *Contexts that matter for teaching and learning: Strategic opportunities for meeting the nation's educational goals.* Stanford: Center for Research on the Context of Secondary School Teaching.

McLaughlin, M. W., Talbert, J. E., & Bascia, N. (Eds.). (1990). *The contexts of teaching in secondary schools: Teachers' realities.* New York: Teachers College Press.

McLaughlin, M., Talbert, J. E., & Phelan, P. (1990). *Report to field sites.* Stanford: Center for Research on the Context of Secondary School Teaching.

Miller, J. (1987, November). *Points of dissonance in teacher/researchers: Openings into emancipatory ways of knowing.* Paper presented at the Bergamo Conference on Curriculum Theory and Classroom Practice, Dayton, OH.

Moir, E., & Garmston, S. (1992). *A guide to prepare support providers for work with beginning teachers.* Sacramento: California Department of Education and Commission on Teacher Credentialing.

Moll, L. C., Amanti, C., Neff, D., & Gonzalez, N. (1992). Funds of knowledge for teaching: Using a qualitative approach to connect homes and classrooms. *Theory into Practice, 31*(2), 132–141.

Murphy, J., & Hallinger, P. (Eds.). (1993). *Restructuring schooling: Learning from ongoing efforts.* Newbury Park, CA: Corwin.

Myers, M. (1985). *The teacher-researcher: How to study writing in the classroom.* Urbana, IL: National Council of Teachers of Education.

National Board for Professional Teaching Standards. (1991). *Toward high and rigorous standards for the teaching profession* (3rd ed.). Washington, DC: Author.

National Center for Education Statistics. (1993). *The condition of education 1993.* Washington, DC: U.S. Department of Education.

National Commission on Excellence in Education. (1983). *A nation at risk: The imperative for educational reform.* Washington, DC: U.S. Government Printing Office.

National Commission on Time and Learning. (1994). *Prisoners of time: Schools and programs making time for students and teachers.* Washington, DC: U.S. Government Printing Office.

National Council of Teachers of Mathematics (NCTM). (1989). *Curriculum and evaluation standards for school mathematics.* Reston, VA: Author.

National Council of Teachers of Mathematics (NCTM). (1991). *Professional standards for teaching mathematics.* Washington, DC: Author.

Nisbett, R., & Ross, D. (1980). *Human inference: Strategies and shortcomings of social judgment.* Englewood Cliffs, NJ: Prentice-Hall.

Nolan, J., & Price, K. (1992). Changing perspectives on curriculum and instruction. *Supervision in transition: The 1992 ASCD Yearbook.* Reston, VA: Association for Supervision and Curriculum Development.

O'Brien, T. (1987). *Some thoughts about treasure-keeping.* Unpublished manuscript, Southern Illinois University, Teachers' Center Project, Edwardsville, IL.

Organisation for Economic Co-operation and Development. (1990). *Teacher demand and supply: The labor market for teachers.* Paris: Author.

Pate, G. S. (1988, April/May). Research on reducing prejudice. *Social Education, 54*(4), 287–289.

Pellegrin, R. J. (1976). Schools as work settings. In R. Dubin (Ed.), *Handbook of work, organizations and society* (pp. 343–376). Skokie, IL: Rand McNally.

Perrone, V. (1991). *A letter to teachers: Reflections on schooling and the art of teaching.* San Francisco: Jossey-Bass.

Peters, C. W. (1991). You can't have authentic assessment without authentic content. *Reading Teacher, 44*(8), 590–591.

Peterson, P. L., Fennema, E., Carpenter, T. P., & Loef, M. (1989). Alternative perspectives on knowing mathematics in elementary schools. In *Review of research in education, Vol. 15* (pp. 57–150). Itasca: F. E. Peacock.

Philadelphia Schools Collaborative. (1989). *Notes from the seminar on teaching and learning.* Philadelphia: University of Pennsylvania Press.

Philadelphia Teachers Learning Cooperative. (1984). On becoming teacher experts: Buying time. *Language Arts, 6*, 731–736.

Piaget, J. (1973). *To understand is to invent.* New York: Grossman.

Piaget, J., & Inhelder, B. (1969). *The psychology of the child.* New York: Basic Books.

Pincus, M. (1993). Conversion of a skeptic. In M. Cochran-Smith & S. Lytle (Eds.), *Inside/outside: Teachers, research and knowledge* (pp. 249–255). New York: Teachers College Press.

Polanyi, M. (1958). *Personal knowledge: Towards a post-critical theory.* Chicago: University of Chicago Press.

Porter, A. C. (1989). A curriculum out of balance: The case of elementary school mathematics. *Educational Researcher, 18*(5), 9–15.

Prawat, R. (1992). Teachers' beliefs about teaching and learning: A constructivist perspective. *American Journal of Education, 100*(3), 354–395.

Project START. (1989). *Notes from teacher–student teacher seminar on learning to teach.* Philadelphia: University of Pennsylvania Press.

Puget Sound Educational Consortium. (1988). *Teacher leadership: Commitment and challenge.* Seattle: Author.

Puget Sound Educational Consortium. (1989). *Teacher leadership: New skills— New opportunities.* Seattle: Author.

Pulaski, M. (1980). *Understanding Piaget.* New York: Harper & Row.

Putnam, T. M., Lampert, M., & Peterson, P. (1990). Alternative perspectives on knowing mathematics in elementary schools. *Review of Research in Education, 16*, 57–150.

Resnick, L. B. (1987). *Education and learning to think.* Washington, DC: National Academy Press.

Richards, J. (1991). Mathematical discussions. In E. von Glasersfeld (Ed.), *Radical constructivism in mathematics education* (pp. 13–51). Dordrecht, The Netherlands: Kluwer Academic Publishers.

Richardson, V., & Anders, P. (1991). The relationship between teachers' beliefs and practices in reading comprehension instruction. *American Educational Research Journal, 28*(3), 559–586.

Richardson-Koehler, V. (1988). Barriers to the effective supervision of students: A field of study. *Journal of Teacher Education, 39*, 28–34.

Rogoff, B. (1993). Observing sociocultural activity on three planes: Participatory appropriation, guided participation, apprenticeship. In A. Alvarez, P. del Rio, & J. V. Wertsch (Eds.), *Perspectives on sociocultural research.* New York: Cambridge University Press.

Rosenholtz, S. (1991). *Teachers' workplace: The social organization of schools.* New York: Teachers College Press.

Rudduck, J., & Hopkins, D. (1985). *Research as a basis for teaching: Readings from the work of Lawrence Stenhouse.* London: Heinemann.

Russell, S. J., & Corwin, R. B. (1993). Talking mathematics: "Going slow" and "letting go." *Phi Delta Kappan, 74*(7), 555–558.

Ryan, K. (1970). *Don't smile until Christmas.* Chicago: University of Chicago Press.

Sarason, S. B. (1982). *The culture of the school and the problem of change.* Boston: Allyn & Bacon.

Schaefer, R. (1967). *The school as a center of inquiry.* New York: Harper & Row.

Schifter, D. (1993). Mathematics process as mathematics content: A course for teachers. *Journal of Mathematical Behavior, 12*(3), 271–283.

Schifter, D. (Ed.). (1996). *What's happening in math class?, Volumes 1 and 2.* New York: Teachers College Press.

Schifter, D., & Fosnot, C. T. (1993). *Reconstructing mathematics education: Stories of teachers meeting the challenge of reform.* New York: Teachers College Press.

Schifter, D., & Simon, M. S. (1992). Assessing teachers' development of a constructivist view of mathematics learning. *Teaching and Teacher Education, 8*(2), 187–197.

Schwartz, J. (1988). The drudgery and the discovery: Students as research partners. *English Journal, 77*, 37–40.

Senge, P. (1990). *The fifth discipline: The art and practice of the learning organization.* New York: Anchor/Doubleday.

Sergiovanni, T. (1992). *Moral leadership: Getting to the heart of school improvement.* San Francisco: Jossey-Bass.

Shedd, J., & Bacharach, S. (1991). *Tangled hierarchies.* San Francisco: Jossey-Bass.

Shulman, L. (1986). Those who understand: Knowledge growth in teaching. *Educational Researcher, 15*(2), 4–14.

Shulman, L. (1987). Knowledge and teaching: Foundations of the new reform. *Harvard Educational Review, 57*, 1–22.

Shulman, L. (1989, January). *Teaching the disciplines liberally.* Paper presented at the third annual meeting of the Holmes Group, Atlanta.

Simon, M. S., & Schifter, D. (1991). Toward a constructivist perspective: An intervention study of mathematics teacher development. *Educational Studies in Mathematics, 22*(5), 309–331.

Siskin, L. S. (1991). Departments as different worlds: Subject subcultures in secondary schools. *Educational Administration Quarterly, 27*, 134–160.

Siskin, L. S. (1994). *Realms of knowledge: Academic departments in secondary schools.* New York: Falmer.

Sizer, T. R. (1984). *Horace's compromise: The dilemma of the American high school.* Boston: Houghton Mifflin.

Sizer, T. R. (1992). *Horace's school: Redesigning the American high school.* Boston: Houghton Mifflin.

Smith, H., & Wigginton, E., with Hocking, K., & Jones, R. E. (1991). Foxfire teacher networks. In A. Lieberman & L. Miller (Eds.), *Staff development for education in the 90s* (pp. 193–220). New York: Teachers College Press.

Smyth, W. I. (1987). *A rationale for teachers' critical pedagogy: A handbook.* Victoria, Australia: Deakin University Press.

Southern Maine Partnership. (1985–87). Unpublished minutes of group meetings, University of Southern Maine.

Southern Maine Partnership. (1993). Mission statement. (Unnumbered document).

Steffe, L., Cobb, P., & von Glasersfeld, E. (1988). *Construction of the arithmetical meanings and strategies*. New York: Springer-Verlag.

Stodolsky, S. S. (1988). *The subject matters: Classroom activity in mathematics and social studies*. Chicago: University of Chicago Press.

Stodolsky, S. S. (1993). A framework for subject matter comparisons in high schools. *Teaching and Teacher Education, 9*, 333–346.

Stodolsky, S. S., & Grossman, P. L. (1992, April). *Subject matter as context*. Paper presented at the annual meeting of the American Educational Research Association, San Francisco.

Strieb, L. (1985). *A Philadelphia teacher's journal*. Grand Forks, ND: Center for Teaching and Learning.

Sykes, G. (1985). Teacher education in the United States. In B. R. Clark (Ed.), *The school and the university* (pp. 264–289). Los Angeles: University of California Press.

Talbert, J. E., & Ennis, M. (1990). Teacher tracking: Exacerbating inequalities in high school (Technical Report No. 90–121). Stanford, CA: Center for Research on the Context of Secondary School Teaching, Stanford University.

Talbert, J. E., & McLaughlin, M. (1994). Teacher professionalism in local school contexts. *American Journal of Education, 102*, 123–153.

Teacher leadership: Contributions to improved practice. (1990). Seattle: Puget Sound Educational Consortium, University of Washington.

Teacher Leadership: New Skills—New Opportunities. (1990). Seattle: Puget Sound Educational Consortium, University of Washington.

Téllez, K. (1992). *Impotent, flawed, and loco: The public schools' response to Latino gangs*. Paper presented at the meeting of the National Association of Chicano Studies, San Antonio.

Téllez, K., Hlebowitsh, P. S., Cohen, M., & Norwood, P. (in press). Social service and teacher education at the University of Houston. In J. Larkin & C. Sleeter (Eds.), *Developing multicultural teacher education curriculum*. Albany: State University of New York Press.

Tharp, R. G., & Gallimore, R. (1988). *Rousing minds to life: Teaching, learning and schooling in social context*. Cambridge, England: Cambridge University Press.

Thompson, A. G. (1991, July). *The development of teachers' conceptions of mathematics teaching*. Paper presented at the annual meetings of the International Group for the Psychology of Mathematics Education, Assisi, Italy.

Traugh, C., Kanevsky, R., Martin, A., Seletzky, A., Woolf, K., & Strieb, L. (1986). *Speaking out: Teachers on teaching*. Grand Forks: University of North Dakota Study Group on Evaluation.

U.S. Department of Labor. (1986–1987). *Current population survey*. Unpublished data.

von Glasersfeld, E. (1983). *Learning as a constructive activity*. Proceedings of the fifth annual meeting of the North American Chapter of the International group for the Psychology of Mathematics Education, Montreal.

Vygotsky, L. (1978). *Mind in society*. Cambridge, MA: Harvard University Press.

Wasley, P. (1991). Stirring the chalkdust: Changing practices in essential schools. *Teachers College Record, 93*, 28–58.

Weber, L. (1991). *Inquiry, noticing, joining with, and following after*. New York: City College Workshop Center.

Wehlage, G., Smith, G., & Lipman, P. (1992). Restructuring urban high schools: The new futures experience. *American Educational Research Journal, 29*(1), 51–93.

Weiner, L. (1993). *Preparing teachers for urban schools*. New York: Teachers College Press.

Westerhoff, J. H. (1987). The teacher as pilgrim. In F. S. Bolin & J. Falk (Eds.), *Teacher renewal* (pp. 190–201). New York: Teachers College Press.

Wiggins, G. (1987). Creating a thought-provoking curriculum. *American Educator, 11*(4), 10–17.

Wigginton, E. (1985). *Sometimes a shining moment: The Foxfire experience*. Garden City, NY: Anchor.

Wiske, M. S. (undated). *Teaching geometry through guided inquiry: A case of changing mathematics instruction with new technologies*. Cambridge, MA: Educational Technology Center, Harvard Graduate School of Education.

Wiske, M. S., & Houde, R. (in press). From recitation to construction: Teachers change with new technologies. In J. L. Schwartz, M. Yerushalmy, & B. Wilson (Eds.), *What is this a case of: A geometric supposer reader*. Hillsdale, NJ: Erlbaum.

Wong-Fillmore, L. (1991). When learning a second language means losing the first. *Early Childhood Research Quarterly, 6*(3), 323–347.

Wood, D. (1992). Teaching narratives: A source for faculty development and evaluation. *Harvard Educational Review, 62*(4), 535–550.

Wood, D., & Einbender, L. (in press). *An authentic journey: Emergent understandings about authentic assessment and authentic practice*. New York: National Center for Restructuring Education, Schools and Teaching.

Wood, T., & Cobb, P. (1991). Change in teaching mathematics: A case study. *American Education Research Journal, 28*(3), 587–616.

Zeichner, K. (1986). Preparing reflective teachers: An overview of instructional strategies which have been employed in pre-science teacher education. *International Journal of Educational Research, 7*, 565–575.

Zumwalt, K. (1982). Are we improving or undermining teaching? In L. N. Tanner (Ed.), *Critical issues in curriculum: The eighty-seventh yearbook of the National Society for the Study of Education* (pp. 148–174). Chicago: University of Chicago Press.

About the Editors and the Contributors

Milbrey W. McLaughlin is a professor of education and public policy at Stanford University and director of the Center for Research on the Context of Teaching. Her interests focus on policy implementation, contexts of teaching and learning, and educational settings for nontraditional students. Her recent books include *Identity and Inner City Youth* and *Urban Sanctuaries: Neighborhood Organizations in the Lives and Futures of Inner-City Youth*.

Ida Oberman is a doctoral student in the history of education at Stanford University and researcher for the Pew Forum on Education Reform. She has been a teacher in both Germany and the United States. Her research focuses on educational change from a cross-national and historical perspective, with special concentration on the dissemination of reform initiatives in America.

Edwin Bridges is professor of education and director of the Prospective Principals' Program at Stanford University. Prior to joining the Stanford faculty, Bridges held academic appointments at the University of California–Santa Barbara, the University of Chicago, and Washington University, St. Louis. He is co-author with Philip Hallinger of *Implementing Problem-Based Learning in Leadership Development* and *Problem-Based Learning for Administrators*.

Martin G. Brooks is superintendent of schools in the Valley Stream, New York, Union Free School District 13. Brooks was the founder of the Association for Supervision and Curriculum Development's Network on Understanding Educational Change. He is co-author with Jacqueline Grennon Brooks of *In Search of Understanding: The Case for Constructivist Classrooms*.

Marilyn Cochran-Smith is associate professor and director of Project START (Student Teachers as Researching Teachers) at the Graduate School of Education, University of Pennsylvania. Cochran-Smith's research focuses on children's early literacy development, research on teaching, and teacher education. She is author of *The Making of a Reader* and *Learning to Write Differently*. Cochran-Smith and Susan L. Lytle's volume, *Inside/Outside: Teacher Research and Knowledge* (Teachers College Press), was the recipient of the AACTE 1995 Award for Outstanding Professional Writing in Teaching and Teacher Education.

Myrna D. Cohen is the director of field experiences and a visiting assistant professor of curriculum and instruction at the University of Houston. Her research interests include second-language instruction, teacher education, cooperative learning, and distance learning. Cohen's teaching experience is varied, encompassing higher education, elementary, middle, and high school levels, as well as years of teaching in Israeli public schools.

Stephanie Dalton is associate director of the Center for Research on Cultural Diversity and Second Language Learning at the University of California–Santa Cruz and co-principal investigator of the Center's Native American research project. Following a period of research teaching and consulting for the Kamehameha Elementary Education Program (KEEP), she co-developed and served as coordinator of the University of Hawaii's alternative teacher education program, Pre-Service Education for Teachers of Minorities (PETOM), built on KEEP principles with inquiry-based, interdisciplinary curricula, and field experience suitable for preparing teachers to assist culturally and linguistically diverse student populations in Hawaii. Dalton coordinated PETOM's annual program evaluation design. She has served as a teacher education task force leader in Goodlad's National Network for Educational Renewal and as a Holmes Group Member. She received her B.A. from the University of Maryland, M.Ed. from the University of Miami, and Ed.D. from the University of Hawaii at Manoa.

Linda Darling-Hammond is William F. Russel Professor of Education at Teachers College, Columbia University, and co-director of the National Center for Restructuring Education, Schools and Teaching. Her research focuses on issues of teaching quality, school restructuring, and educational equity. Her recent books include *Professional Development, Schools: Schools for Developing a Profession, A License to Teach: Building a Profession for the 21st Century Schools*, and *Authentic Assessment in Action: Studies of Schools and Students at Work*.

Beverly Falk is associate director for research at the National Center for Restructuring Education, Schools and Teaching (NCREST) at Teachers College, Columbia University. Currently an adjunct assistant professor at Teachers College and the City College of New York's School of Education, she has taught in early childhood through graduate education settings, has been the director of an early childhood center, the founding director of a public elementary school, and a program coordinator and consultant for several school districts. Falk's present work focuses on reform initiatives pertaining to learner-centered curricula and authentic assessment. She is co-author, with Linda Darling-Hammond and Jacqueline Ancess, of the forthcoming book *Authentic Assessment in Action*, is the editor of the Fall 1994 volume of *Educational Forum*, and is the author of several articles and monographs about educational leadership and school reform.

Jacqueline Grennon Brooks is on the faculty of the State University of New York at Stony Brook, where she is also the director of the Biotechnology Teaching Laboratory and the Discover Laboratory. Grennon Brooks is co-author of *In Search of Understanding: The Case for Constructivist Classrooms*.

Pamela Grossman is an associate professor of curriculum and instruction at the University of Washington. Her research interests include the content and processes of teacher education, teachers' knowledge and beliefs, and secondary school teaching. She is currently working on a research project designed to create a community of learners among high school English and history teachers.

Philip Hallinger is associate professor of educational leadership at Peabody College, Vanderbilt University, and holds a joint appointment at Chiang Mai University in Thailand. He also directs the Vanderbilt International Institute for Principals. Hallinger has written extensively on the effects of principal leadership, on national and international topics of school improvement, and on leadership development. Hallinger's current research focuses on the cultural foundations of leadership.

James K. Hammerman is senior research associate at the Center for the Development of Teaching at Education Development Center, Inc. He holds an A.B. degree in psychology and social relations and an Ed.M. in teaching curriculum and learning environments, both from Harvard University. Hammerman worked for several years at the SummerMath for Teachers program at Mt. Holyoke College as an instructor and classroom consultant. He also developed materials for secondary and middle school mathematics curriculum projects. Hammerman's current work is with a four-year, systematically embedded, National Science Foundation-funded project called Mathematics for Tomorrow. There his focus is on teacher education and the role of communities of inquiry among teachers in promoting changes in knowledge, beliefs, and teaching practice.

Kate Jamentz is the director of the California Assessment Collaborative (CAC). The CAC works with teachers in more than 25 school districts to develop performance assessment strategies, focusing on a wide variety of subject areas and grade levels. Jamentz holds a B.A. from the University of California–Santa Cruz, an M.A. from the Monterey Institute of International Studies, and an M.Ed. and Ed.D. from the Harvard School of Education. She has served as both a teacher and principal in secondary and elementary schools.

Charles Taylor Kerchner is the Hollis P. Allen Professor of Education at the Claremont Graduate School. He has studied teacher unionism for more than a decade and is the co-author with Douglas Mitchell of *The Changing Idea of a Teachers' Union*. Before coming to Claremont in 1976, Kerchner was on the faculty at Northwestern University, where he received his Ph.D. and was a member of the Illinois Board of Higher Education. He is currently collaborating on a book about the implications of teacher unionization in the postindustrial era. In addition, he is studying the relationship between urban education reform and the building of American cities.

Ann Lieberman is professor and co-director of the National Center for Restructuring Education, Schools and Teaching at Teachers College, Columbia University. Her books and articles have been used from the statehouse to the school house. She is the author of *Building a Professional Culture in Schools*, *Staff Development for Education in the 90s*, and *The Work of Restructuring Schools: Building from the Ground Up*.

Susan L. Lytle is assistant professor of education in the language in education division at the Graduate School of Education, University of Pennsylvania, and director of the Philadelphia Writing Project and of the Program in Reading/Writing/Literacy. Lytle's research focuses on the professional development of teachers, teacher/practitioner inquiry, literacy learning in adolescence and adulthood, alternative assessment, and the literacies of women. She is co-author with Marilyn Cochran-

Smith of *Inside/Outside: Teacher Research and Knowledge* (Teachers College Press) and the author of several monographs and many articles on literacy and teacher education. A former high school English teacher, Lytle works with communities of experienced teachers and other practitioners—from K–12 schools, colleges, universities, and adult literacy programs—committed to inquiry and educational reform.

Lynne Miller is professor of education at the University of Southern Maine, where she directs the Southern Maine Partnership, a school–university collaboration that involves 22 school districts, three private schools, the Maine College of Art, and the University of Southern Maine. Miller was a high school English teacher, alternative school director, building-level administrator, and assistant superintendent before entering higher education. She is a member of the Rockefeller/Carnegie Commission on Teaching and American's Future and on the advisory committee of OERI's study on systemic change in education. She is co-author with Ann Lieberman of *Teachers, Their World and Their Work*, *Staff Development for Education in the 90s*, and *Teachers, Restructuring Their World and Their Work* (in press).

Ellen Moir is the director of teacher education at the University of California–Santa Cruz. She has been a supervisor of teacher education at UCSC since 1979, where she teaches courses in literacy, bilingual methods, and beginning and intermediate student teaching. She is also the director of the UCSC-led New Teacher Project, which has served over 350 new teachers in Santa Cruz County Schools since 1988. She has produced three video documentaries: *Partnership in Education: Helping New Teachers Succeed, Passage into Teaching: California New Teacher Project*, and *Bilingual Education: An Inside View*. She has a master's degree in elementary education and a bilingual specialist teaching credential. Moir is recognized nationally for her work with beginning teachers.

Cynthia O'Shea is the principal of the Narragansett School in Gorham, Maine. She and Lynne Miller have co-authored "Learning to Lead: Portraits in Practice," published in the *National Society for the Study of Education Yearbook* (1992).

Barbara Scott Nelson is senior scientist and director of the Center for the Development of Teaching at Education Development Center, Inc. She holds a B.A. from Mt. Holyoke College, an M.A.T. from Johns Hopkins University, and an Ed.D. from Harvard University. As program officer at the Ford Foundation in the 1980s, she designed the Urban Mathematics Collaborative Program and Quantitative Understanding Amplifying Student Achievement and Reasoning (QUASAR), a mathematics reform program for inner-city middle schools administered by the Learning Research and Development Center at the University of Pittsburgh. Her current work includes direction of the Center for the Development of Teaching at the Education Development Center and a National Science Foundation grant, "Mathematics for Tomorrow," which looks at the systemic implications of a mathematics teacher enhancement program based on a constructivist view of teachers' intellectual development. She co-chairs a national working group of researchers studying teacher change in the context of mathematics education reform, sponsored jointly by the Center for the Development of Teaching and the National Center for Research of Mathematical Sciences Education.

Margaret Szabo is the executive director of the California Center for School Restructuring, generating leadership and support for the 150 schools engaged in California's restructuring initiative. She is a former filmmaker, public school teacher, administrator, and director of the Bay Area Region Coalition of Essential Schools. In these capacities, she has designed and led numerous school change strategies and learning institutes around such topics as constructivist curricula and pedagogy, whole-school change, authentic assessment, and outcome-based school design. She earned her doctoral and master's degrees in education from Stanford University and her B.A. in sociology from Stanford. Her research interests include organizational socialization, conditions supporting new teachers, and processes and practices that support reculturing and organizational change.

Edith S. Tatel received her doctorate from the University of Maryland and is currently the director of teacher education at the American University School of Education in Washington, D.C. She has taught English to middle and high school students in urban public and private schools.

Kip Téllez is assistant professor in the department of curriculum and instruction at the University of Houston. His research interests include second-language education, urban education, teacher education, and pragmatism. His teaching experience includes elementary English as a second language and high school fine arts and English. He is currently at work on a foundations of education text, focused on the contributions of the progressives.

Index